THE PHILOSOPHY OF VIVEKANANDA

THE PHILOSOPHY OF VIVEKANANDA

Edited by

REKHA JHANJI

ARYAN BOOKS INTERNATIONAL
New Delhi

THE PHILOSOPHY OF VIVEKANANDA

ISBN-81-7305-320-0

First Published in **2007** by:
ARYAN BOOKS INTERNATIONAL
Pooja Apartments, 4B, Ansari Road, New Delhi - 110 002 (India)
Tel.: 23287589, 23255799; Fax: 91-11-23270385
E-mail: aryanbooks@vsnl.com

Computer Typeset and Printed in India at
ABI Prints & Publishing Co., New Delhi.

Dedicated to my mother who aroused in me the spiritual quest by introducing me to Ramakrishna Vachanamrita

Dedicated to my mother who inspired in me the spiritual quest by introducing me to Ramakrishna Paramahamsa

Acknowledgements

This book is a collective venture, many people have played an important role in its emergence. I am grateful to all of them for their cooperation. Some of the articles in this volume were presented during the lectures and seminars organised by the U.G.C. sponsored Centre for Vivekananda Studies in Panjab University, Chandigarh. I am grateful to the Panjab University and University Grants Commission for providing the infrastructure for undertaking a study of Swami Vivekanada's life and works. Professor K.N. Pathak, the former Vice-Chancellor of Panjab University was specially helpful in carrying on the activities of this Centre. Without his encouragement and cooperation, this book could not have been published.

I express my gratitude to my colleagues, research scholars and all other authors for contributing articles to this volume.

The greatest inspiration for carrying out this task has come from Swami Brahmeshananda, the Secretary of the Ramakrishna Mission, Chandigarh. He has always helped me in planning and executing different activities of the Centre. Brahmachari Bhaskarchaitanya of the Ramakrishna Mission, Chandigarh has also been very helpful in cross checking the citations from the different works of Vivekananda included in this volume. Prof. Dharmanand Sharma, the present Coordinator of the Centre for Vivekananda Studies has been very helpful in finalising the manuscript of this volume.

I am also grateful to Mr. Deepak Semwal, the secretarial assistant of the Centre for the effort he has made in typing out the manuscript.

Contents

Section Two
Nature of Man, Creativity, Language and Art

Section Three
Indian Philosophical Systems

List of Contributors

Bhagwan Josh
Professor, Centre for Historical Studies, Jawaharlal Nehru University, New Delhi.

Dharmendra Goel
Former Professor and Head, Department of Philosophy, Panjab University, Chandigarh (38-A, Swastic Vihar, Panchkula - 134009).

Raghunath Ghosh
Professor, Department of Philosophy, University of North Bengal, District Darjeeling - 734430 (West Bengal).

Indu Sarin
Professor, Department of Philosophy, Panjab University, Chandigarh - 160014.

Veena Kapoor
Professor, Department of Philosophy, Panjab University, Chandigarh - 160014.

Pabitrakumar Roy
Senior Fellow, Indian Council of Philosophical Research, New Delhi.

Geeta Manakatala
Professor, Department of Philosophy, Panjab University, Chandigarh - 160014.

Swami Brahmeshananda
Secretary, Ramakrishna Mission Ashrama, Sector 15-B, Chandigarh - 160015.

Asha Maudgil
Former Chairperson, Department of Philosophy, Panjab University, Chandigarh - 160014.

Pankaj Srivastava

Research Scholar, Department of Philosophy, Panjab University, Chandigarh - 160014.

Kuldip Dhiman

Research Scholar, Department of Philosophy, Panjab University, Chandigarh and Chief Designer, The Tribune, Chandigarh (#581, Sector 10D, Chandigarh - 160011).

Rekha Jhanji

Former Professor, Department of Philosophy and Co-ordinator, Centre for Vivekananda Studies, Panjab University, Chandigarh - 160014 (#733, Sector 11B, Chandigarh - 160011).

Manjulika Ghosh

Professor, Department of Philosophy, University of North Bengal, District Darjeeling - 734430 (West Bengal).

Godabarisha Mishra

Professor, Department of Philosophy, University of Madras, Chennai.

C.V. Babu

Former Research Scholar, Department of Philosophy, Panjab University, Chandigarh (Senior Research Fellow, Indian Institute of Technology, Hauz Khas, New Delhi - 110026).

Introduction

It is a Herculean task to write something on a personage like Swami Vivekananda. It is like measuring the ocean. His depth of vision cannot be fathomed by an ordinary human mortal but since his message is for ordinary beings like us, it is important to talk about it so that we can imbibe his ideals in our lives. Romain Rolland compared his life to the music of Beethoven

He was the living embodiment of the harmony of four *yogas* propounded by him. His actions give one a clear testimony of the *Karma Yoga* of *Bhagwad Gītā*. His devotion to God and the emotive sensitivity to the divine in the poorest of poor – the *Daridra Nārāyaṇa* is a clear sign of his perfection in *Bhakti Yoga*. His final detachment from all his projects towards the last part of his life shows how deeply entrenched he was in *Jñāna Yoga*. His passing away in *samādhi* shows his mastery of *Rāja Yoga*.

How can an ordinary mortal fathom the depth of such a multi-faceted personality like Vivekananda? Nag Mahashaya's statement would help us to see our limitations in understanding this dynamic personality. He said to Vivekananda:

> who will understand you? Unless the inner vision opens, nobody can understand you. Only Sri Ramakrishna understood you; all else have simply put faith in his words, but none has understood you really.

The papers in this volume are a result of this desire to understand this great stalwart. The title of this book may seem incongruous because Vivekananda was not a philosopher in the sense in which the term philosophy is seen in our times.

For the last half a century philosophy in India is essentially seen in its Anglo-Saxon connotation – a critical enquiry into the different dimensions of our knowledge of the world based on conceptual and linguistic analysis. Indian philosophy as it is seen in the traditional sense is essentially regarded as a *darśana* – a vantage point to see Reality. Such a vision of reality transforms one's being. As Swami Nikhilananda puts it:

> In the Western world a student of philosophy is expected to cultivate truthfulness about facts and intellectual integrity, his aim being to acquire knowledge. But the goal of a student of Indian philosophy is not only to know Reality but to realise it and mould his life according to Reality.[1]

Vivekananda's life is an exemplar for students of Indian philosophy. It was his mission to establish coherence between theoria and praxis. Summarising his whole life's task Vivekananda writes:

> The abstract Advaita must become living-poetic in everyday life; out of hopelessly intricate mythology must come concrete moral forms; and out of bewildering yogi-ism must come the most scientific and practical psychology and all this must be put in a form so that a child may grasp it. That is my life's work.[2]

His philosophy is deeply embedded in a spiritual quest that was his life-long mission. He did not see it solely as an analytical study of concepts. He was by no means lacking in critical and analytical thinking but he did not see it as an end in itself. Since the purpose of human existence is self-knowledge, analytical thinking was useful for him only to the extent it helped in achieving that objective. He was well aware that the path of self-knowledge cannot be pursued by cowards. That is why he laid so much emphasis on being courageous. He wanted the Indian youth to be manly. Manliness for him is not gender-related but it stands for courage, vigour, enthusiasm, love and compassion. He put his paradigm of manliness clearly to his disciples:

> you must try to combine in your life immense idealism with immense practicality. You must be prepared to explain the intricacies of scriptures now, and the next moment to sell the produce of the fields in the market. The true man is he who is strength itself and yet possesses a woman's heart.[3]

The first section of this book is devoted to an exposition of Vivekananda's views on religion and ethics and their significance for Indian society and nation. Sister Nivedita says that:

the Shastra, the Guru and the Motherland are the three notes that mingle themselves to form the music of the works of Vivekananda.

To give a sample of this music we thought it would be better to start with Vivekananda's views on religion and society. The first paper in this volume is devoted to an historical account of the emergence of Swami Vivekananda in the 19th century India caught up in the exigencies of British rule. Prof. Bhagwan Josh has given a detailed historical background of those times, the impact of Raja Rammohun Roy and Keshav Chandra Sen on Vivekananda and his emergence as a *sanyasi* through his relationship with his guru Ramakrishna Paramhamsa.

Prof. Dharmendra Goel's paper also focuses on the state of Indian society in the 19th century. He has tried to highlight the internal tensions in the Indian society in those times, even the struggle for independence was not seen by different segments of Indian society with a sense of solidarity. He states that it is not due to multi-culturalism but due to the fact that different ideologies that flourished non-contemporaneously prevented the fusion of a common objective. He emphasises Vivekananda's role in critiquing the casteism of Indian society. However, he holds that Vivekananda's *Daridra Nārāyaṇa* does not fascinate the subaltern imagination. We need to note here that the fault does not lie with Vivekananda, but with us who did not live up to the ideal of the worship of *Daridra Nārāyaṇa.* That is why the poor and the low castes in India feel that these sublime ideas have remained only at the level of ideation. Raghunath Ghosh's paper on Vivekananda and Youth Forces, highlights the significance of Vivekananda's message for the young generations.

Since Swami Vivekananda's central message is related to the need for experiencing religion in its essential sense, four of the articles in this volume focus on his conception of religion. Pabitra K. Roy's article, "The Religion is, the Religions are", is based on Vivekananda's concept of the inherent unity of all religions. Vivekananda saw reality and unity in coeval terms. He upholds that all religions are in essence one but diverse in manifestation. Vivekananda's concept of religion is realisation of oneness of the humankind based upon love. He advocates the idea of practical spirituality.

Vivekandna's concept of real and apparent religion has an oblique reference to the twofold nature of man. The real man is the eternal *atman* while his apparent form is the ego bound by space, time and causality. Religion in the real sense is the religion of the *atman*. This needs to be experienced. Here the author compares Vivekananda's concept of unity of religions with Dalai Lama's exposition of the possibility of inter-faith understanding based on the pervasive condition of human suffering and the need to come out of it.

While the relativist would agree with Vivekananda's account of the diversity of religions, he would not accept his idea of the primordial essence manifesting itself in diverse forms. The author does not decide the issue between relativists and absolutists he holds that Vivekananda's reasons for essentialism are no less important than the relativist's for no answer is possible to satisfy all the contenders. Geeta Manaktala's article on universalising universal religion highlights the equivocal character of the concept of religion by citing several conceptions of religion propounded by different thinkers. Swami Vivekananda saw an inherent oneness in the diversity of religious practices. He advocated the idea of a universal religion that transcended all these limitations. She points out that it is the religious sense within the various religions that can help to free people from the feeling of absoluteness of any particular religion. But world religions have not united human beings despite their common goals. She is doubtful of the contemporary relevance of this universalising tendency.

In her article on "Religion as Foundation of Morality", Indu Sarin also focuses on Vivekananda's conception of unity of religions and its significance in inculcating values in human beings. Indu Sarin referes to the four *yogas* and then moves on to a discussion of Vivekananda's views on God. Vivekananda rejects the possibility of giving any proofs for the experience of God because God is not a fact that can be proved or disproved. He rejects both natural and revealed theology. For Vivekananda religion and morality cannot be separated from one another. Morality for him lies in unselfishness. In the moral sphere the centre is "thou" not I. If one has an awareness of divinity this faith spontaneously generates moral actions. To be religious means having faith in oneself, and this faith breaks the gap between theory and practice thus overcoming all moral weakness.

Like Indu Sarin, Veena Kapoor also highlights the significance of religion in ethics. In her article "Realising Perfection through Self-Abnegation". The quest after perfection is actually motivated by the search after our true self. The real self can be realised only by going beyond the ego. Only unselfishness can generate purity. The quest for personal interest separates one from others while selflessness generates unity. She also gives an exposition of Vivekananda's critique of utilitarian ethics and emphasises the need of religious basis of ethics. In no other way can the pursuit of good be justified. All these papers highlight Vivekananda's holistic approach to life. For him virtuous life is based on the belief in the essential oneness of all creation. The pursuit of virtue is seen as identical with the quest of perfection. To know what perfection means, one has to explore the purpose of human existence because that alone can give one an idea of the direction one needs to take to achieve perfection. For Vivekananda the purpose of human existence is the attainment of knowledge and not pleasure. He lays down four paths for the attainment of knowledge – *karma* (action), *bhakti* (devotion), *jñāna* (knowledge) and *rāja yoga* (silencing the mind through psychological and physical discipline). All these four *yogas* aim at freeing the individual from the clutches of their limited psycho-physical being and realising the oneness of all existence. This knowledge generates freedom from suffering. Vivekananda's concept of the essential oneness of all existence is in tune with the *Vedāntic* view of Brahman and the doctrine of *pratītiyasamutpāda* in Buddhism.

Pankaj Srivastava has highlighted the role of religious symbols in the realisation of divinity. He distinguishes between sign and symbol. While the former points to something other than itself, the latter participates in that which it symbolises. He points out the distinctive character of religious symbols from all other symbols because they are replicas of the personal journey of individuals. Seen in this light they can lead to inner transformation. Vivekananda recognised the importance of religious symbols. That is why he also emphasised the need of understanding their real meaning.

The second section of this volume contains papers focusing on Vivekananda's concept of human nature and its manifestation in different forms of culture like language, art and literature. Our understanding of Vivekananda's concept of religion cannot be clear without going deeper into his view of human nature. In his paper on the "Nature of Man in Vivekananda", Swami Brahmeshananda elucidates the different definitions of man in the Western tradition which range between homo-sapiens, homo-sexualis and homo-economicus. As against these Swami Vivekananda highlighted the divinity of man. This is a concept of man that liberates a human being from narrow identities. However, it is difficult to experience our divinity and impart it to others. Swami Brahmeshananda points out the difficulties involved in the realisation of the divinity. Each individual has his own concept of divinity. Vivekananda preached this divinity of man to bring out the best in all human beings. Despite the turmoil, it is better to struggle for realising a higher concept of ourselves than to accept a degraded concept and become brutes.

In her paper "Self: Appearance and Reality", Asha Maudgil highlights the need to realise one's real nature. She has drawn parallels between Vivekananda's and Wittgenstein's thought: both see the self as apart from the mundane world. In my paper on Vivekananda's aesthetics I have tried to bring out his creativity in the arts and his deep understanding of world art. Vivekananda had the strong conviction that to visualise God it is necessary to appreciate the beauty and sublimity of nature and art. For only then is one capable of realising the divine which is the manifestation of the highest sublimity and beauty. He compared great art to a lily which springs from the ground but is untainted by it. He saw art as a pursuit of the beautiful, the grotesque having no place in it. Vivekananda was both a critic and an artist. His music and poetry give one a glimpse of his exquisite aesthetic sense. Kuldip Dhiman has highlighted the power of Vivekananda's language. He combined in it a modern idiom with the metaphors and similies from the epics. Despite the criticism of his language by contemporary writers and critics, he continued with his ideal of simplicity in communication because he was convinced that to address the masses he needed to use simple colloquial language. Through his powerful language he inspired Indians to strive for political and spiritual freedom. We can see the impact of his language on many of the leaders of the movement of India's independence as well as on spiritual aspirants. His impact on the youth is noteworthy. His *mantra* "Arise, Awake and stop not till the goal is reached" has such a charismatic power that one immediately gets charged with energy on hearing it. Raghunath Ghosh has focused on Vivekananda's role in arousing the youth forces. He points out that Vivekananda aroused the youth to realise their spiritual power for he was convinced that they alone can save India and liberate her from the tyranny of blind materialism.

The last section of this volume is devoted to an exposition of of Vivekananda's views on traditional Indian philosophies. Vivekananda had a deep understanding of different schools of classical Indian philosophy. However, he did not look upon these philosophies merely as theoretical exercises but saw in them possibilities of realisation. C.V. Babu's article "Sages of ages" attempts to see Vivekananda's study of *Śrutis* in terms of a continuous revelation of eternal truths. Manjulika Ghosh's article is based on Vivekananda's comments on Buddha and Buddhism. He looked upon the Buddha as a true *Karma Yogi*. She points out that the real antagonism was not between the Buddha and Samkara but between him and Kumarila Bhatta, the latter found the Buddha's repudiation of the *Vedas* as ignoble. Samkara did not repudiate the Buddha though he did have some animus against his followers. Similarly, both Vivekananda and Ramakrishna had great admiration for the Buddha. Vivekananda's study of Buddhism is based on Pali Buddhism. He was critical of Tantric Buddhism because he was not sympathetic towards esoteric religious ideas. Godabarish Mishra's paper "Vivekananda: An Advaitin" delineates Vivekananda's innovative interpretation of *Advaita Vedānta* and distinguishes it from Samkara's view of *Advaita*. He points out that Vivekananda's brilliance lies in the practical application of *Vedānta* to one's mundane life in society. The *Vedāntic* view of the individual's identity with God is interpreted by him in its true spirit which implies that the real worship of God is the worship of mankind. Unlike Samkara who emphasised the transcendence of Brahman, Vivekananda laid stress on the immanence of Brahman. My article on Vivekananda's *Rāja Yoga* is based on his exposition of Patanjali's *Yoga Sūtras*. *Rāja Yoga* as a means of realisation is particularly relevant for the present times because we are living in times dominated by a body-centric vision of the world. Yoga does not deny this vision but alleviates it. It begins with the body and helps one to become a witness of the body-mind complex.

All these papers show the multi-faceted personality of Vivekananda and his genius in creatively understanding Indian religion, society and art. But to my mind the real greatness of Vivekananda lies in his power in helping his readers to enlighten their existential journey through wisdom. Even to this day there are people all over the world who are guided by his spiritual vision. He learnt from his guru the need to accept and respect religious diversity. This needs to be practised the world over. Only then can we overcome religious bigotry. His emphasis on the need to cultivate selfless service and sacrifice is the only way to overcome tensions and depressions generated in interpersonal relationships.

Some of the contributors to this volume have pointed out the contradictions and inconsistencies in Vivekananda's views. I have already stated that Vivekananda was not a philosopher in a purely theoretical sense. That is also the reason why for him theoretical consistency was not a value in itself for that is a purely rational approach. Vivekananda's writings and speeches show that he was a great admirer of rationality but he was also aware of the limits of reason. That is why he did not feel hesitant to acknowledge inconsistencies in his views. His position is similar to that of Walt Whitman who says in his "Song of My Self":

> Do I contradict myself?
> Very well then I contradict myself
> (I am large, I contain multitudes.)

NOTES AND REFERENCES

1. The Upanishad in New Translation by Swami Nikhilananda, Vol. II, Ramakrishna Vedanta Centre, New York, 1990, p. 206.
2. *Vivekananda: The man and His message by his Eastern and Western Disciples,* published by Swami Muktananda, Advaita Ashram, Kolkata, 1995, p. 46.
3. *Ibid.,* Vol. 2, p. 456.

SECTION ONE

RELIGION, SOCIETY AND ETHICS

1

Making of a New *Sannyasin*: Outline of a Historical Approach

Bhagwan Josh

The economic changes and the educational system introduced by the colonial power led to the creation of a sizeable number of a new middle class by the second-half of the 19th century in India. Over the years this middle class has continued to absorb various sorts of ideas coming from the West: liberal, humanitarian and radical ideas of the French revolution. Ideals of equality, democracy and rule of law had begun to take possession of the minds of many of them thereby unsettling their deeply held beliefs, views and rituals. Also, these new currents of thought were unfolding in an atmosphere where the fierce and intemperate attacks were being made on Hindu religion, customs and traditions by the missionaries.[1]

This led to a process of re-thinking as well as roused the spirit of nationalism stimulating a defensive and protective attitude to Indian ideas and ways of living. There emerged vigorous movements directed towards the reconstruction of new cultural mores involving both reform and re-invigoration of the inherited modes of living and thinking.[2] Following the pattern of European history, this early period of modern history was labelled as the period of Renaissance by earlier historians. Nowadays historians have ceased to use this label because of the serious implications of colonial context.[3] Here, I am deliberately avoiding the traditionally used pair of binary opposites to label the messy history of this period, i.e., reform and revivalism. The messiness and complexity of the historical period, where the ideas, views and sentiments not only criss-crossed but also seem to be inseparably entwined, was overlooked through the deployment of two mutually exclusive simplified categories. This binary was then translated by the historians into another pair of binary opposites labelled as "progressive and reactionary" trends in the 19th century.[4] The process of their transformation did not stop here. Soon they came to be labelled as "nationalism and communalism" during the anti-colonial struggle and finally to "secularism and communalism" in independent India. This process is indicative of two clear cut dichotomous histories of modern India. Needless to say that this kind of history writing has vitiated the political and academic scene in this country.

The multi-pronged contact with the West had led to the creation of a new psychological situation where the sentiments of national pride were enmeshed with the processes of rethinking about the contemporary situation. The Christian missionaries, apart from denouncing Hinduism, also preached a gospel of equality which they claimed had transformed their societies with more humane political practices and norms.[5] While these norms of equality and political practices could not be found in Hindu religion.

> ... While almost all sections which asserted their reaction to this onslaught on their religion and culture were quite progressive in education, economic and political matters, some took up a conservative attitude in matters of religion, others a liberal and reformist attitude, while yet others revolted against the past and broke away from its shackles.
>
> An illustrious example of the conservative school was Radha Kanta Deb, who was one of the founders of the Hindu College and the helm of its affairs for over 30 years from 1817 to 1850. He opened a Sanskrit College in 1851 and the Hindu Metropolitan College in 1853 after he had resigned form the managing committee of the Hindu College on account of differences with the English Chairman. He was a conservative Hindu and fought hard against the conversions that were taking place to Christianity from Hinduism.
>
> Then there was a group of radical young men moulded by their brilliant professor of English, Henry Derozia, who started journals like *Parthenon* and *Bengal Spectator*, which became the mouthpiece of the group known as "New Bengal". These journals were outspoken in their criticism of Hindu religion and social customs. The spirit of inquiry and free thinking generated by the times led to some spectacular protests against orthodoxy with young men flouting taboos against eating and drinking and some even repudiating Hinduism itself and indeed all religions. Between the two extremes of invigorated orthodoxy and radical revolt

against Hinduism, there was a middle path initiated by Raja Rammohun Roy.[6]

This situation could be characterised as a crisis of identity for the newly emerging intelligentsia. The manifestation of this crisis was itself a complicated process.

There were sections in the intelligentsia that were impressed by these new currents of thought. Their attitude was to understand the significance and meaning of these ideas and their likely implications for the society in which they were located. Some of these individuals not only accepted the inevitability of social change marking the beginning of a new era but also stressed desirability of this change along certain lines. The range of experiences they were undergoing cannot be captured through the simple and popular paradigm of "challenge and response" because many of them seem to have looked at this context more as an opportunity and less as a challenge.

The educational context created by the colonial power resulting in accessibility to scientific knowledge produced by Europe was certainly a welcome development, while the same institutions practising racial discrimination could not but be resented. Attacks on Hindu religion, customs and traditions not only led to a process of rethinking but also roused the patriotic spirit. Raja Rammohun Roy, a linguist and a student not only of Hindu religion but also of the Christian and Islamic faiths, was a member of this section.[7]

The most significant aspect of this new credo was its repudiation of polytheism in favour of monotheism and it was claimed that it was derived directly from the *Vedas*. This reconceptualisation of Hinduism created a new social divide between the *bhadralok* and *chhotolok* who practised folk Hinduism. Roy's followers set up a new organisation which had a distinct church-like character, with chapels and sermons and hymns. This Christian streak within the Brahmo Samaj was most pronounced in Keshub Sen, the Brahmo who finally acted as a conduit between Ramakrishna and the *bhadralok* society. The *Indian Christian Herald* mourned his death in the following words: "Christians look upon him as God's messenger, sent to awake India to the Spirit of Christ."

Keshub was a thinker who seemed to be struggling to bring his patriotic feeling in conformity with his other conviction that the reading of the *Bible* and the figure of Christ was of great importance for his country in the "present transition stage". He solved this problem by drawing a distinction between Christ and Christianity and then transforming "Western Christ" into an Oriental one. But truth was not the monopoly of the Orientals. Again he had to distinguish between "the outward Christ" and "the inward Christ". Even when "the outward Christ" was Asiatic, the inward Christ was universal. Given this kind of striving for resolving his intellectual and emotional crisis, drove him, and many others, to the personality of Ramakrishna yet not placing their faith in him. This act of fully placing one's faith in Ramakrishna involved going beyond the limits of rationality and thus constituted the last and final obstacle which could not be surmounted without at least making a partial break with the Brahmo Samaj.

Ramakrishna's profound exposition of the basic tenets of Hindu faith and mystic experience singled him out from all other religious men of his time. As a practitioner of God-realisation and his tolerance of all faiths and complete self-realisation by renunciation of ego, accompanied by love and compassion, he came to be recognised widely. His firm faith in the self-evident truths of his tradition and compassion for all humanity, made him a charismatic personality in the eyes of Bengali intelligentsia riddled with the misgivings of identity crisis.[8] Like many other members of the *bhadralok* group Naren too came to see Ramakrishna in 1881. What was his state of mind at this time? This is a difficult question to answer as the biographies of all great individuals, constructed retrospectively, tend to place the seed of their future greatness at the very beginning of their story. What is certain is that during his college education he had studied Western philosophy, ancient and modern history of different nations. Like his contemporaries, he must have been familiar with Herbert Spencer, Kant, Schopenhauer, Auguste Comte, Hume and John Stuart Mill, especially with his "Three Essays on Religion". This reading seems to be sufficient to fill one's mind with numerous questions for a lifetime. A historical survey of his interactions in later life tells us one very important psychological fact about his *svabhāva*, i.e., his personality had a streak of impatience and impulsiveness. An account of Naren's first meeting with Sri Ramakrishna is available from both, the guru and the disciple.[9] Sri Ramakrishna said of this meeting:

He seemed careless of his body and dress and unmindful of the external world. His eyes bespoke an introspective mind as if some part of it was always concentrated upon something within. I was surprised to find such a spiritual soul coming from the material atmosphere of Calcutta.[9a]

Naren sang few Bengali songs at his request which made Sri Ramakrishna lose control of himself and fall into an ecstatic mood. What seems to me as the most important element of this first encounter between them is the "song" and the "act of singing". It is common knowledge that there are individuals in all walks of life, including politics, who conceptualise effective communication as establishing relationship between two hearts. Who does not know that the staple Indian cinema formula has always been that a single song can emote sensitivities much better than dialogues consisting of thousands of words. A song is always a short-cut to spontaneity, a state of mind conducive for innermost experiences. Perhaps without this sort of communication Naren would not have been able to connect with him at a deeper level and ask him his favourite question, a question he had asked without success of so many holy men: "Have you seen God, Sir?". To his utter surprise came the answer:

Yes, I see Him just as I see you here, only in much more intense sense ... God can be realised, one can see and talk to Him as I am doing with you. But who cares to do so? People shed torrents of tears for their wives and children, for wealth and property, but who does so for the sake of God? If one weeps sincerely for him, He surely manifests Himself.[9b]

God comes to those who seek Him and show how badly they need Him. All religions were but different ways to reach the same God. Do not, therefore, revile any religion. God was both Personal and Impersonal and yet He is beyond any intellectual or theological dogmas. He is manifest in the soul's own innermost realisation.

Next year, series of meetings between them brought them closer. This capability (i.e. singing) of Naren must have helped him not only to bring him closer to Ramakrishna but also provided him with a state of mind to directly experience the spiritual energy transmitted by Ramakrishna.

One day Ramakrishna turned round to some of his devotees and said:

Well, if Keshab is possessed of one mark of greatness which has made him famous, Naren has 18 such marks. In Keshab and Vijay I saw the light of knowledge burning like candle flame, but in Narendra it was like a blazing sun, dispelling the last vestige of ignorance and delusion.[10]

True, Narendra protested and asked him not to say such things. But it must have bolstered the ego and self-conceit of a young man. Naren was convinced of the master's utter sincerity, and greatly admired his renunciation and his child-like simplicity. But he was not prepared to accept his *Vedāntic* tenet of one universal reality which existed not only in every human being but also in everything else around him. Soon Ramakrishna realised the fact that when convictions on both sides are deep seated, argument is futile. One day after one such futile argument Ramakrishna touched Naren and he immediately fell into a *Samādhi*. This is how Naren describes this incident:

The magic touch of the master that day brought immediately a wonderful change over my mind. I was stupefied to find that really there was nothing in the universe but God. I saw it quite clearly but kept silent, to see if the idea would last. But the impression did not abate in the course of the day. I returned home, but there too, everything I saw appeared to be Brahman. I sat down to take my meal but found that everything – the food, the plate, the person who served and even myself – was nothing but that .... I realised that I must have had glimpse of the Advaita state. Then it struck me that the words of the scriptures were not false. Therefore I could not deny the conclusions of Advaita philosophy.[11]

The wall of reason had been breached but yet it did not collapse completely. This was to happen very soon. Naren's other bone of contention with his master was the latter's worship of Kali as the Divine Mother and continuously quoting Her as if he was actually seeing Her everyday and conversing with her. Naren constantly argued with Sri Ramakrishna against image worship. Sri Ramakrishna brought home to his disciples the profound truth that recognition of One in the many did not prevent the individual from exercising his own judgement according to reason when it came to matters of daily conduct.

In early 1884, Naren's father died suddenly. He found that his father had spent more than he had earned and had left him without resources and with the responsibility of maintaining his large family. From comfort he was suddenly thrown into poverty.

This is how his biographers describe his existential crisis:

In college he was the poorest of poor. His friends, now and then, invited him to their houses. He would chat happily with them for long hours, but when food was offered, the vision of desolation at home would come before his eyes and prevent him from eating. He would leave with the excuse that he had a pressing engagement elsewhere. The Datta family was proud in a lordly way, and concealed its misery under the cloak of pride. His friends, sons of wealthy families of Calcutta, drove up in the magnificent carriages to Naren's home to take him for drives and trips, never suspecting that his wasting away physically was due to any other cause than an exaggerated grief at the loss of his father.[12]

Vivekananda States:

Even before the period of mourning was over, I had to knock about in search of a job. Starving and barefooted, I wandered from office to office under the scorching noon-day sun with an application in hand, one of two intimate friends who sympathised with me in my misfortunes accompanying me sometimes. But everywhere the door was slammed in my face. This first contact with the reality of life convinced me that unselfish sympathy was a rarity in the world – there was no place in it for the weak, the poor and the destitute. I noticed that those who only a few days ago would have been proud to help me in any way now turned their face against me though they had enough to spare. Seeing all this, the world sometimes seemed to me to be the handiwork of the devil. Sometimes when I found that there were not enough provisions for the family and purse was empty, I would pretend to my mother that I had an invitation to dine out and remain practically without food. Out of self-respect I could not disclose the facts to others. My rich friends sometimes requested me to come to their homes or gardens and sing. I had to comply when I could not avoid it. I did not feel inclined to express my woes before them nor did they try, themselves, to find out my difficulties. In spite of all these troubles, however, I never lost faith in the existence of God nor in His divine mercy. Every morning taking His name I got up and went out in search of a job. One day my mother overheard me and said bitterly, "Hush, you fool, you have been crying yourself hoarse for God from your childhood, and what has He done for you." I was stung to the quick. Doubt crossed my mind. "Does God really exist," I thought, "and if so, does He really hear the fervent prayer of man? Then why is there no response to my passionate appeals? Why is there so much woe in His benign kingdom? Why does Satan rule in the realm of the Merciful God?" I was exceedingly cross with God. It was also against my nature to do anything secretly. So it was quite natural for me now to proceed to prove before the world that God was a myth, or that, even if He existed, to call upon Him was fruitless. Soon the report gained currency that I was an atheist and did not scruple to drink or even frequent houses of ill fame.[13]

Naren, however, had still the problem of maintaining his family. By working in an attorney's office and translating a few books, he earned just enough to live from hand to mouth, but there was no fixed or stable income to maintain his family. Naren then remembered that it was Sri Ramakrishna who had dissuaded him from taking *sanyas* at once and persuaded him to stay on in the material world. He also remembered the Master telling him that God listened to his prayers. So he hurried to Dakshineshwar and asked him to make an appeal on behalf of his starving family. Sri Ramakrishna told him that he could not make such demands and said: "Why don't you go and ask the Mother yourself?" Sri Ramakrishna told Naren that, "All your sufferings are due to your disregard of Her." Naren had loudly proclaimed his disbelief in idol worship in the past and had rebuked Rakhal for bowing before the image of Kali and desisted only after Sri Ramakrishna's intervention. How could he now go to that Kali and ask Her for a favour? So he again pleaded with the Master to pray to Her on his behalf. Sri Ramakrishna replied that he had done so repeatedly, but She did not grant his prayer because Naren had not accepted Her. He told Naren,

> Today is Tuesday, go to the Kali temple tonight, prostrate before the Mother and ask Her any boon you like. It shall be granted. Everything is in Her power to give.[14]

At this Naren's life-long resistance to idol worship broke-down. His own pressing need not only to find sustenance for his family but also to get freedom to renounce the world was urging him to follow Sri Ramakrishna's advice. Also, he had a profound belief in his Master's spiritual strength as also in his affection for him. So he agreed to do what he had been told. Once the decision was taken, disbelief gave way to belief in an almost instantaneous fashion and a strange sense of excitement filled him. What happened then is best told in Naren's own words:

> About nine o'clock the Master commanded me to go to the temple. As I went, I was filled with a divine intoxication. My feet were unsteady. My heart was leaping in anticipation of the joy of beholding the living Goddess and hearing her words.[15]

Days passed and his mind continued to waver between doubt and certainty. And then there took place an experience that was to settle his doubts and set him firmly on the path that had been chalked out for him by fate. It is best to quote Naren himself on this matter:

> One evening, after a whole day's fast and exposure to rain, I was returning home with tired limbs and a jaded mind; overpowered with exhaustion and unable to move a step forward, I sank down on the outer plinth of a house on the roadside. I can't say whether I was insensible for a time or not. Various thoughts crowded in on my mind, and I was too weak to drive them off and fix my attention on a particular thing. Suddenly I felt as if by some divine power the coverings of my soul were removed one after another. All my former doubts regarding the co-existence of divine justice and mercy and the presence of misery in the creation of a Blissful Providence were automatically solved. By a deep introspection I found the meaning of it all and was satisfied. As I proceeded homewards, I found there was no trace of fatigue in the body and the mind was refreshed with wonderful strength and peace. The night was well-nigh over. Henceforth I became deaf to the praise and blame of worldly people. I was convinced that I was not born like humdrum people to earn money and maintain my family. I began secretly to prepare myself to renounce the world like my grandfather.[16]

In the above narrative there is this interesting line: "Henceforth I became deaf to the praise and blame of the worldly people." To me, this seems to be only a partial recollection of his path towards being a *sanyasi*. Read on the surface, it only conveys his sense of disgust he had felt during those days. The deeper layer of this sentence suppresses the pain and bitterness it had caused. Much before we see this young man of a poor family in that state of being, i.e., as a *sanyasi*, he went through a process of self-empowerment, seeking self-worth and recognition of his spiritual stature, of his knowledge of scriptures, from the wealthy and powerful of the land. The memories of humiliation had drawn a faultline between his old self and the one struggling to be born. It was his self-assertion against that world of Indian elite which had despised him and in the process had deeply wounded the self-respect and pride of a poor young man. Also, I would like to suggest that his decision to go to Chicago to attend the Parliament of Religions was the culminating event of the same process of self-empowerment and self-assertion.

After the death of the Master, Naren, now in a *sanyasi's* attire, left Calcutta to roam around the various parts of India. He met the Maharaja of Alwar and brought home to him the falsity of the belief that what the Hindu was worshipping was stone or metal, while what he was really worshipping was the spirit of which it was a symbol. The Maharaja of Alwar, Shri Mangal Singh, became his devoted admirer. At Jaipur he met Sardar Hari Singh, the Commander-in-Chief of that state, who being a strong *Vedāntin* did not believe in images. He gave him a practical lesson why image-worship was important. From Jaipur, the Swami went to Ajmer and then to Mount Abu. There he met the private secretary to the Maharaja of Khetri who insisted on taking him to his prince. The Maharaja became a dedicated admirer and the Swami had to initiate him as his disciple. He spent several weeks at the palace teaching him not only philosophy but also inducing him to take interest in scientific training and research for the development of the country. One of the few instances of the Swami granting a personal favour was his agreeing to the Maharaja's request for a blessing that a son may be born to him.

At Porbandar, he spent 11 months helping its *Dewan*, Pandit Shankar Pandurang, to translate the *Vedas* and also started learning French. It was at Porbandar that the idea first came to him to go to the West to give them the message of his master. It was Pandit Pandurang who told him:

> Swamiji, I am afraid you cannot do much in this country, you ought to go to the west where people will understand you and your worth. Surely you can throw a great light on eastern culture by preaching the Sanatan Dharma.[17]

Towards the end of August 1892 he was in Poona where he was the guest of Bal Gangadhar Tilak. From Belgaum the Swami went to Bangalore where he met the *Dewan* of Mysore, Sir K. Seshadari Iyer, and was his guest for three to four weeks. Seshadari was so impressed by his spirituality that he said: "He must have been born knower of religion, otherwise how could he at such a young age have gained all this knowledge and insight? He introduced him to the Maharaja, Sri Chamarajendra Wadiyar. The Swami now became the guest of the state and spent considerable time closeted with the Maharaja. From Trivandrum, the Swami went on to Rameshawaram, stopping on the way at Madurai to meet the Raja of Rammand, for whom he had a letter of introduction. Swami reached Hyderabad on February 10, 1893. At the railway station about 500 people assembled to receive him including Nawab Bahadur Khurshid Jah, brother-in-law of the Nizam. The Nawab was so impressed by the Swami's discussion on the *Vedānta* that he offered him 1000 rupees to help him in his projected mission. He also met the Prime Minister of Hyderabad, Ashmen Jah, Maharaja Krishna Bahadur and Maharaja Shiv Raj Bahadur and all the three promised their support for his proposed mission to the west. The same afternoon, the Swami delivered a public lecture at the Mehboob College. His eloquence came as a revelation to his audience. More than 1000 persons came to the railway station to bid him farewell. He was only thirty years old. After his performance at the Mehboob College he lost his diffidence about his ability to sway large assemblies. On the birth of a son, the Maharaja of Khetri received the Swami prostrating himself before him in the presence of all the guests who had gathered to participate in the festivities. From the point of view of the Swami, I would like to suggest, this was a rare gesture which would have certainly enhanced his sense of pride in his knowledge of the scriptures, if not the spiritual attainments. At last, I would suggest, Swami could now afford to entertain the belief that India had finally seen the glimpse of a man whom Ramakrishna had told that he was a "blazing sun." This prostration of the Raja must have been the biggest boost to his ego. It is at this moment, I would like to stress, when one of the most important incident of his life occurred which completely deflated his ego.

One evening, the Maharaja being entertained with music by a rustic nautch-girl, sent a request to the Swami to join him. But the Swami declined on the ground that as a *sanyasi* he could not come. The singer, who was told this, was deeply grieved and sang, as though in reply, Surdas's famous *Bhajan*.

The power of the song could not have been resisted; and he joined the party. Perhaps it had suddenly brought back gushing the memories of his association with Ramakrishna, the true renouncer. Once again, his mind was illuminated with the power of his master's message. His desire for recognition and ambition to carry the message of *Vedānta* to the Western world had dimmed the radiance of his *bhakti*, even if momentarily. Why did he say "no" to Maharaja's message? Just because this woman, not looked upon respectfully by the society around her, was doing a job not to a Swami's liking? Or was it the fact that she was a woman? The Swami had forgotten his spiritual lesson.

The desire to seek the recognition of the powerful in Indian society and the ambitious idea of going to Europe seems to have overwhelmed Swamiji's thoughts.

Speaking of this incident later, the Swami observed: "That incident removed the scales from my eyes." He had also assumed the name of Vivekananda at the instance of Maharaja and retained it for the rest of his life.

The Parliament of Religions opened at the Art Institute, Chicago, on 11th September 1893. There were of course no orthodox Hindus and the only *sanyasi* present was Vivekananda. His simple words – "Sisters and Brothers of America" – evoked an outburst of enthusiasm that was fantastic.[18]

After his triumphal return from America and foundation of the Mission he warned fellow monks to have nothing to do with the rich but to treat the poor with loving care and to serve them joyfully:

> To pay respect to the rich and hang on them for support has been the bane of all monastic communities of our countries. A true sanyasi should scrupulously avoid them.[19]

The Swami had consistently struggled against his desires by carefully introspecting even the subtlest of his motivating impulses. As a result he was getting closer to fully imbibe the teachings of his Master. This led him to utter the profoundest of truths about human nature:

> I have long given up my place as the leader.... Behind my work was ambition, behind my love was personality, behind my purity was fear, behind my guidance my thirst for power.[20]

Naren's becoming of *sanyasin* in modern India should be viewed as an intellectual's struggle to evolve his love for the poor, insulted and humiliated, exploited and oppressed in a hierarchical and caste-ridden society. His mental tug-of-war to overcome his aloofness and generate compassion should be understood through a historical perspective, i.e., as a real struggle through the power relations of a society. The process unfolds as a series of shifting equilibriums of contradictory psychological forces within an individual's mind, many a times moving one step forward and then two steps backwards. His life had a paradigmic significance for the coming generations of political workers. Without imbibing something of this "Sanyasi Syndrome" none of these political workers would have prepared themselves to face the sufferings which participation in the national movement entailed. To be a true *sanyasin* is not only to be someone who was all the time aware of his deeper motivations but also someone who constantly struggled to liberate himself/herself from the inner shackles woven by the desire for worldly success and power.

As a college student, he came under the influence of Brahmo Samaj and its protest against certain features of orthodox Hinduism such as polytheist image-worship, divine incarnation, and the need for a guru, offering in its place a monotheistic religion without an intermediary. Naren was a tough rationalist. The movement had also espoused progressive social reforms such as the break-up of the caste system, recognition of the equality of man, education and emancipation of women, and raising the age of marriage. He became a member of one of its splinter groups known as Sadharan Brahmo Samaj. Till this point he could argue for the deliverance of the world from unreason through equality, liberty and fraternity.

The "rational Hinduism" constructed from the textual Sanskrit sources by Raja Rammohun Roy may have succeeded in facing up to the onslaught of the missionaries and other officials in the officialdom, but it had left many of his contemporaries completely dissatisfied. The leaders of Brahmo Samaj (founded in 1828) had accepted some of the criticisms of those who were carrying on polemic against Hinduism. Specifically, the denunciation of idolatory was one such criticism. The underlying assumption of such a project was a sort of schism, perhaps this could be even called colonial modernity, between the "intellectual make-up" and the "emotional make-up" of the newly emerging individual whose educational experience and rational knowledge had driven a wedge between his newly-acquired enlightenment reason and his inherited cultural traditions. In a sense, such an individual was faced with the threat to become a permanent outsider vis-à-vis his own cultural traditions. Instead of expounding and extrapolating a particular cultural system's inherent rationality from within, a task which was to be performed later on by Sri Ramakrishna and Gandhi, this educated individual, more or less, assumed its complete absence. But he could now posit the existence of such a rational cultural system in pristine purity in the distant past and then explain its contemporary absence through a process of historical degeneration. This new class of educated individuals had acquired history writing as a mode of thinking and had accepted its claim of discovering the truth about the past. The writings of the Orientalists produced with the help of Indians, mostly Brahmins who knew Sanskrit, led to the creation of a mental picture of a society in the distant past where there was hardly any disjunction between its theory and practice. Here was a time in the distant past when almost all the members of society lived according to *Dharma* and harmony prevailed. Obviously, it was a Utopian picture. But we all know too well the power of Utopia. All the deformities of cruel customs and ceremonies in contemporary society could now be understood and explained as successive distortions from this original state through a long period of history. Thus, the profoundly emotional experience of *Bhakti* did not and could not find a place in this reconstructed Hinduism strictly conforming to the criteria of instrumental rationality.

Actually this "split" was not and is not a simple one. Its complex composition embodies within it the impact of European enlightenment on the educated classes through the mediations of colonial rule and the intellectual domination of the West. In fact, this "split" is very much central to the very definition of a modernised individual in Indian society. This break in our consciousness due to contact with the West has led to the loss of our "cultural innocence". This encounter with the West is "historic", in the sense that now, we, the educated middle classes of this country, cannot experience impulses of the religious traditions of India by delibrately by-passing this frame-work. The presence of Ramakrishna was the only living and organic link this middle class had with the past. For many of them and this applies to us also, to uphold modernity or objectivity and impartiality of scholarship, was and is to uphold the psychological frame where the significance of this "emotional make-up" (sometimes dubbed as subjectivity or "the irrational") is almost minimised. This is how Edward Thorton had formulated this idea in a provocative manner: "As soon as (the Indians) become first-rate European Scholars, they must cease to be Hindoos."[21]

This sort of rational intellectual construct of Hinduism did not place any value on spirituality as a singularly personal and universal experience. The inspirational and solace-giving powers of this rational Hinduism could not but be very limited. As Gandhi used to say: "Great causes like these (a sustained struggle for swaraj) cannot be served by intellectual equipment alone, they call for spiritual effort or soul force." In other words, only a great source of spiritual power could have helped large numbers of this newly-emerged middle class, and Nehru returns to it again and again, in restoring its faith in the validity of the devotional scriptural traditions of its ancestors.[22] Only this could have overpowered the arrogance of instrumental rationality acquired from the contact with the West and provide an anchorage to its wavering and uncertain identity. What was required, for the defence of a many visage Hinduism, was not the rejection of its variety through logical systematisation into another monotheistic system on the model of Christianity. Such an effort involved the claim of the historical method to be able to furnish a criteria of selectivity which enabled the scholar to separate the pure principles of a religion supposed to be present at the point of its origin in the distant past. Contrary to this, what was required was the defence of this diversity and devotional spirituality. This is where Sri Ramakrishna comes into the picture.

This leads us to formulate India's contemporary predicament: Dogmatic Hindutva rejects it in the name of "Hinduism" and "cultural nationalism" while "hollow secularism" underplays its existence in the name of "separating religion from politics".

The shift from Brahmo ideas and ideals to the views of Vivekananda, i.e., from 1820s to 1890s occurs through two double moments: one internal and the other external. The external moment is born out of the realisation that the British rule involved racial discrimination, that they were being treated as inferior subjects if not as slaves. Exploitation of Indian resources and the many changes brought by its administration had caused famines thereby ruining the peasantry. 1,40,000 died of hunger and disease in the famine of 1864. It was during this time that Bankim was writing his first novel in English which was later on published as *Raj Mohan's Wife*. His sudden abandoning of this novel in English and shedding his ambivalence to produce a new novel in Bengali *Durgeshnandini* (1865) is considered as a sign of new emotion sprouting in the minds of Bengali youth. By 1874, we are told by many sources, that the government was no longer interested in recruiting Bengalis in the administration. Daily interaction with the administration left many of them humiliated. The nationalism born of their injured pride and emotional hurt, in turn, demanded a relatively more strident expression of nationalist sentiment from the intelligentsia. This shift in the tone of emerging nationalism, in turn, generated a new mood.

The internal moment seems to have been caused by the observation that reformed Hinduism in practice had led many of them to become only Christianised Hindus. This way of coming to terms with the religious traditions of their ancestors came to be considered more as an apology in the face of missionary onslaught. This analytical separation between the two moments did not mean that this is how they existed in the minds of the actors. In their experience they were certainly fused and entwined. Thus, the reconceptualistion of religious traditions by Vivekananda as distinguished from Brahmoism, could not be separated from the emerging national sentiment. In its very birth the thought of Vivekananda occupied wider spaces, considerable parts of which were laced with a sort of cultural nationalism, to the extent he passionately sought to answer the critics of "Hinduism". It is in such contexts that he seems to reconstruct Hinduism almost as a national religion.

Let us return to his biographical trajectory. For Vivekananda, this shift away from Brahmonism may have been caused by a deepening sense of frustration with other members of the intelligentsia but this alone cannot explain the making of a *sanyasin*, as Vivekananda came to be known later on. The widely recognised spiritual authority of Ramakrishna not only helped him to resolve his identity crisis but also enabled him to recover his faith in the validity of the religious traditions of India.

Ramakrishna (1836-1886) was born in a poor Brahmin family of Kamarpukur and apparently had mystic experience at a young age. He came to Calcutta in 1852 and in 1856 reluctantly took up the charge of priesthood at a new Kalighat temple. According to the "Gospel of Sri Ramakrishna" he was initiated into monastic life by an individual whose name was Totapuri. According to other sources, he immersed himself in ascetic traditions of popular Hinduism, under the tutelage of a woman known simply as the Bhairavi Brahamani, and a Punjabi Naga Sadhu by the name of Totapuri. It is said that it was during the experience of his spiritual visions that he completely identified with a personal deity, in this case, Kali and began to call himself, "a madman of God". In the popular traditions of India, *sadhus* have been credited with such extraordinary experiences since time immemorial.

Most sources agree that Ramakrishna acquired the bulk of his more famous disciples in the years between 1879 and 1885, a few years before he died. No one could have foreseen that he would, one day, become the Guru of *bhadralok* youth and icon revered by middle and even upper-class Bengalis. Obviously, the question comes to mind: what was it that made the *bhadralok* youth, who had enthusiastically imbibed the critical and scientific thinking under the westernising influence of the Company Raj, turn its face towards Ramakrishna Paramahansa?

In terms of mode of worship, Raja Rammohun Roy and the Brahmo Samaj had rejected what they call idolatry while, with the help of Ramakrishna, Vivekananda sought to come back to the same mode of worship. He criticised the excessive elevation of rationality to the exclusion of emotional legacy of his inherited cultural traditions. Thus, in two generations Indians of the Hindu fold had traversed a "circle of reason". What was a "reasonable" rejection for Rammohun, once again became an "unreasonable" attitude for Vivekananda. Once again, he sought to build a bridge between "the intellect" and "the emotion" by shifting the centre of gravity of Indianness within the indigenous cultural fields. This was also an attempt to restore equilibrium within the fractured modernity so that individuals could also bear their misfortunes in this world with equanimity. With his life and thought he managed to provide a new paradigm which could be employed as a counterpoise to human mind's unlimited secular consumerist tendencies. Let it not be misunderstood, I am not using this word "fractured modernity" in a disparaging manner. On the contrary, what I am suggesting is that this is perhaps the only way Indians could have become "modern" by cutting themselves completely from their cultural moorings. Thus, the emergence – or should one say the re-emergence – of a new and alternative Reason embodied in Vivekananda was now critiquing the instrumental rationality as well as re-asserting its validity in conformity with the religious traditions of India. Thus, the two "Reasons" were entwined in unity and struggle. This created a tension between two "reasons" at times, perhaps, even a split, within an individual psyche and outside in the society, when the dialogical character of this tension is either rejected or misunderstood. To counterpoise Raja Rammohun Roy to Vivekananda would certainly be a misunderstanding. They must be conceptualised as two points on the same "circle of reason" produced by specific experience of colonial modernity.[23] In the twentieth century these two "points" were called Nehru and Gandhi. India cannot fully express its uniqueness in the modern world or realise its full potential through only one of them. Historically speaking, the powers of these "two Reasons" have always contended and continue to contend even today for the heads and hearts of Indian middle classes, thereby causing shifts in their moods and sympathies. But these two discourses of modernity remain tied to each other despite their differences as long as they continue to uphold a dialogic relationship without being disrupted by violence in word and in deed. "Secular limits to cultural nationalism" go hand-in-hand with "cultural limits to secular politics".

NOTES AND REFERENCES

1. A.R. Desai, *Social Background of Indian Nationalism*, Bombay, Asia, 1959; Bipin Chandra, *Rise and growth of Economic Nationalim in India*, PPH, Delhi, 1972.
2. Karl W. Deutsch, *Nationalism and Social Communication: An Inquiry into the of Nationality*, Cambridge, MA, MIT Press, 1953; Vasudha Dalmia and Heinrich Von Stietener on *Representing Hinduism*, New Delhi, Sage, 1995; Madeleine, *Hinduism: The Anthroplogy of a civilization*, Delhi, OUP, 1989.
3. Carol A. Breckenvidge and Peter Vander Veer, *Orientalism and the Post-colonial Predicament: Perceptions on South Asia*, New Delhi, OUP, 1994.
4. John R. McLane (ed.), *The political awakening in India*, Englewood Cliffs, Prentice Hall, 1970.
5. B.R. Purohit, *Hindu Revivalism and Indian Nationalism*, Sagar Sathi Prakashan, 1965; P. Spratt, *Cultural and Personality: A Psycho-Analytic Study*, Bombay, Manaktalas, 1966.
6. V.K.R.V. Rao, *Swami Vivekananda*, Publications Division, Government of India, New Delhi, 2001, p. 6.
7. For details about the life and activities of Raja Rammohun Roy, see the following:

   Iqbal Singh, *Rammohan Roy*, Asia Publishing House, New Delhi, 1983.

Iqbal Singh, Asia Publishing House, New Delhi, 1987, Vol. 2 & Vol. 3.
Sophia Doloson Collet, *The life and Letters of Raja Rammohun Roy,* Sadharan Brahmo Samaj, Calcutta, 1962.
Bruce and Carlisle Robertson, *Raja Rammohun Roy: The father of Modern India,* OUP, Calcutta, 1995.
Hari Hara Das and Sasmita, Mahapatra, *The Indian Renaissance and Raja Rammohun Roy,* Pointer Publishers, Jaipur.
Satischandra Chakravarty (ed.), *The Father of Modern India* commemoration volume of the Rammohun Roy Centenary celebrations, 1933, Calcutta, November, 1935.

8. Swami Gambhirananda, *History of the Ramakrishna Math and Ramakrishna Mission,* Calcutta, Advaita Ashrama, 3rd edition, 1983. Isherwood, Christopher, *Ramakrishna and His Disciples,* Advaita Ashrama, 1965.
9. Makarand Paranjape (ed.), *Swami Vivekananda: Reader,* Penguin Books, India, 2005, Preface.

9a. V.K.R.V. Rao, *Swami Vivekananda, op. cit.,* p. 19.

9b. *Ibid.,* p. 20.

10. *Life of Swami Vivekananda by his Eastern and Western disciples,* in two volumes, Advaita Ashram, Kolkata, Volume 1, p. 88.
11. *Ibid.,* Vol. 1, p. 96.
12. Swami Nikhilananda, *Vivekananda: A Biography,* Calcutta, Advaita Ashram, 1971; Rajagopal Chattopadhyaya, *Swami Vivekananda in India: A corrective Biography,* Delhi, Motilal Banarsidass, 1999.
13. V.K.R.V. Rao, *op. cit.,* pp. 30-31.
14. *Life of Swami Vivekananda by his Eastern and Western Disciples,* Vol. 1, p. 127.
15. Quoted in V.K.R.V. Rao, *Swami Vivekananda, op. cit.,* p. 34.
16. *Ibid.,* p. 32.
17. *Life of Swami Vivekananda by his Eastern and Western Disciples,* Vol. 1, p. 295.
18. For address at the Parliament of Religions, see Makarand Paranjape, *Swami Vivekananda: Reader,* Penguin Books, India, 2005, pp. 40-60.
19. V.K.R.V. Rao, *Swami Vivekananda: The Prophet of Indian Socialism,* Ministry of Information and Broadcasting, New Delhi, 1979, p. 107.
20. *Ibid.,* p. 111.
21. Quoted by Gauri Viswanathan in *Masks of Conquest,* p. 21, Edward Thornton, Parliamentary Papers, 1852-53, 31:36).
22. Amiya P. Sen, *Swami Vivekananda,* New Delhi, OUP, 2000. Basu Shamita, *Religious Revivalism as Nationalist Discourse: Swami Vivekananda and New Heumanism in Nineteenth Century Bengal,* New Delhi, OUP, 2002; Arun Kumar Biswas, *Swami Vivekananda and the Indian quest for Socialism,* Calcutta, Firma KLM, 1986; William Radice

(ed.), *Swami Vivekananda and the Modernization of Hinduism*, New Delhi, OUP, 1998.

23. The life of Vivekananda embodied the message that religion could help people to appropriate the ideals and enthusiasms of modernity by translating them from an alien secular idiom into a larger mythology and spirituality that they could understand and make their own.

2

Vivekananda: His Religious Vision and Indian Society

Dharmendra Goel

In this note I shall seek to put together in brief outline the pivotal concerns of Swami Vivekananda, his religious vision, passion and mission. He rekindled the flame of awakened Indian society, that had been reeling under accumulated sins of atrophy, cruel fossilisation of *Vedāntic* tradition and alienation generated by the onslaughts of medieval Muslim and recent English rulers.

Let it be recognised steadfastly that in his day Vivekananda had no political agenda of either arousing the Indian society against the British sovereign, or to abolish the different social and political restraints that the Raj had sedulously imposed since it took control of Indian life, economy and polity. It was a gradual expansion from the British-captured Bengal in 1757 after planting Mir Zafar as the Nawab of East, after Clive's victory of Plassey. By the time Vivekananda was born in 1862, Bengal had lived with the English rule, much ahead of the rest of India, by almost a century. So the predecessors of his community had been exposed to the ways of English education, administration and commercial practices in which they had been allowed to share as junior partners. Most leaders of the Bengal renaissance looked towards the great stirrings in their age owing to the bounties of rule of law, orderly conduct of functioning of administration, and possibility of sharing authority by acquiring English education in addition to classical learning. Unlike the peasant recruited from the upper gangetic plains, the Bengali *Bhadraloka* looked upon Christian missionaries and their evangelism as some new leavening that could enrich their own somewhat stagnant social practices and beliefs. This is as much true of Raja Rammohun Roy, as that of Maharishi Debendra Nath Tagore, Pt. Ishwara Chander Vidyasagar, Keshab Chandra Sen and last but not the least even of the great master of Bengali language – Bankim Chandra Chatterji![1]

Once the Raj had firmly stabilised the Indian society after the Mutiny (1857) by the royal proclamation of Empress Victoria (1858) assuring every Indian equal right as subject of the British Crown and fullest liberty of religious conviction and freedom of its observation, consistent, of course, with morality and good sense, these Anglo-philes in the *Bhadraloka* fell for Westernising their faith in the shadow of Christian ideas. Brahmosamaj desired to shape older *Vedāntic* traditions in the light of Christian doctrines. A point that slowly emerged that ordinary Hindu sensibility revolted against such overlaying of Christian beliefs about man and God.[2]

Despite recognising the merits of Western ideas, a split was soon visible even among the educated Bengalis.[3] The youthful preacher Keshab Chandra Sen, Christian convert Benimadhav Upadhyaya and the still louder radical Michael Madhusudan Dutta and D. Rozario wished to hit the orthodox *Pundits* hard, to an extent that seemed to abolish Sanatana Hinduism lock-stock and barrel while Debendra Nath Tagore, Vidyasagar, Bankim Babu wanted this heady wine to be mellowed by *Vedāntic* wisdom and accepted only such ideas of modernity as could help Hindu society out of its various old ills.[4]

In the midst of these perfervid debates appeared the titan figure of Ramakrishna Paramahansa, who with his ecstasies and transparent piety lent a lustre to the ancient wisdom and won most of his contemporaries, with his benign humanism.[5]

To him came one day the bright starry-eyed Narendra Nath Dutta asking point blank, could the Savant make him realise God? Unhesitatingly Paramahans nodded, "Yes". He pushed the lad's head under Ganga's current till he felt choked, indicating to him the degree of struggle, needed to know God. It must match the intensity of effort required to get over choking. That day was born the prime disciple of the humble *Rishi* and *Paramahans Bhagwan* Ramakrishna, the formidable Swami Vivekananda.[6] Rest is folklore of Hinduism.

Let me refer to the year 1893, the year the legendary Hindu Swami Vivekananda had attended the World Congress of Religions, at Chicago and made his captivating and triumphal address at the Congress and subsequently at other audiences in the United States, and elsewhere. The folklore and the voyage gave great cheer not only to the *Bhadraloka* in Bengal but it generated deep vibrations amongst middle class urban centres throughout the sub-continent. Even the *mofussil* masses of common people ruled by Indian princes in states innocent of rule of law felt his glory as their own. Swamiji had been a great wayfarer. He had before going for this Congress at Chicago and after his world travel crossed and recrossed the sub-continent from Srinagar, Almorah to Kanyakumari and from Sindh to Assam more than once. In his short life this itinerant preacher made his vibrant young voice the call of an ardent Hindu. He had the greatest desire to see the reawakening of the Hindu soul to a new dawn.[7]

Swamiji was no elitist scholar, though a voracious *pundit,* he was moved by the most intense desire to see his countrymen come out of their utter casteist distortions and superstitions. He hated abject serfdom to the colonial civilisation and the merciless penury that feudal oppression had imposed on peasantry from times immemorial short of being an incendiary or a subverter. He was no idle quiescent *Rishi* like Paramahans or several others. He was probably an early version of Gandhi, who was still in the making![8]

Yes, fortuitously, the year 1893 saw another small event far away from the spotlights of world society. A certain coolie Barrister Mohandas Karam Chand Gandhi on an assignment from his Gujarati Vora clients boarded a first class railway coach at Pietr Maritzburg to reach Durban. Another co-passenger got infuriated to an uncontrollable anger on seeing a black man, belaboured the frail Barrister from the Queen Victoria's Inner Temple Courts, and threw him on the dirt track along with his bags despite firm protests about his rights as a British subject and his valid first-class ticket. Nobody came to succour this young person in the dread of this dark night of his soul. It is such quirks of History that disclose how humanity transcends all premeditated ruts. Yes, this frail lad must have undergone a million inner transformations, to be reborn as the *Satyagrahi,* who was to change the millions later over the globe and pull down an Empire on which sun used never to set.[9]

Let me underscore yet another quirk of this very interesting year 1893. An outstanding holder of first rank in Classical Tripos

(Greek & Latin) as well as the bright topper of the coveted Indian Civil Service of that year from University of Cambridge was denied his appointment by the Secretary of State for India, U.K. for flimsy reasons. He made his tryst with destiny by going to a *mofussil* College (newly started by Gaikwad of Baroda), threw away his European being, sought to be a reborn Hindu, wearing coarsest cotton, lying on an iron cot, seeking mystery of being, *Vedas* and Brahman, I mean Yogi Aurobindo.[10]

In the obscure periodical[11] the young *Sadhak* was pouring out his heart, mind and soul to restore the lost glory of the Aryan race and the Holy Mother; while equipping himself with the sacred traditions of *Veda*, *Vedānta*, Yoga, and *tantra* in the late nineties, before he was to launch the great fight for his *Bande Mataram* from Kolkata.

Yogi Aurobindo still in early youth had a resolute working agenda for his three clear targets: to see God face to face; to feel as part of his own physical body as one and all his fellow Indian men, women, and children; and lastly to see Mother India liberated of every trace of White Imperialism.

No doubt, with that sort of will, heart, mind, intellect and soul Sri Aurobindo could dazzle and astonish men, scholars, patriots and saints alike everywhere by his scintillating addresses, even by his meanest of comments in his writings.[12] He was a revolutionary amongst intellectuals, and the highest seer among political activists of Hindustan, such as Sachin Sanyal, Lala Lajpat Rai, Hardayal and Bal Gandadhar Tilak. He could set the Hooghly on fire to let scores of revolutionaries plunge into fire at one little swish of his pen; yes, it literally happened.

One who had mastered his own mother tongue quite late in his life, he could excel in almost any Indian language he picked up in amazingly short period – be it Sanskrit, Gujarati, Hindi or Marathi. Of course, Western literary critics like Gate-keeper of England, Victorian Culture recognised qualities of his English poetics. Tagore himself, though senior to him by almost a decade composed poems in his honour, a testimony of his high esteem (Ravi Babu had been liberal in this; he had written panegyrics for Gandhi and Guru Gobind, Sivaji and Subhas as well). But soon Sri Aurobindo escaped into his *Sādhanā* to integrate his historical personality into the supra-mundane.[13] That is another riddle of that man's quest.

* * *

Having underlined the episodic value of the year 1893 in grasping Indian society in the life of 20th century, and the three perspectives of Swami Vivekananda, Gandhiji and Sri Aurobindo who provided very pivotal though distinctive impulses to it, it is important to have some real understanding of India under the Raj at its high noon.

Politically and socially it was an age's servile submission to the white imperialists by both rising middle classes, in areas of older British settlements around metros of Bombay, Madras and Calcutta, as well as docile Indian princes in the rest of India. The fate of the under-classes everywhere was miserable in extreme. But for some higher intellectual pursuits most aspiring civil and military middle class was mesmerised by the slogan of the Raj: "You Indians decide whether you wish to be ruled by the sword OR by the Pen, British Lion is capable of the both."

Sir Henry Lawrence – (Lahore Equestrian Statue at the Mall)

It was equally believed by most educated Bengalis with the great Bankim Babu that it was providential that we got English to let our rude and coarse medieval society emerge in the light of Western science, ideas of human dignity and above all equality under law. Most sincerely not only Bankim Babu, Raja Rammohun Roy, Pt. Vidyasagar, but persons as different as Sir Saiyyed of Aligarh (who felt threatened by Bengali exodus into Ganga Jamni Doab), Pundita Ramabai, and Jyotirba Phule later Gopal Krishna Gokhale and Dr. D.D. Karve sought redemption of their differently oppressed constituents through supplications of British patronage and their guidance.[14]

All believed in graduating to earn the good grace of administration that could alone ensure safety of the lamb along with the various kinds of rapacious wolves of whom the earlier generations of 18th century Indians and even before Ghadar of 19th century had traumatic memories.[15]

A brief review of the last quarter of 19th century shows it didn't matter to most, such aspiring *Bhadraloka* that everywhere if Indian handicrafts were ruined, millions of Indians had been carted out as indentured *coolies* across the seas to the Empire's work-stations. While other millions were oppressed by planters to cultivate on their lands, tea, jute, indigo and coffee for European planters to promote their global commodity trade. In addition to these hundreds of thousands peasants perished by starvation over recurring famines since 1871, when the British had the first census King George V had his "Dilli Darbar" in 1911. A decimation of almost 25 per cent of all Indians alive in 1871.[16] It could not stir favour seekers of among the rising genre of patronage in the Raj establishment be at the lowest levels of *mabaalnabis* and *subedar* in the constabularies of the Empire.[17] Nobody could be more callous than our Raj underlings as and when it dealt with the dirt poor of the Mofussil.[18]

The above, of course, is very insufficient representation of India on the Diamond Jubilee of Queen Empress Victoria of the state of the subalterns. One has to sieve through loads of records and facts that cannot be done here. But one could just refer to the horrifying conditions of widows as portrayed by rta Ramabai,[19] and Pariahs by Abbe Dubois and Shudras as best recognised in that period by Jyoti Rao Phule and later by Dr. B.R. Ambedkar.[20] It is to no purpose here ever to try record the issues that are being debated by idealists like Gandhi, Aurobindo, Bhagwandas, Vivekananda, Tilak, Coomaraswamy throughout 20th century against subaltern spokespersons like B.R. Ambedkar, Ramaswami Naicker, R.M. Lohia and Kancha Alaiah, who fail to see any merit either political, social or ethical in the espousal of *Varna* concepts for justifying unequal stratification of Hindu caste-mentality. It was even worse in the days of Vivekananda; he was appalled by it more and more as he saw with his own eyes the havoc of untouchism as the hallmark of degenerate caste-system (*Collected works*, Vol. I, p. 44). Yet Vivekananda was like Gandhi, fully convinced of the virtues of *Swadharma* (see, Vol. 5, p. 214) and the possibility of a Pariah and *Chandal* graduating to rise to the highest Brahmin by spiritual evolution. Moon shine, indeed. All this kind of moonshine, unity lately very popular with Manu's followers, now it stands wholly denied by Ambedkar, who thinks it to be the ideology of the Tyranny of the twice-born.

* * *

It is perhaps time to compare Swami Vivekananda, his *Bhadraloka* renaissance mentality with still regressive thoughts of people elsewhere in other parts. This shows the deep differences in the ways of Bengali society that had accepted English hegemony and identified it with the gateway to its redemption in catching up with Western enlightenment and probably gaining preference in lower echelons of authority after long period of subordination under the Moghuls. Mostly it was seen as the gateway to cultural rebirth, through ideas of reason, utilitarianism and human progress as the ruling impulse of industrialism of Europe against time-warped traditions of agrarian privilege and suppression of peasantry by feudal privileges amongst indigenous states.

This shows how, despite several generations of the onslaught of Western civilisation, the diverse mental dispositions of significant cultural groups had remained widely disparate. Of course, besides such multi-tiered mind-sets we have to recognise the deep fissures in pursuit of sectional interests as noticed in the course of 1857. Neither the martyrdom of Mangal Pande[21] of Barrackpore, nor the great heroism of Lakshmi Bai could evoke a response among the people of South, Bengali *Bhadraloka* or amongst the Punjabis. No response then, not even now, among all of them.[22] Sardars, perhaps, had a legitimate grievance against Hindustanee troopers, who had been campaigning against Khalsa *Durbar* in previous decades under Company Bahadurs, with great insensitivity; that Sardars, after being inducted by Lawrence *Sahib* in British service, paid back Hindustanees – or *Purbias* – in their own coin, or at last this is what WOGS so legitimise for their later flunkeydom to this day in 21st century. So were other Indian princes.

Quite contrary to the attitude of 19th century, Bengali intellectuals as well as even writers after a century today who have highly distorted reading of the our First War of Independence. They usually extol the virtues of English enlightenment and cautious *Babudom* in even fiction written after the events in the 20th century[24] by them.

Be this as it may, the attitude of Swami Dayanand Saraswati, the founder of Arya Samaj, was highly robust and contrary to most middle class pusillanimity that marks our cultural history. It is known that as a young *Vedic* scholar he had actually fought with rebels in 1857. An important interaction, as recorded between him and the rebel Rana Benimadhav on the bank of Ganga in Avadh who was then being hunted by Colonel Neal's pursuing troop's informers – Rana asked the sage what sins Aryan race had committed that it was being so licked by *Firangis*?

It is reported that Swamiji, had responded laconically: "untouchability, and female infanticide,".[25]

It thus goes to establish a point about our Indian social reality, that it is not merely the case of cultural difference or multiculturalism alone. But it is the time-warped fragments of non-contemporaneous ideologies of different epochs that are confronting against their own will by forces of colonial history to subsist and distort each other and prevent true fusion. Such superimposition of different time-warps are not capable of providing even a viable syncretism, what to speak of *Advaitic Tadatmaya* as Swami Vivekananda or other Brahmo's inspired renaissance hoped to forge.[26] After talking briefly of Swami Vivekananda's idea of realisation and social reform I would appraise his long-term impact on such cultural importunities as we face, even today, despite all the great veneration and idolisation he had commanded amongst Hindu – nationalists in the 20th century and after.

* * *

ADVAITA, REALISATION AND PARAMAHANS

Romain Rolland writes in his life of Vivekananda: "with Vivekananda everything is a paroxysm of pride, of faith, or of love; under each of his words can be felt the brazier of the burning *Atman* – the Soul God. It is then easy to understand that exalted revolutionary individualism to use this flame in social incendiarism and this is a danger that the successors of the great Swami who have charge of his heritage have often had to avoid.... Further, the tenacious and unwavering of Gandhi's action mixed up with politics sometimes becomes their leaders, but Vivekananda's heroic passion (that of Krishna was battle) rejects politics... the followers of Ramakrishna have kept themselves aloof from the campaigns of Gandhi." In fact, there was no such danger after all as noted earlier was a committed follower of Advait – despite the lure of activism (a la – Tilak, Gandhi and Aurobindo). He writes in his *Karma Yoga Mayavati*, (1954, p. 406)

> ... So long as the dream that you are a body exists, you are bound to see yourself as being born and dying and so will the dream vanish that you are being born and dying, but as soon as that dream vanishes will the other dream that there is a universe vanish that every thing we now see as Universe will appear to us as God ... and God will appear to be internal as our own self.[27]

This shows how Swami Vivekananda had the duality in his spiritual heritage, while he wished to see Indian social life regenerated; he could not for a moment live without the luminosity he had encountered in his spiritual awakening with Ramakrishna.

Swami Vivekananda would love to encapsule the various strands that he admired in the vast pantheon of Indian spiritualism, from the hoary Buddha, Kabir, Nanak, or the recent Bengal *savants* like Raja Rammohun, Bankim Babu, Keshub Sen, his friend Bandhu Madhav Upadhyaya and the social activist and great scholar Pt. Ishwar Chandra Vidya Sagar.[28] Apart from *Vedāntic* idealism, Vivekananda also was fully aware of *Tantrism, Raj Yoga,* and other forms of *Bhakti Yoga, Sakta* sacrifices, popular Vaisnavism, and even animistic cults of popular grass root Hinduism. He was, unlike Dayanand, allergic to refute any of these. In that sense, he was a true Henotheist.[29]

Vivekananda wanted to integrate the vast strands of Hindu traditions, within which he visualised Buddha, Kabir, Gaurang, Nanak, even Islam, popular grass-root animistic faith of masses, as well as the traditions of *Tantra, Raj Yoga,* Vaishnavism and thousand local cults of Hindu communities. He saw them as part of *Vedānta*. This is so natural to the Oriental mind as has been noted that different gods have been seen to hold the highest rank by turns. It is not possible to insist on consistency of monistic rigourism as in the Judeo-Christian theology. Vivekananda and his own mentor Ramakrishna had such flexible veneration true to the later spirit of Gandhi's "Sarva Dharma Samabhava".

Quite anticipating the arguments of Gandhi, Aurobindo, Ananda Coomaraswamy by almost a generation or two, and unlike Dayanand, Vivekananda was for purging the caste of its aberrations (Vol. IV, p. 299-300). He writes: "I have no partiality for any party this caste question, because I know it is a social law and is based on diversity of Guna – Karma." (See Vol. VI – 394-5). He wanted reconstruction of *Varnas*. He was aware as he candidly records:

> No religion on Earth preaches the dignity of humanity in such a lofty strain as Hinduism, and no religion on Earth treads upon the neck of the poor and the low in such a fashion as Hinduism.

(Vol. V, p. 15). He was fully conscious of contemporary Hindu degeneracy and categorically castigates:

We are neither Vedantists, most of us now, nor Pauranikas, nor Tantrikas we are just "Don't Touchists". Our religion is in the Kitchen. Our God is the cooking pot, and our religion is "Don't touch me, I am holy". And if this goes on for another century every one of us will be in lunatic asylum (Vol. IV 298).

He writes,

My heart ached when we think of the poor, the low, in India ... they feel the blows showered upon them by a cruel society ... They have forgotten they too are men ... Religion is not at the fault ... Logical development of Hinduism-Buddhism ... nerved with Lion's courage by their sympathy for the poor and the fallen and the down-trodden- ... go down the length and breath ... the gospel of equality... (*op. cit.* 15) ... if you cannot do this then fie upon your education and culture, and fie upon your studying Vedas and Vedānt. (*ibid.*, p. 381).

He is such a revolutionary hued in the garb of a *Sanyasin*, no wonder so many – Romain Rolland (*op. cit.*), Shamita Basu (*op. cit.*) and Tapas Raychowdhury (Radice *op. cit.*) – see him as someone who saw the gleanings of Gandhi's *Daridra Nārāyaṇa* early. He was fusing *Advaita, Raj Yoga* and highest social activism.[32] Yet he was not willing to give up Hinduism for all its faults, even by a millimetre. He would himself be the paragon of Vedic renaissance. He disagreed completely with *Pundita* Rama Bai in Boston in 1894 a discussion on women. In fact, Sister Nivedita, his disciple, defends Hindu traditions on widows. Despite her own services to their cause, she had inculcated immense Hindu pride by pointing out to the great widows like Lakshmi Bai and Ahilya.[33]

Swamiji was a great upholder of ideas of *Swadharma, Sevabhava* and the sacred order of *Vedic* tradition. He was not willing to let the Hindu spiritualism die for any modern rationalistic theory,[34] (Vol. III, pp. 173-74).

* * *

As written earlier, Swami Vivekananda fired the down and out middle class Indians to a high sense of cultural eminence. Perhaps, a certain degree of slowly emerging sense of nationalism quite outside the limits of Bengali *Bhadraloka* also accompanied his liberal, rationalistic humanism which refused to denigrate various cults and practices of the population of the continent. He gave his peers a cultural identity.

No doubt, he very definitely cracked through deep schisms that divided at least caste Hindus in different regions of British India. Perhaps, after 1893, and before Tilak, Aurobindo and Lala Lajpat Rai fired a spirit of independence in the wake of the division of Bengal. Swami's speeches and movements between 1893 and turn of the century till he passed away in 1902 articulated most significantly a high sense of Hindu pride and nationalism.

But after one hundred years, now, I fully agree with Tapas Raychaudhuri (*op. cit.*) that votaries of jingoistic *Hindutva* are wholly unjustified in appropriating his own universal nationalism that embraced much of Islamic civilisation as well. While he did invoke *Raja Yoga, Advaita* and the cults of Bengal Vaishnavism, he was opposed to Brahmanic hegemony in every sense. He was often branded as a Kayastha and a Sudra for crossing seas, for sporting *Sanyas* and generally being critical of archaic Brahmanical social practices. He was not at all a revivalist. He was a humane voluntarist, who loved every bit of his people and their past. Unlike Keshub Sen, Raja Rammohun Roy, Michael Madhusudan Dutta, his old college friend Bandhu Madav Upadhyaya, he wanted reassertion of *Vedāntic* Hinduism purged of strictly familiar rituals and casteism that had restricted the public domain to the minimal and issues concerning Indian social sphere confined to casteist affiliations only. He could not have accepted Dr. Albert Schvitzar's denunciation that the Hindu idea of *Moksha* was life-denying and overall egoistic. Be as it may, he was not willing to concede that Christian Mission could be the sole votary of the oppressed and could not but loudly denounce like Gandhi and Tilak after him even such noble efforts of a person like Pundita Ramabai in Boston, where he was dared by her regarding the state of Hindu women. Of course, he had great admiration for the nobility of her mission but would have agreed with the obituary note of regret on her passing away which saw her as someone who succumbed to the temptation of the missionaries:

> ... such an intelligent determined and enterprising woman's achievements helped not the Hindu Society but foreign missionary organisations ... she could have proved her capacity for organisational work while remaining a Hindu. But unfortunately this was not to be! (11th April 1922, *Kesari*).

This shows the cracks in the very distinct paradigms of rising Indian middle classes. Gandhi and Tilak and Aurobindo would also denounce social reforms if it came from colonial sources.[35] Tilak, unlike Phule, did not agree to ask the white masters to divide lower classes against Brahmins.

The seductions of abiding Sanatan Dharma and its hoary glories had captivated a large number of highly honest and dedicated *Savants,* yet we cannot fail to set aside the hard and cruel treatment meted out by the patriarchical ideology of Brahmins, especially as far as untouchables and women are concerned. This juxtaposition of warped mind-sets of old times and civilisation continued to distort the new social awareness. For the period of whole of 20th century this struggle of paradigms has continued and continues even today.

Ambedkar denounced the traditions of ancient epics in the following candid manner in: (works, Vol. 4, p. 156) *The State of Aryan Society,*

> This practice prevailed so extensively that the Devas came to regard prelibation in respect of Aryan Women as their prescriptive Right ... Avadam. The laya Hoame which is performed in every Hindu Marriage ... in the Ashwalyan Grahya Sutras ... Devas if they were dissatisfied with the compensation could claim the woman ... there was no rule of chastity of maidens. A girl could have sexual intercourse with and also progeny from anybody ... Surya cohabiting a Mare, the most hideous instance is that of the woman having sexual intercourse with the horse in the Ashwamedha Yajna (p. 157).

No doubt the myth of Sanatana Hindutva was being questioned right in Swami Vivekananda's own decades. Let me quote the views of Jyotirao Phule, admired by D.D. Kabeise, M.G. Ranade and G.G. Agarkar, a prominent social thinker and colleague of Tilak and Gokhale in Pune.

D. Keer writes (*op. cit.*) of Phule:

> Frankly and boldly he preferred British rule to Brahmin Rule he had such a dread and hatred of Brahmin Rule that he totally failed to look at the revolution from the broader angle ... he ageed with *Aitihasik Prastawana* of V.K. Prajwade (p. 356) ... Rajwade condemned the leaders of that generation as worthless men who were disgrace to the society and nation! At the same time be branded the revolutionary leaders as a brand of thoughtless men who were of more philosophic and world negating bent, than realistic ....

Agarkar agreed with Phule (*Essays*, Part I, p. 151):

the existing times were favourable for social reforms God was merciful lent thought to the Shudras, that he frustrated the attempts of Nanasaheb Peshwa.

Jyotirao felt: "It was God's wish, he observed that Nanasaheb Peshwa was defeated in the Revolt of 1857" (p. 119, Keer, *ibid.*).

... Later Dr. Ambedkar waged a war with the orthodox in India for two decades and more over the abolition of untouchability and the establishment of Social equality (*ibid.*, p. 39).

Phule was socially more revolutionary than Gandhi.

... he led peasant and barber's agitations. Both were truth seekers ... Truth alone Triumphs. Jyotirao was as harsh as TRUTH itself. He would not allow any of his lieutenants to compromise truth. (*ibid.* 237).

What has been seen by Pundita Ramabai, Jyoti Rao Phule, G.G. Agarkar and B.R. Ambedkar was the broken column of *Sanatan* Hinduism that was being propped by artificial life support systems rhetorically provided by Aurobindo and Vivekananda. It didn't work then; today it is passe.

This juxtaposition of the fractured inheritance in the subcontinent with warped and distorted mind-sets has not yet settled even in 21st century. In the 20th century as the British historian C.A. Baylay (*Indian Society and the Making of the Indian Empire, Cambridge,* 1988) argues:

It was to be India of a mercenary army whose career as an overseas "fire-brigade" for the British Empire had already begun in earnest with the campaign in China and Southasia (p. 134) ... movements for self-respect amongst lowly people appealed to and were forwarded by well placed and relatively prosperous farmers whose activities only became visible once the infant vernacular press began to report them ... other categories such as Hindu or Muslim revivalism. Still others began quite early to contribute a rural popular base to what it is inadequately called Indian Nationalism ... which consolidated through the great changes ... (p. 206).

For the last half a century since 1947, Ambedkar and his Dalit Neo-Buddhist struggled against Harijan syndrome of classic *Sanatan Dharma* of Gandhiji. R.M. Lohia,[36] in his own inimitable manner, pushed for other backward castes – the Bahujans – against the overarching *Manuvadi Sanatan* Hinduism. Some of these certainly contain Swami Vivekananda's radical *Advaita* up from the grass-roots. However, Gandhi's *Harijan* and Vivekananda's *Daridra Nārāyaṇa* fail to fascinate the subaltern imagination. They wish to blast through any façade of the hegemonic Brahmanism – so as to let poor, indigenes, women, sudras, minorities, and Tribals to declare "Buddham Sharnam Gachhami".[37]

NOTES AND REFERENCES

1. See, *The Indian Middle Classes* (Their Growth in Modern Times), B.B. Misra, Royal Institute of International Affairs, Oxford University Press, London, 1961, Chapter VI and VII, pp. 147-210. The Educated Middle classes, Author Records Missionaries" agenda, "... the cause of Christianity ... reported its progress by an endeavour to exploit their poverty ... measure the extent of their success by the number of converts so Gained ... p. 201.
   On the other hand, Raja Rammohun Roy in his *Memoirs* was convinced of the wretched state of his contemporary Hindu ethos, as well Bankim Chandra Chatterji who in his classic *Anand Math* makes his *Sanatanas* extol the virtues of white man's science and civilisation, to be avidly emulated by author's readers.
   On the contrary, the Imperialist Agenda candidly set out to make " ... a class of persons who may be interpreters between us and the Millions whom we govern, a class of persons Indian in Blood and Colour but English in tastes and opinions, in morals and intellect...." p. 729, Macaulay's *Minute to Governor General* ... 7th March 1935 = Macaulay's Prose and Poetry selected, G.M. Young Rupert Hort Davies, Solo Square, London, 1952. He was wholly contemptuous of Oriental wisdom: He wrote, "A single shelf of a good European Library was worth the whole native literature of India and Arabia," p. 722, (Third para, *op. cit.*). His remarks on *Babus* and Bengali *Bhadraloka* were even more derisive. It appears highly ironic and derogatory to Indian's sense of national pride that our Renaissance *Savants* were over-eager to get into some reflected shine of their white overrulers!
2. J.N. Farpihar's Herford Lumson Lectures, "Modern Religious Movements in India", Macmillan, 1929, reviews the different currents and response of different sections of Brahmo Samaj, see Shivnath Shastri's *History of Brahma Samaj* and Pt. Sita Nath Tattvabhushan's *Social Reforms in Bengal*", pp. 16, 21.
   Ibid., p. xxi, Farquhar refers to great deeds of early missionaries like David Hare, in service to Lepers, Mr. D.W. Bettune's to girl's education, and Mountstuart Elphinstones" work of education in

Mumbai in early 19th century. See the turmoils and troubles over overlay of Christianity in Keshab Sen's New – dispensation and Maharishi Tagore's innate *Sanatanist* vision, p. 44 (Nab Bishan), see Keshab Ch. Sen's *Lectures in India*, p. 299.
(*Ibid.*) Tarquhar argues on p. 65, that Keshab died in 1884, a Christian.

3. When Keshab Sen in 1881 presented himself as a prophet the Brahmo Samaj lost most of its Hindu admirers who accepted the mellow wisdom of Ramakrishna at Dakshineshwar, see *ibid*. p. 57.
4. *Ibid.*, pp. 65, 69.
5. Bankim Chatterji, Maharishi Tagore, Shivnath Shastri, Pt. Ishwar Chandra Vidyasagar, and host of other Hindu stalwarts accepted modernity and English education. Still they wanted to enrich the ancient *Vedic* roots that had been maimed in the Medieval Age. By no means they were willing to let radicals like Derozio and Michael Madhusudan Datta Gibe the *Sanatan Dharma*.
6. The attitude of Vivekananda towards Paramahans Ramakrishna was ecstatic, nothing shorter than that he regarded him the complete *Avtar*. See *Biography of Vivekananda* – by Swami Nikhilananda, Cal., 1987, p. 296.
7. See *Bibliography of Vivekananda*, by Swami Nikhilananda, pp. 288, 290. He was for integrating all the communities living on the Indian sub-continent. He believed that: "for our Motherland a junction of the two great systems, Hinduism and Islam: Vedānta's Brain and Islam's Body is the only hope."
He wanted a synthesis of all religions including that of *Koran* and *Bible* into *Vedānta* as redemption, *Collected Works* Vol. II, p. 333. See Romain Rolland.
The Life of Vivekananda, Punjab Lectures in 1897, Footnote 1...." Religion being realisation and not any doctrinal affirmation." It is natural that the same verity changes when it is adapted to the different needs of the most diverse human natures." p. 188, see also (*op. cit.*) p. 236, wherein Romain Roland finds him nearer Gandhi.
8. See *Collected Works*, Vol. V, pp. 145-46 (Vol. VII, p. 150). In these lectures Swamiji characterises himself as a socialist.
9. The mystery of Gandhi's transformation from a Barrister to the *Satyagrahi* is an axial event that has dominated 20th century global consciousness. See its portrayal in R. Attenborugh's celebrated movie "Gandhi", or Shyam Benegal's "Making of the Mahatama" – the fullest documentation is in a Hindi text "Pahla Girimitia" by Giriraj Kishore, 2000, Bhartiya Gyan Peeth, New Delhi.
10. This great yogi has been the moving stars of the resistance to Banga-Bhanga and the Young Messiah at Surat Congress in 1907

amongst senior statesmen such as "Bal-Pal-Lal" of the extremist section that brought the split from the constitutionalists like G.K. Gokhale, S.N. Banerjee, Feroze Mehta. See *A Memorial*, the novel text of his first student Kanihyalal M. Munshi who eventually became the famous writer and the legal Luminary, "Swapna Drasta".

11. Aurobindo's early writings (*Collected Works*, Vol. I and II) show his vast compassion and dedication to his mother land – a quality of mind rarely equalled among poets and philosophers, that he was. He wrote a column in an obscure weekly from Pune for Several years starting 1893, till such time as he left for Kolkata to edit his own *Bande Matram* in 1904 – These pieces in Indu-Prakash titled "New Lamps for the Old" speak of the breadth and depth of his vision of Maa Bharati and more the lofty thoughts, even after a century and over they first appeared. So were his miscellanies in *Bande Matram* that were given highest accolades even by the gate-keepers of Imperial Culture, i.e., editors of *Times*, London.
12. One can swown on his breath-taking imagery in *Savitri*, or philosophical profoundity, in *Life-Divine*, or literary grace and precision in his future of poetry. He was a political seer, a dreamer of dreams as wrote his masterly essays on *Gita* and generously worshipped his colleagues such as Dayanand, Lajpat Rai, Tilak, Gandhi and even a philosophy teacher R.D. Ranade. No doubt only one who had overcome his own ego so completely could do such things. For don't we know he could compose verses in Greek and Latin while still at school in Eton. He took to life of spirit true to the manor born.
13. What happened to Sri Aurobindo after he was acquitted in the sedition trial in 1910, is a mystery. Why, how he withdrew from the national struggle in favour of others particularly Gandhiji after his famous Uttarpara Address. He stayed in Pondicherry for almost 40 years before *Samādhi*, writing highly recondite spiritual works and poetry – questioning for absolute and claiming to change the course of human history. Gandhi in his itinerant trips, once was refused admittance in his *Asram*, supposedly as the Yogi was in trance. Gandhi had his doubts, as man of strong common: "sense, "perhaps rebels were not welcome!" he wrote to a friend.
14. The best is Gopal Krishna Gokhale's pregnant remark that "what Bengal thinks today, rest of India thinks tomorrow". As one reads Bankim Babu's *Atma Chanit* one sees his great veneration for his service masters besides what he has put in the mouth of his characters of *Anand Math*. Sir Saiyyed while trying to build an independent patronage for upper class *Shurfa* (land owners) analysed the causes of Ghadar in his *Asbab E Baghavat-e-Hind* and desired to seek an Anglo-Muslim rapport at Aligarh like there was

in presidencies of the metros. Whether it Pt. Vidyasagar, or S.N. Banorji, Tagore, R.C. Dutta or early Bengali civilians they wished to keep their *Bhadraloka* the front-runners in the rat-race. See J.H. Broomfield's *Elite Conflicts in Bengal in 19th century* – It was this that led to the infamous division of Bengal by Curzon. Op. B.B. Misra (*op. cit.*) p. 229.

15. See Sir Jadunath Sicar's on Shivaji, and his laments on the periodic Raids of Mavthas to the south-west Bengali district adjoining Orissa till the end of 18th century.
16. The materials are too vast, but just to refer to some crucial studies: B.M. Bhatia's *Famines* in 19th century, Asia, 1960, See Sir Richard Temple's *Famine Commissions' Reports*, Dadabhai Naoroji's *Poverty and Unbritish Rule in India* (London), R.C. Dutta's *Economic History of India*, Vol. I, II. Charles Digby: *The Poor, Record of Families*. Hugh Tinkers: The Second Slavery – The *Indentured Labour*, Macmilan, London, 1973, Also see the total absence of any single discussion of such plights in the I.N.Congress, since 1885, formed under the Aegis of Sir Alan Octavius Hume, Weddborn, Munro, Hist of I.N. Congress, P. Sittaramyya.
   One and only one soul was stirred by infamous exactions over Indigo Culivators i.e. "Deenbandhu Maitras Tragedy-A Bengali Play Neel Darpan – whose pathetic portrayals led Pt. Vidyasagar to get emotionally distraught. Yes Pundita Ramabai also records in her works Ed. by Meera – Kosambi, Oxford, Delhi 2000, pp. 250-260; the human misery of The Poor under Famines.
17. See B.B. Misra (*op. cit.*), pp. 250-278. Cp. With Sita Ram Pande's – Auto-biography, "Sipoy to Subedar" Ed. Philip-Mason, translated from Avadhi by General Norgate, for Sandhurst in 1885.
18. See, Bhartendu Harish Chandra's Farce "Andher Nagari Chopatt Raja".
19. "The Cry of Indian Women" Kedagoon, Archives, Mukti Mission, June 1882, she wrote, "One could fear the shock of a Thunderbolt falling on the head but it requires a very hard heart to bear with ease the drop of tears falling down the eyes of the helpless widows.... In former days the practice of Suttee (burning widows), p. 113. Cp. D.D. Karves Report. On Raja Rammohun Roy's sister in Law being pushed in the funeral pyre of his Brother, Jagmohan, pp. 45-46, D.D. Karve, D.D. Chanda Warkar, Pubcs. Dn. Ministry of Information, G.O.I., New Delhi.
20. The reality of Caste Society and its horror – making attributes were noted in contemporary Records, most-famous are there of Abbe Duboi's who wrote in eary 19th Century about South Indian Hindus, translated by H.K. Beanchamp, from M.S. (French's Roopa, 1980, see pages 727-747. Compare appraisals by Jyoti Rao

Phule's who writes around (1890) he was so angered by the Brahmins that he saw English as Redeemers of Mahars and writes, "... Ramdas and Dhyaneshwar did not have courage to condemn the wicked acts of the Brahmins ... it was God's wish, he observed, that Nanasaheb Peshawa was defeated in the Revolt of 1857", pp. 119-125, Priest and Kshatriya always oppressed shudras in Medieval World. Dr. Ambedkar, and recently Kancha Alaiah has endorsed this stratified character of Caste hierarchy and note how Buddhist ideology was more geared to advance equality., pp. 219-222. (God as a Philosopher – Buddha's Challenge to Brahman – Somya – 2000) *op. cit.*, with the classical work of Louis Dumont on The Homo – Hierarchicus.

Tilak, Vivekananda as well as Anand Coomaraswami all extolled Varna Theory when cured of dehumanisation of the sub-alterns.

21. The best record is provided by contemporary Bengal fiction, how the *Bhadralok* in and around Kolkata in 1857 was involved in pursuit of its own Middle class perceptions, unmindful of the great tide and distant drums of war peeling the fires, after happenings in upper India. I refer to great fiction of Sunil Gangopadhyaya "Shedin". Legitimisation of a Bengali Babu. Jivan of the gory death of Mughal Princes in Puranakila in the "Lal-Kila" – by Pramathnath Bishi.

    Of course, sensitive fiction of Mahashweta Devi hardly, reveals any empathy either with Lakshmi Bai, Sundari – Mundari her soul mates, but makes long remarks to establish soul distortions of a Brahmo when faced with cruel oppressions by Col. Neal's 1858 troops, See AMRITA SANCHAYA.

    Except for Sarat Chattarji's "Savya Sachi" Bengali fiction has not written much about Revolutionaries. See *Pather Davi*. Even Bankim Chatterji otherwise so full of praise for Hindu chivalry and Author of *Bande Mataram*, the national Anthem had precious little to empathise with Nana, Kunwar Singh, Tatya, or Zafar Bahadur Shah.

22. See S.N. Sen and R.C. Majumdar, the official Indian Historians of 1857. Both show that the uprising could not evoke response anywhere outside Oudh and Central India, not even in Maharashtra or Rajashtnana; South was indifferent, so was Punjab and Bengal.

23. As far Sikhs, S. Khushwant Singh in his apologia for the mercenary treacheries that his fore bearers had done in cruelly suppressing purbias in Oudh offered in his "Sikhs", the argument, that these sipoys of Bengal Army had fought for Company Bahadur in Sikh Wars that led to losses of Lahore Durbar and end of Khalsa Raj only a few years later (1847). Naturally Sikhs saw this as a good Revenge opportunity to suppress their so-called Ghadar.

24. See Mahashweta (*op. cit.*)
25. J.N. Farquahar p. 170 (*op. cit.*), Life of Dayanand Saraswati – Acharya Ramdev Lahore see also, J.F.T. Jordan OXU p. 1978, p. 85 – Dayanand Life and Times. And K.C. Yadav p. 31. Autobiography, Manohar 1978.
26. My own Essay: Idea of Tradition – P.U. Journal of Medieval Studies, 1982, Cp. O Spengler's Decline of the Next. Vol. II, George Allen & Unwin, London, 1922.
27. The whole question of Vedant Quietism is Central. It can be true of life of Guru Raman Maharishi, as much as of Paramahans. Even later the firy Revolutionary Aurobindo got Quiescent as noted and cloistered in Pondicherry: See Raman Maharishi. The living Guru, A.R. Natarajan, Raman Maharishi Centre, 1996, Bangalore, p. 41. "that joy of Abidence is in the Wonderland of Silence"
    "When the ego which separates, is merged in its source one becomes aware of one each successive moments for these is no part, no future, no thoughts of dead yesterdays and unborn tomorrows ... the mind is silent, universal love bursts forth embracing all life in its vastness". Cp. Life of Sri Ramakrishna, Ashram Mayavati Almorah, Himalays, 1924. Such transcendental Realisation is nugatory of the Historical Activism despite its passionate advocacy by Swami Vivekananda, this shows how the accepted the Indian Religions, with abundant perversions of Tantrik Orgies, Vaishnavite excess, Caste and Untouchability, Deoda, Kulinship and widowhood, and its tantrums. Of course, in his 39 years he struggled to service – he establishes Rama Krishna Mission, his devoted disciple Sister Nivedita lived for two decades carrying that Mission of Mercy. But, to a Yogi, it was only incidental. This tension and paradox of Moksha with History remains; See *Insights into Hinduism*, R.N. Dandekar, Selected Writings on Moksha is neither Prapya (to be reached) nor utpodya (to be created) nor Vikasya (modified change) nor Samskarya (some perfection...) ... Moksha is native – but covered with Avidya, p. 59.
28. See Farquhar J.N. *op. cit.*, pp. 80-110, his lectures Vol. 1-8, cp. S.K. Chatterji, Sivani V.World Figure Cent. Vol. 1963, Col. Ed. R.C. Majumdar pp. 231,
29. In his collected work Vivekananda wished to assimilate and integrate Vedas, Upaniṣads and Smritis into the universal religion of Spirit, See Vol. III, pp. 193-94.
    "... For our Motherland a junction of the two great systems, Hinduism and Islam – Vedant brain and Islam – Vedānta brain and Islam Body is the only hope ..." VI, 415-16, *op. cit.* S.K. Chatterji piece Vivekananda Com. Vol. 1963, Cal. Ed. R.C. Majumdar. He shows on p. 231, how Vivekananda wished to embrace all the

myriad ways of Religion from the most primitive sakta sacrifices to the highest elevation of Samādhi as held by Ramakrishana aphorism "Jato Mata toto Path" As many opinions, so many ways. A recent study by Shamita Basu – 2002, New Delhi, Religious Revival in Nationalist Discourse – S.V. Nand in 19th century – O.U.P. shows:

"... He was attracted of Enlightenment ... Rammohan Ray, Keshab Sen's Brahmo movement, ... however, through Ramakrishna that he was the eclectic possibilities of Hinduism ... twin syncretism and the principles of universalism of Advaita philosophy.... He proposed a new inflection of the tradition – Modernity dichotomy", p. 197, see p. 87 also when Nivedita refers to his last vision of Jesus as Brahman as in Jan 1897, without losing his moorings in Ramakrishnan's in such ideas of oriental Christ. He sought to Hinduise Christianity, pp. 90-2.

30. Vivekananda, Vol. III, pp. 173-74, See R.G.Bhandarkara "Vaishnavism ...." Cp. P.V. Kane's Monumental work on History of Dharma Shastras – note M.N. Srinivas : Studies in Change in One's own Society"., 1972, Cp. D.N. Dandekar (*op. cit.*), p. 66, on Karma and Freedom his specious analysis of Satya Kama, Jabala, Chandogya Upanishad IV, a. on treatment of Shudras. Cp. Also Swami Aghelanand Bharati. On Tantra and Sexual Mudras – and then Orgies – religious accepted by Hinduism – p. 248 – O Chre Robe, Allen Unwin, London, 1961.

    See S. Vivekananda and Medern Hinduism William Radice ex. See Dalima reporting Dayanand struggled Orthodox Pandits of Banaras in 1880s against Vallabhacharya, Tantras and Bhartendu Harish Chandra Defence of Murti Pooja, Gtanthawali, Vol. 3, 689-98, B.R. Das Banaras.

31. While he was severe on "touch menotism" of Hindu Brahminic priests, he wished to be saved from alienation of his co-religionists, unlike Christ-leaving Brahmos, Vol. III, pp. 219-22. Of course, he would ridicule pundits who would respect a Bhangi as soon as he got baptised otherwise all treated him worse than beasts, Vol. V, 15 and Vol. I, p. 5, Cp. This to Abbe Dubois (*op. cit.*) how Brahmins in South India treated Sudras worse than animals, p. 72 see also. Dil Keer: Life of J. Rao Phule (1827-92), p. 79, who wished Brahmini (Tyranny to be curbed by Raj, Popular Prakashan. Mumbai, 1964, Cp. B.R. Ambedkar, (Works), as well Kancha Ilaiah Saumya – 2000, where we criticised Gandhi, Vivekananda and Aurobindo for seeing virtues in Varna-dharma.

32. All of these authors argue that Vivekananda was influenced by Enlightenment and utilitarian rationalism was a liberal see (*op. cit.*) Int. p. IX. Basu (*op. cit.* p. 89) and R. Rolland (*op. cit.*, p. 236) where he finds him closer to Gandhi than to Ramakrishna.

33. See her works, Vol. II, foot falls of Indian History – p. 170, also see p. 191, where she justifies exploitation of Widows by House owners, see Web of Life – p. 236 – an idealisation of Hindu practices.
34. In contrast see Jyoti Rao Phule, (*op. cit.*), D.D. Karve, Pt. Ramabai The Cry of Indian Widows as Follows, "In India there are 21,000,000 mamied and widowed and it is likely that cry of these helpless will not be vainly spent"., "it is difficult to bear the drops of tears falling down of the helpless Widows"... , p. 107-111.
Cp. D.D. Karve, G.L. Chandrawarker 1962" (*op. cit.*), where he recounts the sad plight of Sister-in-law of Raja Rammohun Roy in being forced to be Sati – in 1812. He, Jyotirao Phule, Dr. B.R. Ambedkar – were for subalterns and critics of Hindu Revivalism of Tilak, Gandhi, Aurobindo.
35. See R.N. Dandekar (*op. cit.*) on casteist Hindu Mind, pp. 98-99, as opposed to Renaissance accepted beliefs, Tilak, Nivedita, Bhagwandas who always vaxed eloquent of Varna-dharma. Aurobindo and Even Scholarly Anand Coomaraswami eulogised its high preserving qualities. See Sister Nivedita's Web of Life, p. 110, in passim. It compares well with studies of Sri Aurobindo on Swabhava and Swadharma in his Essays on Gita, and other works, like wise Tilak Gandhi and his scores of disciples have marvelled on the enduring qualities of Varma-Ashrama. As noted earlier, Dayanand denounced caste, female in fanticide and Pauranik Image Worship of degradation of Arya-Satya. (See Satyarth Prakash).
36. Dr. R.M. Lohia was a subaltern Gandhian rebelled against Nehruvian Gandhian legacy, and advocated a grass-root fusion of tribals, landless peasantry, sudras and Backwards – he wrote and worked for subalterns incessantly – most creatively for socialism where caste was also seen as class, and of course he championed the most debased Dalit Women. See his "Wheels of History", Marxism, Capitalism, Gandhi, (Mankind, Hyderabad) as well see his Hindi = Chokhambha Samaj (Kashi Vidyapeeth, 1956).
37. See Kancha Ilaiah: God as a Political Philosopher (Buddha's Challenge to Brahmanism) Somya, Kolkata 2000, 16, Southern Avenue,
It is he and others in 2002, that have issued the Dalit Agenda, at Bhopal, against Hindustan Ideology. He holds, that for the first and the last time it was in Buddhist Sangha where truly free and open debate was democratically permitted and even Buddha's own opinions were modified in view of free and fair Debate – Against earlier Brahmnic authoritarian orthodoxy see pp. 114-5 and p. 174.

3

Swami Vivekananda and Youth Forces

Raghunath Ghosh

The other day a young man of Calcutta had gone to Dakshineswar to satisfy the curiosity whether God exists or not. This young man had gone to the Unmeasured Man, Ramakrishna, with this enquiry. With the magic touch of this Unmeasured One the divine eye of this young man was opened. The young man to whom Sri Ramakrishna was completely revealed is Swami Vivekananda, the representative of youth forces. Sri Ramakrishna's divine power had taken him a long way – the way of transformation – as a result of which he was able to organise the youth forces with the single *Mantra*: *Uttisthata Jāgrata prāpya varānnibodhata,*[1] i.e., "Awake, arise and stop not until the goal is reached...." Like young Nachiketa Swamiji also realised the essence of life and he had taken this *Mantra* as an ideal to organise the youth forces.

In the present day society young men are fearful, cowardly, lacking self-confidence and are self-centred. Hence, it is time to follow the above-mentioned *Mantra* uttered by Swamiji to bring youth forces in order. It is very much relevant so far as the present situation is concerned.

At first the young men are advised to arise (*uttisthat*). "Arising" means "arising from one's inertia (*Jādya*), which is taken to be a curse. An individual becomes non-desirous of doing action if there is inertia in him. When an individual engages in action, he is not touched by inertia. When someone adopts a narrower attitude or becomes infatuated, it is the result of this inertia. Arjuna, a young warrior, became blind with infatuation resulting in narrower attitude, self-centredness, etc. after seeing his relations in the battle field of Kurukshetra. This situation led him to the world of inertia. That is why it is the injunctions of the divine teacher to forsake inertia and to initiate action. Because, it is not befitting for a young man like him. The main object is to promote the philosophy of action. Infatuation, etc. are the result of ignorance (*avidyā*). In this *Mantra, uttisthata* means "arising from the veil of ignorance", as observed by *Śamkara* (*anādyavidyāpraṣuptā uttiṣthata he jantavah).*[2] After forsaking ignorance one is advised to turn one's attention to the knowledge of the Self (*ātmajñānābhimukhā bhavata*).[3] It is Swamiji's call to young generations, who are in inertia, who think themselves weak. It is a venture to bring the young men to the path of self-knowldege and action after leaving behind inertia, the result of *Tamoguna.* Because, to him it is *Karma* alone which brings the meaningful existence of man. It is not true that the doctrine of *Vedānta* has no practical relevance as it is generally thought. On the contrary, it is very much practical and is useful in our day-to-day life. Hence, *Vedānta* as understood by Swamiji inspires an individual to the path of action not inertia. It is *Vedānta* which has taught us to perform *Karma.*

Mere "arising" is not sufficient for the youth, but "awaking" is also essential. One should awake from the sleep of wrong conceptions about oneself. One should awake after awakening the Divinity existing in oneself. An individual should realise the truth of the *Mantra, Tattvamasi* (i.e., That art thou). In each and every situation young persons should have the conviction that he is Bliss Eternal. Vivekananda says:

> There was a man in India, a *Sannyasin,* who used to repeat *Shivoham*– "I am Bliss Eternal" – and a tiger jumped on him one day and dragged him away and killed him, but so long as he was living the sound came, *Shivoham, Shivoham....* The weak will never reach the *Atman*. Never say, "O Lord! I am a miserable sinner. Who will help you? You are the help of the universe.... You are the God of the universe, where can you seek for help?" These are the words that will burn up the dross that is in the mind, words that will bring out tremendous energy which is within you already, the infinite power which is sleeping in your heart.[4]

An individual is asked to awaken his infinite power by which his prayer is answered. For Vivekananda, to keep complete faith in the Self is *Āstikatā* in the true sense of the term. Those who do not believe in their selves are *Nāstikas,* i.e., non-believers in God.

According to Vivekananda, an individual is already Brahman himself. Hence, there is no question of becoming Brahman. It is not the case that an individual is going to be God and perfect, but he is already perfect. When someone thinks that he is not Brahman, it is a delusion. It is a delusion that we are not perfect and hence, we have to practise for the same. This delusion is dispelled as soon as an individual hears *Tat tvam asi*. After hearing this he will have a flash by which this world of delusion vanishes and real nature reveals.[5]

That the attainment of Brahman is not a new achievement as it is already in man is observed by Dharmarāja Adhvarindra in his *Vedāntaparibhāṣā*. He has adopted a beautiful metaphor to explain this situation, which I feel tempted to mention in order to highlight Vivekananda's thought. To Dharamrāja this realisation of the Self or Brahman is not new, but the attainment of what is already attained (*Prāptasya prāptih*). An individual, after keeping a pen in his pocket, may be in search of it outside. When someone points out that the pen is already in his pocket about which he was not aware, it is nothing but the attainment of the object already attained. Such is the case with the Divinity which is already in man. This is possible if there is real awakening of the Divinity which is emphasised by Vivekananda to the young generation. His address to the youth force is as follows:

> young man of Calcutta arise, awake, for the time is propitious. Already everything is opening out before us. Be bold and fear not. It is only in our scriptures that this adjective is given into the Lord – *Abhih*, *Abhih*. We have to become *Abhih*, fearless, and our task will be done.... It is the young men that will do it. "The young, the energetic, the strong, the well-built, the intellectual" for them is the task. And we have hundreds and thousands of such young men in Calcutta .... In other parts of India, there is intellect, there is money, but enthusiasm is in only in my motherland....[6] That must come out, therefore, arise, young men of Calcutta with enthusiasm in your blood.[7]

The young men are specially worthy of this instruction – *uttisthata,* etc. because Vivekananda believed that "from the youth of Bengal will come the power which will raise India once more to her proper spiritual place".[8]

This faith on the youth would be in vain when they become fearful. Because fear is the great cause of misery in the world. The man who does not feel himself as infinite becomes fearful and hence he is always in woe. The fearlessness can bring heaven in a moment.[9] This fearlessness or immortality should be the goal which is to be achieved. A young man should take initiation from his teacher till he realises the Divinity in himself (*Prāpya varānnibodhata*).

The above-mentioned view will find support in the *Śamkarabhāṣya* on this *Mantra*. Śamkara says that "awaking" means "destruction of the sleep of ignorance, the root of all harms" (*Jāgratājñānānidrāyā ghorarūpāyāh sarvānarthavījabhūtāyāh kṣayam Kuruta*).[10] As soon as the ignorance is removed, an individual realises himself as infinite. This realisation is possible if he approaches the seer-teachers (*Prāpya upagamyavaān prakṛṣṭānācāryānstadvidastadupadiṣṭam sarvāntaramātmānamahamasmiti nivodhatāvagacchata*).[11]

So long as an individual does not realise infinity in him, he is weak. According to Swamiji, all sins and evils follow from weakness. It is weakness which is the source of all selfishness. Vivekananda laid great emphasis on cultivating the spirit of sacrifice. He said that we should throw, everything even our own salvation, and go and help others.[12] When Vivekananda requested Ramakrishna to give him salvation he told him that he should not seek his own salvation like a selfish man. He will have to be like a banyan tree under which others would find salvation.[13] Swami Vivekananda had worked for the sake of others during his whole life and hence he was capable of advising the young men.

> Arise and awake and be perfectly sincere. Our insincerity in India is awful; what we want is character, that steadiness and character that make a man cling on to a thing like grim death.[14]

The young generation of the country is requested to arise and awake to protect the spirituality of the world. But it should be clearly borne in mind that spirituality is not to be taken in a traditional sense, but "bringing down of the Advaita into the material world".[15] The spirituality without the association of the material world is of no use. For him is first bread and then religion[16] which is similar to *Śarīramādyam khalu dharmasādhanam*. This interpretation of the *Advaita* doctrines is to be followed by the youth. If they are introduced to such interpretation, each of them will love others and think for the welfare of others. One will sacrifice for the good of many and for the happiness of many (*Bahujanahitāya bahujanasukhāya*).[17] If someone fails to perform this, he is to be taken as a coward. One should forsake one's fear and cowardice, which is against the *Advaita* position. The *Advaita*

Vedānta alone is the source of morality. An individual should not care what becomes of him, but should care for the whole world. The feeling that we are all enjoying bliss at the same time and there is none to kill us is morality which is given by *Advaita Vedānta* alone.[18]

For this the controlling and calming of mind is highly essential. Hence, the youth forces are intiated into *Titikṣā* forbearance, bearing all miseries without any word. The steadiness of mind, towards external sense organs, *Titikṣā,* etc. come into being if an individual thinks himself as the abode of infinite. The highest form of spirituality is revealed in *Titikṣā*. Vivekananda observes:

> Just as the Western ideal is to keep up luxury in practical life, so ours is to keep up the highest form of spirituality, to demonstrate that religion is not merely frothy words, but can be carried out, every bit of it, in this life. This is *Titikṣā,* to bear everything, not to complain of anything. I myself have seen men who say, 'I am the soul.'[19]

Now Let us see the contributions of Swamiji in the philosophical world. First, to Śamkara the whole world and an individual's body, mind, sense organs, etc. become illusory (*māyā*) just after the realisation of the Brahman. In *Advaita Vedānta,* the individual's body and materialistic world is neglected. Vivekananda has given a new interpretation of *Advaita Vedānta*. Swamiji has taken the human body and the material world as the manifestation of Divinity or as real as the Divine but not illusory. Swamiji has described the human body as the abode of infinite where there exists power of being infinite.

Secondly, the terms *uttisthata* and *jāgrata* are taken in a wider sense by Vivekananda. The term *uttisthata* is taken by Śamkara in the sense of turning one's attention to the self-knowledge alone which is narrow. The term *jāgrata* means awaking from the veil of ignorance. But Swamiji has taken the same term as arising from one's inertia (*jādya*), which leads us to the world of action. The term *jagrata* has been taken as awaking oneself to one's divine nature, which is not clearly mentioned in the *Bhāṣya* of Śamkara.

Thirdly, Swamiji has taken the essence of *Advaita* philosophy and has given it a new interpretation. Hence, he is able to advise the young generation to be fearless (*abhih*), to forsake cowardice. This is possible if someone attains spirituality in oneself. When a young man is described as "spirited", it is due to the attainment of spirituality in him. One cannot be "spirited" unless one attains spirituality. In Vivekananda's philosophy, highest dignity is given to a human being. It is man who can extend himself for the service of another man. A man is virtually infinite or God, which is first pointed out by Swamiji so clearly.

NOTES AND REFERENCES

1. *Kathopanisad*, 1.3.14.
   The complete works of Swami Vivekananda, Vol. 3, Advaita Ashram, 1946, p. 318, Henceforth *Complete Works*.
2. *Samkarabhasya* on K.U. 1.3.14
3. *Ibid.*
4. *The Complete Works*, Vol. 3, Advaita Ashram, 1946, p. 26.
5. *Ibid.*, p. 17.
6. Vedantaparibhasa – Visayapariccheda.
7. *The Complete Works*, Vol. 3, pp. 318-19 (Same Edition).
8. *Ibid.*, p. 320.
9. *Ibid.*, p. 321.
10. *Samkarabhasya* on K.U. 1.3.14.
11. *Ibid.*
12. *The Complete Works*, Vol. 3, p. 426 (Same Edition).
13. *Ramakrishnakathamrita*, p. 120.
14. *The Complete Works*, p. 431.
15. *Ibid.*, p. 432.
16. *Ibid.*
17. *Ibid.*, p. 424.
18. *Ibid.*, p. 425.
19. *Ibid.*, p. 17.

4

Religion as the Foundation of Morality

Indu Sarin

We are passing through the dark age where there is so much bloodshed in the name of religion. Seeing this violence one wonders whether religion and morality seem to have any relation to one another. It is the pressing need of the day to understand what religion truly is. Vivekananda's reflections at the end of the 19th century may illuminate our contemporary times as he convincingly pleads for the inherent unity of all regions. He advocates giving up the narrow, limited ideas of religion, which lead to quarrels and disputations. The present paper focuses upon Vivekananda's radical perspective on religion to show its necessity for inculcating moral values in human beings.

Religion is commonly defined in terms of belief in scriptures, prophets, institutions, creeds, sects and gospels. Such elements or a selection of their mixtures make different interpretations in the study of the phenomenon of religion. The formation of different religious categories is an area for theoretical studies of specific religious practices. Each religion confines itself to its narrow shell, propagates its gospel claiming its convictional superiority over that of the other. This attitude breeds hatred and intolerance towards the other religions in hitherto known history of civilisations. The resulting fanaticism has often led to violence and bloodshed. However, the above scenario according to Vivekananda is the degeneration of religion. The purpose of religion is not to divide humanity but rather to unite it. Unity for Vivekananda is the key to religions. The religious institutions, creeds, sects do not define the true nature of religion. They are of secondary importance, "kindergarten of religion" to use Vivekananda's expression.

Vivekananda is not iconoclastic of traditional faith and practices because these may show the way to religion. They are helpful for the common people who are engaged in worldly affairs. The rituals may create a space in their lives to contemplate upon the significance of something supra-mundane. They help them to see how Divine Presence permeates in their daily affairs. Without these concrete supports, people normally do not notice or feel the presence of the Divine. Their worldly life becomes only an exercise of selfishness. But this is only the initial stage of religion. One may have read all the scriptures, visited religious institutions, performed rituals but still may not be a religious person.

The core of religion for Vivekananda is the realisation of divinity – realisation of God in the soul. Realisation means encountering God and getting transformed. The dichotomy between knowing and being breaks down. To know God is to be God-like. It is not a question of what – knowing some or that truth but how to become the spirit. What implies a theoretical enquiry but "how" implies a process of becoming. Vivekananda remarks:

> Religion is to be realised now. And for you to become religious means that you will work your way up, and realise things, see things for yourself.[1]

If one knows about religion, but has not realised it, one is still an atheist. For Vivekananda, mere knowledge is just like a map of a country but it is not the country. Similarly, knowledge of religious scriptures give us the idea of religion but it is not religion itself, which is a living reality. Vivekananda holds the view:

> Religion is realisation; not talk, nor doctrine, nor theories, however beautiful they may be. It is being and becoming, not hearing or acknowledging. It is the whole soul's becoming changed into what it believes. That is religion.[2]

Vivekananda comes close to the Socratic way of thinking – "know thyself" and "knowledge is virtue". For Socrates, knowing something means doing it, thus bridging the gap between theory and praxis, fusing "the givenness" of the world and its content as well as embodying oughts in existential praxis. Religious knowledge is not a set of assertions about the objects. It is rather knowing how to generate meaning and sense of our presence in the world.

The question arises: how is the above realisation possible? Neither the naturalistic approach to self nor the ontology of God succeeds in the above realisation. The realisation of God is possible through controlling nature – internal and external, mind and matter. Nature, Vivekananda argues, is governed by its ordained laws. Mind and matter being in time and space are controlled by the law of causation.

At the naturalistic level, the individual is controlled by his psycho-physical impulses, mental functions on the one hand and external forces on the other. He is simultaneously witnessing the multi-tiered levels of being, such as body's passions, infirmities owing to the potentialities of mind, language, intellect and accumulated creations of growing corpus of human world. The individual becomes a victim of the social milieu. He remains mired in the web of his civilisational networks and seems to circumscribe his life to the externalities of culture, tradition, class, nation and the typical roles imposed through one's station and its duties in the society.

Both the internal and external forces fetter man in bondage and create a chain of causation. Clinging to one's unreal nature and the world around, cover the true nature of the soul. The disclosure of the true nature of the soul is the emergence of freedom. The subtle soul is beyond all materialism and is the centre for the realisation of God. The covering of soul according to Vivekananda is due to the following factors:[3]

1. Ignorance (not knowing the truth),
2. Disturbed state of consciousness (*chitta vritti*),
3. False (ego-centric) consciousness (*ahamkara*), and
4. Desire for possessions (*vasana*).

When the mind is not concentrated on the specific object but drifts away from one to the other, it is called the disturbed state of consciousness. It works for getting motivations from one's psycho-somatic identity (ego), leading to a state of *ahamkara*, since our real being is neither mind nor body but is pure consciousness that is divine in nature; *ahamkara* is the state of falsity. The most of our works in the world are done for the satisfaction of ego not only for gross material desires but very often apparently appreciable works are also done on the initiative of this false identity (ego, *ahamkara*).

Desires (*vasana*) are the alluring occasions which are necessary for the existence of false identity (ego). In fact it is the crazy race for the fulfilment of desires that gives rise to a false identity. To get rid of the trap of *vasana*, is to get rid of ego or the other way round.

Ignorance is the centre of *ahamkara* and *vasana* resulting in disturbed states of consciousness. It is because of ignorance of one's true nature that one falls prey to ego and runs like a crazy person in the cycle of desires (*vasana*). Ignorance appears as idleness and lethargy, which prevents one from making efforts by weakening the will to be on the path of self-realisation. When the ignorance is dispelled by knowledge, the above demerits get dropped by themselves.

Vivekananda holds that there are three instruments of knowledge – instinct, reason and inspiration.[4] Instinct is common to both man and animal. But man has a capacity to go beyond, which distinguishes him from animals. The animal looks downward whereas man looks upward. The quest for spirituality is within the constitution of man. Reason belongs to man and inspiration to God-man. Reason limits itself to the boundaries. If it attempts to go beyond the boundaries, it is regarded as irrational. Inspiration, on the other hand, crosses all the boundaries; it is ecstatic.

Instinct, reason and inspiration are not contradictory, all of them play a crucial role in man's life. Reason is development from instinct and inspiration from reason. Inspiration is not rejection of instinct and reason but is going beyond them. An old man does not contradict the child but develops out of it. Vivekananda takes an integrative approach that harmonises all the dimensions of man.

Vivekananda argues that the lower form of instrument of knowledge be not regarded as the highest. Many times, instinct is confused with the inspiration. Instinct is presented before the world as inspiration and spurious claims of prophecy are made.[5] Religious knowledge is neither the outcome of irrational impulses nor of abstract, calculative, objective reason leading to demonstrability. Rationally arguing for the religious doctrines cannot make one a religious person. Religious knowledge is not a set of assertions about the "objects". It is to generate meaning to enable the person to grip the sense of our presence in the world. Inspiration in contradistinction to both instinct and reason is neither irrational nor rational. It rather belongs to the sphere of non-rational or a-rational going beyond reason without becoming irrational.

Inspiration comes through faith in one's own self, which crosses all the frameworks set by reason. It bestows man with strength and courage through which he is able to stand against all the fret and fume, odds, risks, fears and despair. It is said that "faith can move mountains too". The man of faith is divinely inspired and plunges into voluntary, creative actions, rejecting the rigidness of dogmatic beliefs and much beyond the dry mapping of scientific knowledge as well.

The negative elements of psychological impulses also disappear eliminating the ugliness of horrifying cruelties and beastliness giving rise to the autonomous liberated spirit. It is inching beyond finitudes, absurdities and disorienting otherness. One lives through the "dark night of the soul". This pilgrim's voyage to a surge of liberation and ecstacy uncovers the calm, serene and free soul in ever blessed plenitude.

To have religious knowledge means that the individual is able to discriminate between the sensuous and the supersensuous, empirical and transcendental, profane and sacred, darkness and illumination. What is needed is the power of concentration to see the above distinctions that can check the undesirable impulses, worldly possessions, the narrow self-identity that lead to the disturbed state of consciousness. Concentration for Vivekananda is the essence of all knowledge.[6] Concentration upon any subject means mastering it. This is what Yoga is – "control senses, will and mind to see God". Vivekananda remarks:

1. Each soul is potentially divine.
2. The goal is to manifest this divinity within by controlling nature, external and internal.
3. Do this either by work or worship or psychic control or philosophy – by one or more or all of these and be free.[7]

Vivekananda suggests the path of four *Yogas* – *Raja Yoga*, *Karma Yoga*, *Jñāna Yoga*, and *Bhakti Yoga* for self-realisation. One may follow any one of these *yogas* depending upon one's temperament or combine all of these.

Raja Yoga is the path of self-realisation in which specific physical and psychic methodology is prescribed. *Yoga sutra* of Patanjali holds the view that it is because of the modifications (*vrittis*) of mind the the real nature of pure self is concealed. The aim of *Raja Yoga* is the cessation of the modifications of mind (*yoga-chitta vritti-nirodha*), so that the real self gets manifested.

Karma Yoga is the path to act without desiring for results. Desireless action is the key to *Karma Yoga*. Normally, the individual acts for getting some fruit out of it – to achieve some favourable and to fulfil some desire and avoid misery and pain. *Karma Yoga* teaches us to act without being influenced by the good or bad results.

The basic philosophy of *Karma Yoga* is that the desire with which actions are performed is the cause of bondage. Actions in themselves do not generate bondage. There is nothing in actions which can allow me, seduce me and force me to do this or that. It is my desire with which I perform an action that enslaves me. The highest stage of *Karma Yoga* is the attainment of the attitude of being non-doer. The body is regarded only as an instrument to perform actions. To realise this state is to realise one's nature, which is beyond the influences of causation.

Jñāna Yoga is the path of wisdom (*viveka*) to understand the manifestation of the real nature of the world and our place in it. The identification with the material world in terms of different roles and designations, station and its duties (as discussed earlier), is a false self-identity and does not constitute the true nature of one's being. Through *viveka* and listening to the illuminating teachings of the spiritual preceptors, one begins to see the falsity of the above identity. Consequently, the attachment to different roles and worldly duties begins to disappear. Self-knowledge (*Atma Jñāna*) is achieved through the process of discriminating real from unreal (*sad-asad-viveka*).

Bhakti Yoga is the path of developing an emotional, intimate relationship with one's Lord who is regarded to be the Supremely Divine and is the source of bliss. The intimate, emotional relationship is manifested in every act performed by the devotee (*bhakta*). The latter does not get involved in worldly activities. He ceaselessly feels the presence of God within him.

Vivekananda holds that people adopt different paths depending upon their tastes, temperaments and inclinations. Some persons are more active, some are emotional or others are rational, etc. But no one is either completely rational or emotional and in each of these paths, the element of the other path is incorporated. For example in *Raja Yoga, Iswara* (*Pranidhan*) is necessary for achieving the cessation of modifications of mind. In the path of *Karma Yoga*, understanding and wisdom are also required. In *Jñāna Yoga*, an element of faith at the feet of the preceptor, transforming wisdom into action is also needed. Similarly *Bhakti Yoga* is impossible without leading a moral life, distinguishing good from bad, earthly from supra-mundane. So there is no contradiction involved in different *yogas*. They are rather supplementary.

All the above-mentioned paths lead to the same goal and free one from the material bondages – freedom from pleasure and pain, good and evil, life and death and what happens after the death. Besides the earthly bondage, Vivekananda holds that one should be free from the ideas of heaven. The idea of happiness in heaven is also a vain dream. God is to be realised here and now by the individual himself. Vivekananda says that to be bound by the idea of God in heaven is also a slavery.

The existence of God raises a number of questions: how is God known? What is the relationship of God to man and the universe? Is God a creator of the universe? Why has the perfect Being created-imperfect universe? Why is there problem of evil? In the history of philosophy, so many proofs have been given to demonstrate the existence of God. They are ontological, cosmological, teleological, design and moral arguments, etc. Vivekananda shows the futility of such demonstrations. This will according to him lead to endless debates and logical absurdities. For him, there is no ontological reality of God from the individual's experience.Vivekananda takes for example the design argument, proving the existence of God through the design of the universe. The existence of God is shown through nature. He holds that if God is Omnipotent, He needs no design, no scheme, to plan the universe.[8] It amounts to limiting Him from his Omnipotence. The contingency of the universe does not prove that God is a necessary Being. Vivekananda says:

> The idea that nature in all her orderly arrangements shows design on the part of the Creator of the universe is good as a kindergarten teaching to show the beauty, power, and glory of God... but apart from that, it is not good, and perfectly illogical. As a philosophical idea, it is entirely without foundation, if God is taken to be omnipotent.[9]

Nature, therefore, is not a proof for the existence of God. For Vivekananda, the arguments given by dualism or monism are also not convincing. Dualism regards God and universe to be separate; the universe depends upon God. Monism rejects such kind of dualism between God and the universe. It holds that God is all and universe is lost in God. To explain the reality of world and to save the reality of God from being delimited by the reality of the world, panatheism equates the reality of the two. Vivekananda does not take the position of pantheism because the latter restricts the reality of God to the reality of the world. Moreover, the deterministic position taken by pantheism makes the role of human actions as insignificant. Consequently, there is no moral effort on the part of the individual to bring transformation in one's self as well as in the world.

In order to overcome the drawbacks of pantheism, the transcendent aspect of God is emphasised as wholly other. But Vivekananda cannot accept this view-point also because for him, God dwells within the soul of man. Vivekananda's position may be regarded as panentheism – God is immanent as well as transcendent. He is present in the external world but is also beyond it. He cannot be made an object of knowledge. He is the foundation of man's real being. God is to be realised in the soul. In order to realise Him, the materiality of nature is to be transcended. The attainment of freedom is to break the law of nature.[10] The demand for the proof of the existence of God is meaningless. God is not a fact among other facts that can be proved or disproved.

It is by stopping the "gyrations of the mind"[11] that soul is manifested. Vivekananda is critical of both natural theology and revealed theology. Natural theology holds that the existence of God is proved through rational arguments. According to revealed theology, God is above and bestows grace on the individual. In both the cases, God does not reside in the soul.

The realised individual is the paradigm, the biggest proof of the existence of God. God is revealed through the way the individual lives his life. The rationalistic arguments to prove the existence of God become redundant. Unlike revealed theology, the way is from man to God and not from God to man. What is needed is faith in one's own self, which generates faith in the whole humanity. Vivekananda says:

> ... have faith in yourselves. You yourselves are the proof of God.... But it is not selfish faith ... it means faith in all, because you are all.[12]

Vivekananda argues that the essence of all religions is one – realisation of divinity in man. Therefore, the core of all religions is universal. The universal religion is neither the amalgamation of all religions nor in addition to many religions. It is to point out that all religions lead to the same goal, only the paths are different. All historical religions are variations of the universal religion. The starting point of the individual may be a particular religion with personal God. But as he steps higher, he communes with undifferentiated pure spirit. Every religion has its own mythologies, dogmas, beliefs and gods that can lead to exclusiveness. As the belief in impersonal God is not tied to any particular religion it can bring harmony in all religions.

Vivekananda does not want to subsume all religions under the one religion. Each religion should follow its own practices. His aim is to find out unity in diversity. He is for diversities but diversities should not lead to disharmony and discord. His emphasis is on the harmony of all religions, to a symphony produced by various notes. He sees the universal in and through the particulars.

Vivekananda is critical of conversions imposed by a particular religion, spreading one's own religion at the cost of other religions. One should stick to one's own religion and finds the bond of unity among all religions. The unity is spiritual, which makes one to be open to the other; mere tolerance is not enough but one should whole-heartedly accept other religions. To develop fellow-feeling is common to all religions. Elaborating Vivekananda's viewpoint, Mazumdar says:

> ... toleration must necessarily lead to acceptance and for this the followers of different paths must develop a mutual understanding which results in what may be called a confluence of selves.[13]

The realisation of God does not imply quietism but rather imparts the individual with vigorous action. The individual is required to dedicate his whole life to the service of suffering humanity. Like *Boddhisattva*, he is not satisfied only with his own salvation but works for the salvation of the whole humanity. Love for yourselves means love for all, "for you and all are one". This thought of Vivekananda is the foundation of ethics. He holds that love is truth and unity is the test of truth. Hatred of the other is false because it brings multiplicity with disharmony and discord.

Love establishes oneness with all other beings bringing harmony in the universe.

Vivekananda is arguing for humanism with a glow of diversity within it. It has the widest social relevance beyond the reach of narrow and violent "religious prejudices, frenzies and passions."[14] Usually the concept of humanism is viewed in terms of ensurance of justice and human rights. The external methods are employed to check their violations. Vivekananda's humanism is derived from *adhyatma-vidya*.[15] The divine self is the only sanction for moral life. The manifestation of divinity in praxis brings peace with one's own self as well as with the whole resolving all the complexities of life. To be religious is to be moral and to be moral is to be inspired by religion. Religion is practiced through transing the path of morality.

For Vivekananda, religion and morality are inseparable. Usually a distinction is made between morality and religion. Morality is said to be practiced in the web of human interactions here and now whereas religion transcends the worldly relationship in quest of God. Religion is regarded to be other worldly; human relationships do not play any significant role in the realisation of God. In contradistinction to this viewpoint, Vivekananda shows the close-knit relationship between religion and morality. He argues that religion does not belong to a transcendent realm cut off from the historical realm. God is not in the distant heaven isolated from the individual. In fact, each individual being is divine. Religion is realised by living actively in the world, serving humanity, inculcating fellow-feeling and bridging the gap between the other and oneself.

Vivekananda defines morality in terms of unselfishness – "that which is selfish is immoral, that which is unselfish is moral".[16] To be moral is to go beyond the naturalistic realm. It is to break the bondages of senses and the material forces working in the world. When one makes an effort to realise this aim, one enters into the sphere of morality.

At the materialistic plane, there is a mad craze for the fulfilment of selfish interests at all costs even by roughing other beings. The result is immoral actions giving rise to vices like hatred, jealousy and violent struggle. For the sake of one's selfish interests, one is ready to go to any extent to harm the other. The materialistic pursuits revolve around the "I". When the centre is "I", it is called *pravritti*, the other is only a means to serve my ends. "Me" and "mine" (*ahamkara* and *mamta*) are the sources of all evils. Vivekananda says:

> Pravritti, which means revolving towards ... is what we call the world, the "I" and "mine"; it includes all those things which are always enriching that "me" by wealth and money and power and name and fame ... always tending to accumulate everything in one centre, that centre being "myself" ... the natural tendency of every human being, taking everything from everywhere and keeping it around one centre.[17]

In the realm of morality, the centre is "thou", which Vivekananda calls as *nivritti* – revolving away. It is to rise above the narrowness of "me" and "mine". *Pravritti* stands for "evil work" whereas *nivritti* stands for good work.[18]

Nivritti is the basis of morality, which leads to self-abnegation to sacrifice one's selfish interests for the sake of the other. The aim of religion is the realisation of freedom that is attained through morality which follows the path of *nivritti*. The latter leads to selfless actions in search of intrinsic values. Love, charity, endurance, self-sacrifice, fellow-feeling, treating others as ends-in-themselves are the moral values to be practiced. Morality consists of "do this" and "do not do this" – positive and negative elements. "Do not do this" puts a check on the desires which enslave the individual and "do this" shows the way to freedom. Through purging one's narrow ego, morality gives birth to the infinite expansion of one's self that embraces the entire mankind. This is universal ethics that is culture-free and is to be distinguished from the conventional morality. Different societies practice different moral codes. Despite the diversities and variation in moral codes, we should see what is universal in ethics. Vivekananda maintains:

> When one sees a man doing good work, helping others, it means that he cannot be confined within the limited circle of "me and mine". There is no limit to, this getting out of selfishness. All the great systems of ethics preach absolute unselfishness as the goal.[19]

Religion for Vivekananda is the groundwork of morality. If morality has a spark of divinity within it, there is spontaneous emergence of moral actions. If the inner being of the individual is transformed, one cannot help being a moral person. To be religious is to have faith in oneself (as mentioned earlier). If one has faith in oneself, the gap between theory and practice breaks down. In that case, there is no room for moral weakness. With religious faith comes the "ocean of infinite power and blessedness". It leads to dropping away of the veils on the soul and the real nature of man gets manifested. One is then able to discriminate between right and wrong, truth and falsity. The ocean of love emerges and hatred vanishes.

According to Vivekananda, two forces are operating throughout the universe – differentiating and unifying. The former separates the individuals while the latter is an assertion of sameness and homogeneity. Love integrates the individuals and "make for that oneness" without leading to homogeneity. It is open and respects the other in his otherness and bring him in brings union with the rest of the world. Vivekananda's view of universal ethics and universal religion propounds unity in diversity.

The upshot that emerges from the above discussion is that neither the naturalistic approach to man nor ontology of God succeeds in the realisation of religion. The subtle soul that is beyond all materialism is the centre of the realisation of God. Vivekananda does not go for any supra-historical spiritual realisation. As he puts it:

> The ordinary sannyasin gives up the world, goes out, and thinks of God. The real sannyasin lives in the world, but is not of it ... lives in the midst of the battle of life. Anyone can keep calm in a cave or when asleep. Stand in the whirl and madness of action and reach the Centre. If you have found the Centre, you cannot be moved.[20]

The spiritual realisation is plunging into the world with self-abnegation enlightening the mankind with the spark of divinity setting aside all the labels of class, race, sex, culture and nation. The enlightened pilgrim wades through existential despair of agnosing forlornness of mutual antipathies breaking through exclusiveness and compartmentalisation. This journey into the elevated interior overcomes the distempers of otherness by assimilating it with one's own self. A new visage emerges which brings meeting of time and eternity, morality and religion opening the gate to freedom. This is intense activity with eternal calmness and blessedness.

NOTES AND REFERENCES

1. S. Vivekananda, *What Religion Is*, edited by S. Vidyatmananda, Advaita Ashrama, Kolkata, 1972, p. 10.
2. *Ibid.*, pp. 41-42.
3. S. Jyotirmayananda (editor), *Vivekananda*, S. Jyotilmayananda, Madras, 1988, p. 113.
4. S. Vivekananda, *op. cit.*, p. 36.
5. *Ibid.*, pp. 36-37.
6. S. Vivekananda, *The Complete Works of Swami Vivekananda*, Vol. VI, Advaita Ashrama, Kolkata, 1995, p. 123.
7. S. Vivekananda, *op. cit.*, p. 1.
8. S. Vivekananda, *The Complete Works of Swami Vivekanand*, Vol. VI, p. 97.
9. *Ibid.*, pp. 131-132.
10. *Ibid.*, p. 100.
11. *Ibid.*, p. 96.
12. R. Rolland, *The Life of Vivekananda and the Universal Gospel*, Trans. E.F. Malcolm-Smith, Advaita Ashrama, Kolkata, 2001, p. 231.
13. *Parliament of Religions – 1963-64*, Swami Vivekananda Centre, Swami Sambuddana, 84.
14. Swami Ranganathananda, *Swami Vivekananda, his Humanism*, Advaita Ashrama, Kolkata, 2000, p. 50.
15. *Ibid.*, p. 11.
16. Swami Vivekananda, *Universal Ethics and Moral Conduct*, Advaita Ashrama, Kolkata, 2001, p. 40.
17. *Ibid.*, p. 33.
18. *Ibid.*
19. *Ibid.*, p. 39.
20. S. Vivekananda, *The Complete Works of Swami Vivekananda*, Vol. VI, 1995, p. 84.

5

Realising Perfection through Self-Abnegation

Veena Kapoor

In this paper I have made an attempt to represent Swami Vivekananda's views on how to achieve perfection in this material world in which people pursue their focal and selfish ends just for the sake of short-lived pleasures and enjoyments which have no intrinsic value. A thing which gives pleasure to an individual at a particular time, if fails to do so at another time or to any other person, cannot be morally esteemed and spiritually desirable. Only an action, having a universal appeal, can be spiritually and morally promoted for all times. On the contrary, an action done from a selfish motive is based upon a limited perspective, and is often indifferent to the kind of means used for achieving the desired results. Such actions cannot evoke universal appeal. Something is sought in its perfection only when it aims at results which are universally desirable irrespective of its occurrence in different spatio-temporal contexts. We can achieve this perfection by overcoming our ignorance through knowledge, and by freeing ourselves from the limitations of the sensuous experience and by expanding our centre of self-consciousness. Perfection lies in the ideal of self-abnegation and understanding that the conception of "I" and "mine" lies along the conception of "thou" and "yours", thus, merging them all together in One, Infinite, Absolute Spirit.

Swami Vivekananda holds that man as a unit from a particular angle is always incomplete, a partial description of that of which he is just a part. But in his absolute nature he is not separate from the whole. But what sorts of actions would help him in realising this Absolute Infinite? Man's ideal lies in achieving perfection through his deeds. Can this perfection be reached by sense-provoked actions? What sort of results will follow sense-based actions? Human perfection needs growth of personality which might not be understood by positive sciences alone. Perfection can be realised only by winning over our desparate longings for material gains. Material gains never satisfy a person, rather they arouse emotions of jealousy, hatred and frustration. The more a person is ambitious to possess material objects, the more he faces miserable situations. Man himself creates situations, miserable or blissful, although no one would say that he is looking for miserable situations. The basic end of life cannot consist in acquiring what one desires or wants at the sensuous level because that will increase his material pleasures but will not bless him with perfection any way. So it is the actions that matter the most. Actions are the means to attain the end. It is only the recogniton and application of appropriate means which will lead to perfection.

Man faces many difficulties at different levels of his life which can be overcome by controlling the mind. No law or legal rules can perfect a man as laws themselves are imperfect because of their ever-changing nature. They are conventions followed by a particular community. But perfection lies in such actions which do not lack anything and are sought by all. To achieve it, one will have to evaluate oneself with reference to others. In this sense, one becomes the other. Vivekananda upholds that religious-oriented morality can alone be the universal code of life. Out of the two tendencies of selfishness and unselfishness, only unselfishness is capable of generating purity. Failures in life also play an important role in the path to pursue perfection. It is only by overcoming ignorance by knowledge that we can achieve perfection. By realising religion we can all unite together as manifestations of the One Absolute. He says Oneness is the rationale of all morality. He strongly objects to the utilitarian view of ethics and shows us the direction in which the Hindu tradition can help us in perfecting ourselves. For him religions do not contradict, rather they complement each other. Perfection for him is to free oneself from the clutches of sensuous desires by self-abnegation (*nivritti*). Consciousness of one is there to control the whole universe and man is capable of it by multiplying his centre of self-consciousness. He believes that blessings and miseries are blows of *Karma* and the *Sanskaras*, the representations of the impressions of past life.

The ultimate goal is to free oneself from the blows of *Karma*. He strongly believes that love is truth and hatred is falsehood because love binds all in One, the Perfect, the Absolute, whereas hatred separates and multiplies which is the root cause of all miseries. Complete renunciation of one's limited self, one's self interests is the only way to seek perfection.

For Vivekananda, the secret to success lies in finding appropriate means to desirable ends. He practically demonstrated this principle. He says that we are so overwhelmed by our ends that we simply overlook the appropriate means to them. Spirit is finest and body is gross. The end of life cannot be realised in particular unless we get hold of our thoughts at the root before they get translated into actions and we will not be able to control ourselves. We will have to understand the finer powers, the finer causes which alone would make us have control not only on ourselves but over every other mind also. A moral man has control over himself. An ethical system is erroneous if it fails to point out the means by which a man could refrain from doing evil. Since all minds are essentially parts of one mind:

> He who knows one lump of clay has known all the clay in the universe. He who knows and controls his own mind knows the secret of every mind and has power over every mind.[1]

Of course, there are many problems, physical and mental, which we can get rid of if we have control on our way of working; and we can avert many failures in life by giving timely care. One can certainly live life in terms of the pursuit of one's narrow selfish goals and enjoy the pleasures associated with them. But one does realise that there is something more to life than simply this pursuit of pleasure. The whole of creation is passing through different stages of development. Vivekananda states it clearly: "There is an end towards which the whole is moving. Let us call it perfection."[2] This perfection is the end of life, a higher part of our life. Man has the power to realise this perfection. So man cannot leave it to nature; for there is no end to the power that a man can obtain to acquire perfection. The power is in the spirit and not in the sword. This power is not a matter to be studied in class-rooms but can be realised fully only through moral and spiritual actions. To acquire this power is not an easy task, for our mind is never steady and stable. Only stable things can be analysed with ease but the mind which is always moving and changing cannot be easily grasped. So, you need firm determination to get hold of it. While judging others we make use of our own set standards and feel as if all that we think about them is the only right judgement. Our world is our ethics, our morality, our sense of duty and our sense of utility. So, there is only my way of evaluating others. We are, here, highly mistaken; for the more we learn, the more we become conscious of our ignorance. In our selfish approach to life we forget the multi-sided nature of man, so we end up having a partial and mistaken picture of man. No one has the right to say that the other is wicked. Same is true with the social and political systems. Without any dispute, perhaps, all will agree that moralising politics will certainly make a nation great. Any social and political system is constructed on moral basis without which its structure will crumble down. One may or may not realise this contention but this is the truth of life. Any political goal is final, because these goals are merely products of certain policies of a particular time. These policies keep on changing and are, thus, modified according to the needs and situations. Laws or legal rules are needed to establish harmony in the conflicting beliefs and situations among people of a particular community. However, there exists an end of life which is not so determined, rather it determines the laws and rules of social and political life. Moral, religious and spiritual thinkers hint at this goal. The ethical code lies with "thou" and not "I". The sensuous life pushes us away from the Infinite, when everytime we signify "I" and not "thou". Senses degrade us down to the animal's level and to get out of this bondage we will have to realise our own nature which is the manifestation of the Infinite. So long as we are bound by the senses we cannot reach perfection. To get out of this complex situation we shall have to look back not to "I" but to "thou". The whole process needs to be reversed by renouncing all that is manifested through the senses. The little self "I" should be renounced totally, for this is the cause of all evil in the world. This is the very beginning of morality. The real self can be realised only by destroying the false small self "I". If at all, we want to merge in the Infinite, we will have to forget our particular. Selves which are finite and the root cause of all our miseries. Swami Vivekananda says that in this universe two forces are working simultaneously: one is selfishness and the other is unselfishness:

"...throughout creation these two forces are working side by side; where you find the one, you find the other too. The one is selfishness, and the other is unselfishness. The one is acquisition, and the other is renunciation. The one takes, the other gives. From the lowest to the highest, the whole universe is the playground of these two forces. It does not require any demonstration, it is obvious to all."[3]

Goodness of man does not lie with seeking one's selfish motives but in good of all. The strength of any law depends upon unselfishness and purity which is the real basis of life. The two forces are directed to preserve love – either love for oneself or love for others. One force renounces love for oneself and the other for others. In neither case, one can deny pursuance of love. The "good" is understood in two different senses – either for the promotion of "I" or "thou". In its exposition of selfishness, the evil is created. The love, so directed by selfishness, becomes limited to oneself, one's relations and one's belongings, forgetting millions of other human beings in the universe. This love can be expanded to all others too who lie outside their limited world of senses. Thus:

> the motive power of the whole universe in whatever way it manifests itself, is that one wonderful thing, unselfishness, renunciation, love, the real, the only living force in existence.[4]

This purity and perfection as the highest ideal of morality has a metaphysical dimension. Human nature is complex and its unfoldment through knowledge alone can expose the divine nature of man.

The ideal of unselfishness is the propelling force in us. Failures are natural which help us in pursuing life with its fullness. Life would not have been worthy of living if there was no struggle. It is only man who makes mistakes. But it is also his failure that shows him the right direction. The goodness lies in all, however, it may be shadowed by selfish motives. But goodness and badness, both are forces in man moving him in particular directions. By realising goodness one can succeed in overcoming his badness and this is so with all. Ignorance leads to the idea of manifoldness, whereas knowledge brings everything to oneness. Separation is not real. It is merely apparent on the surface; in depth there is unity. All are variations of one. The external world is but one part of the whole of phenomenon and is far away from the centre, the common ground. This centre is within us; the innermost core of the human soul is the centre of the whole universe. The religious basis of morality is not to be argued against and disputed. For this we will have to analyse our own souls. Religion does not lie in books and temples; it lives in actual perception. Vivekananda makes it clear that religion, as a mere talk or an intellectual assent, is nothing:

> We often consider a man religious who can talk well. But this is not religion. Wonderful methods of joining words, rhetorical powers, and explaining facts of the books in various ways – these are only for the enjoyment of the learned, and not religion. Religion comes when the actual realisation in our own souls begins. That will be the dawn of religion; and then alone we shall be moral. Now we are not much more moral than the animals.[5]

In fact, we are hypocrites. Once the society makes it free for all to do whatever they feel like doing for their sensuous enjoyments, and free them from any kind of punishment, they will all rush for material goods and will not find any difference between them in this regard. We are all alike and can become truly moral after we have realised religion. Doing good to others is just the manifestation of this oneness. Man has this sense of oneness with the universe which finds expression in love and sympathy. Love and sympathy are the basis of all morality. It is in the unselfish nature of man that we can find that:

> Thou art one with this Universal Being, and, as such, every soul that exists is your soul; and everybody that exists is your body; and in hurting anyone, you hurt yourself; in loving anyone, you love yourself. As soon as a current of hatred is thrown outside, whosoever it hurts, it also hurts yourself; and if love comes out from you, it is bound to come back to you. For I am the universe; this universe is my body. I am the Infinite, only I am not conscious of it now, but I am struggling to get this consciousness of the Infinite, and perfection will be reached when full consciousness of this Infinite comes.[6]

One of the two forces, which are working simultaneously throughout nature, is constantly differentiating while the other is constantly unifying; one is individuating but the other is bringing them together into an Infinite, the sameness in the differentiation. The whole universe is the battlefield of these two forces. One makes men distinct from each other and separates them while the other unifies them by classifying them into species by bringing out similarities in their expressions and forms. The oneness of universe is the perfection and therefore ceasation of the universe; that perfect unity is the perfect annihilation. It suggests that the variation has to remain, for when that stops, everything is gone. Life has a meaning only in variation. However, submitting to this variation we find ethical code in the unity, the sameness. Ethics does not submit to variation; for sameness is required to perceive the variety or vice versa. The unity already exists, and so long as there is life we cannot rule out variation. Life can never be thought about where variation has died down Unity gives a way to dead homogeneity which is not desirable. However, there exists unity as a logical necessity; for there would not be the perception of the finite without the Infinite. Thus, the claim:

> not that this unity has to be made, but that it already exists, and that you could not perceive the variety at all, without it. God is not to be made, but He already exists,[7]

cannot be refuted.

As such, it is not the function of ethics to bring unity by removing variations because it would be bringing death; but it is to recognise the Infinite strength as the property of everyone in spite of the apparent differences and weaknesses. Moral codes are binding because they are rationally justified universal principles and therefore cannot be just human sanctions. Such universal principles must be having eternal sanction that can be found in the infinite Reality that exists in all. The Infinite Oneness of the soul is the eternal sanction of all morality, thus making all one. We all are really one. "This oneness is the rationale of all ethics and all spirituality." Unselfishness is the foundation of all morality. Man grows with knowledge and morality is evolved which brushes aside the idea of separateness. The idea of non-separateness takes over the idea of individuality. This makes me consider that there is no such thing as my good or your good. Your good is my good, and my good is yours. The very idea of oneness, that is that your life is in my life, and my life is in your life, implies to that no one can ever leave one's fellow-beings without helping them. My good consist in good of others. So morality consists in self-abnegation. Individual personalised self is the cause of all struggle, misery, jealousy, hatred and all other evils. Ethics can be explained in one idea only, that:

I am the universe; this universe is one. Or else, where is the reason? Why should I do good to my fellowmen? Why should I do good to others? What compels me? It is sympathy, the feeling of sameness everywhere.[8]

Morality is the abnegation of *Ahamkara* and *Mamata*, the idea of me and mine. Infinite is the true nature of man. Swami Vivekananda strongly repudiates ethical norms which are utilitarian in approach. He stresses upon the realisation of superconscious powers that a man possesses which enables him to overcome his egoistic self. For him, we should hold ourselves last; ethical foundations lay not with "I" but "thou." Self-enhancement is not the motto of ethical discourse, rather it is the non-self. The laws of ethics pronounce that the senses can never have infinite power and can never bring infinite pleasures. Senses speak out for vain ideas of individualism. Infinite is neither possible nor thinkable in the idea of individualism. For Vivekananda:

Thus all codes of ethics are based upon this renunciation; destruction, not construction, of the individual on the material plane.[9]

Man will have to rise above the material plane to seek the Infinite in its depth. While objecting to utilitarian theory of ethics, he attempts to understand the reasons for the need of eradicating selfishness and cultivating unselfishness.

You call yourself a rational man, a utilitarian; but you do not show me a reason for utility, I say you are irrational.... Where is the utility of my being unselfish? My utility is to be selfish if utility means the greatest amount of happiness. What is the answer? The utilitarians can never give it. The answer is that this world is only one drop in an infinite ocean, one link in an infinite chain.[10]

Thus, infinite pleasure through the senses have to be given up. Moral life is based on self-abnegation, and not on acquisition of material things. We cannot have any moral laws from the principle of utility. Perfect self-annihilation or self-abnegation is the ideal of ethics. Ethics consists in the destruction of the individual-self. Considering oneself and others as the same is the only right approach to morals. Ethics cannot be belittled by limiting it to the boundaries of a society. Social norms cannot be eternal as they are merely conventional. Utilitarian theory can function only in present situations. Whereas it is only moral code, derived from spirituality and religion, that can be valid for the whole, infinite man. "...as it applies to the individual and his eternal relations, it must necessarily apply to the whole of society, in whatever condition it may be at any given time."[11]

Vivekananda states clearly that:

> Perfection is one thing and enjoyment another because they have different ends to secure; therefore they engage over differently. He who chooses perfection becomes pure. He who chooses enjoyment misses his true end. Both perfection and enjoyment present themselves to man; the wise man having examined both distinguishes one from the other. He chooses perfection and as being superior to enjoyment. But the foolish man chooses enjoyment for the pleasure of his body.[12]

Apparently, most pleasant things bring misery. One cannot know the truth unless one has conquered his desires for enjoyments, and this idea of renunciation is basic to *Vedic* morality. Our vain desires make us slaves to everything outside, withholding the truth express itself in our habits. Moral code is rooted in spirituality and the idea of Eternal God. Religion based morality expresses that:

> We must not look down upon others. All of us are going towards the same goal. The difference between weakness and strength is one of degree; the difference between heaven and hell is one of degree; the difference between life and death is one of degree, all differences in this world are one of degree, not of kind, because oneness is the secret of everything. All is One, which manifests itself, either as thought, or life, or soul, or body, and the difference is only in degree.[13]

Born in different societies, brought up in different surroundings and circumstances, and the sort of education we receive, we view the truth accordingly. Usually, we view the truth differently in limited spheres, in our own subjective conditions, with our intellect and mind. We grasp the truth as much as we receive it in the purview of our limited capacities and capabilities. And, this makes the difference between man and man, and sometimes it might appear to be giving rise to contradictions; yet, we cannot ignore the fact that we all belong to the same universal truth.

Swami Vivekananda, while supporting Hindu tradition, manners and customs, says that howsoever we may be uneducated, uncultivated and poor, we are not money-makers and self-oriented in the egoistic sense.[14] The traditional customs keep binding us together. In Indian caste system, man is saved from jealousy, hatred and avariciousness which originate from material gains.

However, it has many other ill effects. With Hindus, it is quality and birth which make caste, not money. With well-defined work man finds much time to think about his own divine nature. Caste is not a religious institution but a trade guild. To find God, one must search one's own heart. There are many ways of coming to God; however one thing is common that a truly religious man overcomes petty quarrels of sects and creeds. To be religious implies renunciation of body and believing in a spirit or soul. And this is possible by renouncing material world and body for the realisation of the divine soul. All religions teach us to do good to others. Whichever caste or class a person belongs to, he is supposed to do his duty, to do good to others. There is nothing extra-ordinary in it; rather, it is the only way to live without confrontation. One should not live for ulterior motives. Living means living for perfection, for others. Everything in the universe is for the expansion of life. The moment our attention is centred around our own motives and selfish interests the expansion of life ceases to be and death follows. There are different religions existing simultaneously in the universe. Their variations, their differences are not contradictory; however, we find differences in their rituals, languages and buildings, etc. Instead of contradicting they supplement each other. Thus:

> Each religion as it were, takes up one part of the great universal truth, and spends its whole force in embodying and typifying that part of the great truth. It is therefore addition not exclusion. That is the idea system after system arises, each one embodying a great idea, and ideals must be added to ideals. And this is the march of humanity.[15]

We could say that there can be contradictory views about something, but they all indicate the same thing and that is the truth of life. Vivekananda illustrates this point by giving an example, that,

> Suppose a man is journeying towards the sun and as he advances he takes a photograph of the sun at every stage. When he comes back, he has many photographs of sun, which he places before us.... We see that no two are alike, and yet, who will deny that all these are photographs of the same sun, from different standpoints?[16]

So, we must bear in mind that:

> We are all debtors to the world and the world does not owe us anything. It is a great privilege for all of us to be allowed to do anything for the

world. In helping the world we really help ourselves. The second point is that there is a God in this Universe. It is not true that the universe is drifting and stands in need of help from you and me. God is ever present therein. He is undying and eternally active and infinitely watchful. When the whole universe sleeps, he is working incessantly. All the changes and manifestations of the world are His. Thirdly, we ought not to hate anyone. This world will always continue to be a mixture of good and evil. Our duty is to sympathise with the weak and to love even the wrong doer. The world is a grand moral gymnasium wherein we have all to take exercise so as to become stronger and stronger spiritually. Fourthly, we ought not to be fanatics of any kind, because fantaticism is opposed to love. And further the calmer we are and less disturbed our nerves, the more shall we love and the better will our work be.[17]

In view of the level of knowledge and spirituality, there are various classes of men in this world.[18] First, there are godmen, highest of all men who do good to others even at the cost of their individual self. Then, there are men who do good to others so long as it does not harm themselves. Thirdly, there are men who do good to themselves even by injuring others; fourthly, there can be a class of people who injure others merely for injury's sake. "I" and "Mine" – the *pravritti* is the tendency with most of the people, to accumulate everything in one centre, that centre being "myself". *Nivritti*, on the other hand is abnegation of myself, and is the basis of all morality and religion. Even, in the case of a person, who is uneducated or opposed to religious ideas, if he sacrifices his own good for others, then he must be revered. Man's freedom can be asserted if he does not fall prey to his emotions and desires. *Nivritti* is freedom from attachment. Morality implies freeing oneself from the bondage of matter. Love for others is the ideal of human life. By hurting others you are harming yourself, therefore, no one should hurt others. Thus, for Vivekananda an ethical code can be derived only from the ideal of the impersonal God. Morality is not an end in itself, rather it is a means to free oneself from the bondage of the senses. Everything in this universe is struggling for freedom. By shedding off his selfishness, man acquires infinite expansion. Perfect unselfishness makes a person one with the universe. The unselfish action is directed to the goal of life, that is freedom. "That which is selfish is immoral, and that which is unselfish is moral."[19] Morals, in societies differ. However, there is the idea of duty which does not differ and change. Unity in variety is the plan of creation. People with different minds cannot be treated by the same standard and yet all are expected to do their duty. A *sanyasi* is to be treated as a *sanyasi* and a student as a student. Duty is determined by the circumstances which spell out what should be done or what should not be done. The conception of duty frees one from the selfish bonds.

No utility can judge the rightness or wrongness of an action. If there were no utility of speaking the truth, or behaving honestly then would they not be worthy of apprehension? Of course, we know that all are pursuing happiness. But happiness of an individual in his person, cannot justify the goodness of an action. It is because of ignorance that we think that good resides in personal happiness. In my quest for my personal interest I become separate from others which causes mischief and leads to misery. So misery is the outcome of the selfish nature of man. The world is full of happiness and misery, good and bad. However, happiness and good on the one hand, and misery and bad on the other cannot have interchangeable expression. So to overcome misery, one should try to free oneself from the psychological problems. We learn from the failures of ourselves or others as we learn from our and their goodness. The deed, good or bad, may be on the conscious plane but the cause which affected it may be on the unconscious plane. The negative side of anything always enlightens the positive. Evils do make us realise that why good should be approached and practised. Not only that man learns from good of others, but as a matter of fact he learns more from their evils and failures. Morals have a psychological basis to a great extent. Being in this world and in the process of transaction with worldly beings we develop our convictions stronger and raise the level of consciousness to evaluate and judge actions in a universal sense. However, besides this consciousness, there is a vast store of forgotten thoughts buried in our minds which corrupt our present thoughts. There are mixed and jumbled good and evil thoughts at the unconscious or sub-conscious level. Without our awareness they cause danger to the humanity. So these thoughts should be controlled by conscious thoughts. We often tell children not to steal, but how to do so will really help them. Controlling one's mind is the way to understand things in a better way. It is possible to control feelings and willingness but if the attempt at controlling mind is not voluntary, it may prove to be disastrous.

> The goal of each soul is freedom, mastery – freedom from the slavery of matter and thought, mastery of external, and internal nature ... already existing heavy chain of bondage of past thoughts, past superstitions. Therefore, beware how you allow yourselves to be acted upon by others. Beware how you unknowingly bring another to ruin.[20]

> The extraneous will can function only on a diseased person. "There are two components in every action, the one the subject, the other the object, and the one aim of life is to make the subject master of the object.... Change is always subjective ... that the conquest of evil comes by the change in the subjective alone.[21]

Pleasure can never be the goal of life. However, both pleasure and pain are great teachers. Character of an individual is formed by his actions, good or bad. Man learns more by facing miseries in life. What man learns, is implanted within man; he discovers it or unveils it – the infinite knowledge. All knowledge is in the human mind. In Vivekananda's psychological approach, religions and education have a great role to play in making man strong or weak. With natural gifts of emotions and intellect and what has been taught to man by the world around, he learns to act and create *samskaras* for himself. The more we condemn wickedness and sins of the world to the child, the more we weaken him. He says that we must not condemn wickedness. Rather, we should try to find out the ways to overcome it or replace it with goodness. By teaching children that they are the glorious children of immortality, even the weakest can become strong. Strength is there within us which can be brought on the surface by positive, helpful and strong thoughts. By saying, "I am the Absolute Infinite, I can gather the infinite strength of the world." Sin and misery are the outcome of weakness which is more or less the character-trait that we learn by the education given in our primary years or childhood.[22] Do not let yourself be caught in the nexus of superstitions. Unveil the covering of superstitious ideas over your minds. Let the idea, "I am not separate and different from the Infinite One," reign our minds all the time so as not to let weaker ideas overtake us which cause misery and sin. The goal of perfection may seem to be away and distant but the truth is far from being doubted. The practice of this ideal is not socially bound but a strong society will certainly look for its application. Truth does not need society for its recognition but rather societies need truth as their basis. Man can perfect himself and control the whole universe by multiplying infinitely his centre of self-consciousness:

> Consciousness therefore, is the chief thing to understand. Let us say that here is an infinite line amid the darkness. We do not see the line, but on it there is one luminous point which moves on. As it moves along the line, it lights up its different parts in succession, and all that is left behind becomes dark again. Our consciousness may well be likened to this luminous point. Its past experiences have been replaced by the present, or have become subconscious. We are not aware of their presence in us; but they are unconsciously influencing our body and mind. Every movement that is now being made without the help of consciousness was previously conscious. Sufficient impetus has been given it to work of itself.[23]

Miseries and blessings are the result of *Karma* – the work, the action. Everything that we do, physical or mental, is *Karma* that leaves its marks on us. The greatness of a man can be judged by the common actions he does. He may prove himself great at a particular occasion but not always. "As is *Karma*, so is the manifestation of the will". And, "no one can get anything unless he earns it. This is an eternal law...."[24] Our *Karma* determines what we deserve and what we can assimilate for what we are, and we can also determine our tomorrow. By our present actions we can make our future. So, we have to know how to act. My present acts will determine my future. Usually, we work with various motives, but unselfishness is more paying, not in material terms but in terms of the knowledge of the one Infinite. Unselfishness is the:

> greatest manifestation of power – this tremendous restraint. Self-restraint is a manifestation of greater power than all outgoing action.... This self-control will tend to produce a mighty will, a character which makes a Christ or a Buddha.[25]

We are not far-sighted, and for immediate material gains we become immoral and wicked. This is our weakness, our powerlessness. Any good work should be done for its own sake and never for its results. All that we think and all that we do result in character-building. Man himself is the originating cause of his character. He is what he has created for himself. These impressions or *samskaras* direct a man in his next birth. *Samskaras* do not cease to be and are carried on through *Prāṇa*. *Samskaras* are powerful and remain existent unless they are totally exhausted. Body and mind are just the manifestation of the soul in bondage. The soul cannot be free so long as it is occupied by the material destinies of body and mind. The goal of a man is to free the soul from bodily and mental blows. Mind and body, both perish with the temporal strokes, but soul is never born and never dies; it is eternal. The perishable moving nature makes us believe that the soul is moving; otherwise, the realisation of its being there forever speaks for its being omni-present and free. The soul (*Atman*) in bondage is called individual soul (*Jiva*) of man. In order to understand and communicate the very idea of freedom and omni-presence of the one Absolute Soul, we take recourse to the bondage and say that *Atman* comes and goes. However, this linguistic expression may not cover the nature of the Absolute Soul which is eternal.[26] So:

> Jiva, the soul, comes to higher or lower states. This is the well-known law of reincarnation, and this law binds all creation .... The human soul has joined in lower and higher forms, migrating from one to another, according to the Samskaras or impressions, but it is only in the highest form as man that it attains to freedom. The man form is higher than even the angel form, and of all forms it is the highest; man is the highest being in creation, because he attains to freedom.[27]

There are only a few who grasp this idea of freedom; for the vast majority is running after material things. We are struggling consciously or unconsciously constantly. One can achieve this freedom through the pursuit of unselfishness. A man with self-restraint and self-control learns to act without any selfish motive. Usually our motives are directed by our selfish nature and get manifested in *Samskaras*. *Samskaras* are the representation of the impressions of the past life. Man's character is the sum total of these impressions. *Samskaras* are the irresistible tendencies in man to act in a particular way; what a man is – is the result of these impressions. Man has a power to replace his bad habits by good actions. Character results out of repeated habits, that a man gets accustomed to perform. Past experiences may remain in the sub-conscious mind; they affect our present even when we are not aware of this fact. What we consider today, an effortless movement or action done instantly without being conscious of that, might have been done with a conscious effort. Real activity lies in calmness, in the balance of mind which is never disturbed, whatever may happen. One can do better with a calm mind; losing nerves is to waste one's energy; disturbed mind's output is very little. "It is the calm, forgiving, equitable, well-balanced mind that does the greatest amount of work."[28]

Thus, all our weaknesses are due to ignorance. We have power within ourselves which is to be realised through knowledge and faith in eternal life. The greatest error lies in not having faith in ourselves. The very thought that you are weak, a sinner, a miserable creature, without any power to do this or that, binds you down to ignorance. This is the false life which should be unveiled to manifest its real nature to coincide with life eternal. One should believe in oneself. It is not a selfish belief. It means faith in all because you are all. Love for yourself means love for all, love for animals, love for everything; for you are all one. To discriminate, we will have to know oneness.

> Love is truth, and hatred is false, because hatred makes for multiplicity. It is hatred that separates man from man; therefore it is wrong and false. It is a disintegrating power, it separates and destroys. Love binds, love makes for that oneness.[29]

It is through the self that everything is perceived. All knowledge comes in and through the self. We are weak because we are ignorant. *Vedāntists* believe that God is Infinite Knowledge, Infinite Love and Infinite Bliss, and they regard these three as One. Nothing else is necessary than love, sincerity and patience. To get the higher, renounce the lower. Truth, purity and unselfishness can never let the bearer be looked down upon.

NOTES AND REFERENCES

1. *Complete Works of Vivekananda,* Vol. II, (C.W.) Swapana Printing Works (P) Ltd., 52, Raja Rammohun Roy Sarai, Kolkata, 1995, p. 17.
2. *Ibid.,* p. 18.
3. *Universal Ethics and Moral Conduct* (U.E. and M.C.), p. 12, Advaita Ashrama, Trio Process, Kolkata, 2001.
4. *Ibid.,* p. 13.
5. C.W., Vol. II, p. 164.
6. *U.E. and M.C,* p. 16.
7. *Ibid.,* p. 19.
8. *Ibid.,* p. 25.
9. *Ibid.,* p. 28.
10. C.W., Vol. II, p. 63.

11. *U.E and M.C.U*, p. 31.
12. *C.W.*, Vol. II, p. 181.
13. *Ibid.*, p. 299.
14. *Ibid.*, p. 489.
15. *Ibid.*, p. 365.
16. *Ibid.*, p. 365.
17. *U.E. and M.C.*, pp. 31-32.
18. *Ibid.*, p. 33.
19. *Ibid.*, p. 40.
20. *Ibid.*, pp. 53-54.
21. *Ibid.*, pp. 55-56.
22. C.W., pp. 84-87.
23. *Ibid.*, p. 33.
24. *U.E. and M.C.*, pp. 61-62.
25. *Ibid.*, p. 65.
26. C.W., p. 255.
27. *Ibid.*, p. 258.
28. *U.E. and M.C.*, pp. 72-73.
29. *Ibid.*, p. 73.

6

The Religion is, The Religions are

Pabitrakumar Roy

Vivekananda has passionately and persuasively advanced the thesis that as elsewhere in life and the world, unity of religions persists in and through diversity. There are many ways in which the thesis of unity in diversity could be understood, appreciated and even appropriated. The thesis is difficult and may lend itself to misappropriation if grasped mistakenly. However, I propose to consider the thesis as it might have been intended by Vivekananda in the context of plurality, and even pluralism of religions along with its possible ramifications.

It was in 1893 at the Parliament of Religions at Chicago that Vivekananda proposed the thesis. It appealed to him as "scientific" to look for unity, since that is "the plan of nature". He proposed the concept of *Advaita* to be understood as unity, a qualification that merits consideration. Vivekananda used the word "variety" as a synonym of "diversity". The thesis has been influential in recent Indian history, as such leaders of the Indian renaissance as Tagore, Gandhi and Radhakrishnan employed the thesis as an explanatory device to escape and even eschew the divisive and negative emotions arising out of plurality of religions and our multi-cultural state of affairs. Tagore's *The Vision of India's History* and the poem *Bharat-tirtha* (tr. "India's Prayers") is woven around the thesis of unity in diversity.

Unity is hardly an easy concept. Like "equality" it is not a perceptible element, and Socrates in Plato's *Phaedo* makes the point abundantly clear. Yet we cannot dispense with the term. Unity is a categorical notion with Kant, it is a category (according to quality), and so is plurality (=diversity?). Again, unity may be likened to reality, another category according to quality, and it has its anti-thesis in negation (*Critique of Pure Reason*, B. 106). I do not mean to suggest that Vivekananda has Kant in mind or his view in proposing his thesis. But the Kantian insight could be used with profit in understanding Vivekananda's intention. The plurals tend to negate one another. Yet if they are viewed *sub-specie* unity, one might reach up to reality, and for Vivekananda unity is reality. The unity of the plurals is a richer truth than the isolation and alienation of the plurals themselves. The ancient problem of the one and the many has plagued philosophers here as elsewhere. The monists have tended to discredit the pluralists with any kind of reality, and even existence. It is argued that if we count many leaves, then in addition to the leaves we count there is one thing – a leaf – which they all are. Do we know the thing separately before we can recognise or count the individual leaves? The principle of one over many poses one version of the problem of universals. The particulars are said to inhere in the universal, so goes the *Nyāya* thesis. But *Vedānta* argument against *samavāya* is famous in Śamkara's *bhāśya* on the *Brahma Sūra*. How would Vivekananda get in terms with Śamkara? The refusal to admit the relation of *samavāya* between the universal and the particular might endanger the thesis of unity in diversity. Either unity (in the sense of *advaita*) alone is real, or diversity is. The law of excluded middle may tyrannise the monist condescending the plurals. What does the thesis of unity in variety suggest? Unity as a categorical term is subsumptive in function. Consider Sri Aurobindo's "human unity", which clearly calls for an "ideal", something not yet but very much needed for the future ordering of life and human existence. Vivekananda speaks of "universal religion". Is it another religion apart from the existing ones? Aldous Huxley borrowed an analogy from mathematics to characterise his conception of perennial philosophy, and called it the HCF of the mystical insights of the East and the West. The HCF analogy is not anything apart from the numbers; it pervades them. Does the unity of the plurals, in like manner, pervade the plurals?

Vivekananda's "universal religion" is said to exist, "The Religion is", the intention of the assertion is obviously not to make an existential statement, which the other half of the sentence does. Is it an affirmation of a philosophical faith? If it is something to be achieved, then how? Vivekananda admits that discovering universal features of religions is not an easy task, but adds that "we know that they exist".[1] Is it a case of knowing in the "strong sense"? Vivekananda's master, Ramakrishna is reported to have asserted his God-awareness in the strong sense of having seen God as he saw individual persons. An *āpta purūṣa*, Ramakrishna's assertion cannot be profaned however metaphorical his use of the verb "see" might have been.

Vivekananda's position merits closer attention. He does not discount the variety or the plural in deference to the unity. He recognises unity as well as variation. This is something unique with his kind of monism. He sees beauty no less than human necessity in variety and diversity. Vivekananda upholds the essentialist position that religion is one in essence but diverse in manifestation. He appears to accept the concept of universal religion in the sense of a transcendent essence of primordial unity without undermining pluralism. Since all religions are in essence one, it seems desirable that diverse manifestations of the essence should be encouraged to multiply. Vivekananda has been the philosophical heir to the *anekānta* view of reality of the Jainas, and loves to invoke the *Vedānta* metaphor of the sun reflected in diverse vessels of water. As a propounder of *anekānta Vedānta*, he defends the individuals no less than the reality of unity. Individuals are not bare particulars they are informed by unity, just as the *Vedāntic* metaphor goes, the suns reflected in the diverse receptacles are nonetheless reflections of the sun. He shares the ancient Indian insight that truth may be expressed in a hundred thousand ways, and that each of these ways is true as far as it goes.[2] But what sets Vivekananda apart from previous teachers of the thesis of unity in diversity is his anxiety of its practical application. He is aware that at the conceptual level the thesis might put the logician into unease. But at the level of experience the unity of the diverse is felt; the sense of unity of the variations may so overtake us and in such a manner that our way of looking at life and its ordering may altogether change. The unity waits to be realised, rendered real in experience.

Vivekananda has no patience for theoretical understanding of the thesis, albeit he does not disavow the case. It should be unexceptionable to suggest that the concept of unity in variety is to be regarded rather entertained as a practically regulative notion much like Kant's ideas of reason. It is worth recalling that Kant has remarked that the ideas of reason are either too big or too small for the categories of the understanding. They are required to be made real, i.e., realised in terms of our ways of thinking and action. There is another dimension in which Vivekananda's notion of unity in diversity may be brought in line with Kant's insight. A singular maxim can become a law only if it can be shown to be desirable from the one categorical imperative. In like manner particular religions become worth calling so only when they can be shown as containing elements acceptable to others, or can be shown to be grounded in a universal form, transcending their historical, social, political and cultural contingent characters. It may also be suggested that particular scriptures are but the alphabets of the one language of universal religion.

Vivekananda's another term for "unity" is "harmony". Harmony is an analogy from music, and in that case it has got to be creatively achieved. Harmony is a musical achievement. The intended harmony is not pre-established in Leibniz's sense. Had it been so, then there could not have been anything problematic about the thesis. To persue the musical analogy further, the harmony of point and counter-point is what the composer achieves in his composition. Similarly, the realisation of unity in variety is an achievement of apperception, though not of perception. The *Upanishad* of course says *ekatvam anupaśyata*, should we not take the verb for perception *paśya* in a metaphorical or apperceptional sense? Our dealings with the variations would undergo a sea-change only if we care to deal with them as if they all were represented in their unity, just as all the fruits and flowers of the seasons are insured in the heart of the Absolute, *a la* Bradley.

Vivekananda's thesis is neither a facile generalisation, nor is it easy to generalise the variety. The variations remain, and just because they remain, the sense of their unity is worth looking for. Differentiation of the individuals contributes to the richness, without exhausting it in any manner, of the unity, and the unity imparts a new value to the individuals. For Vivekananda, unity in variety is a principle of life, its practical import is more important than its mere intellectual or theoretical content. It could well be that the thesis is intellectually indemonstrable. One has to grow into the realisation of the truth of the thesis from within. The truth of the thesis is attitudinal or of faith, though not of belief in the epistemic sense.

Vivekananda's thesis is a thesis of philosophy of religion. And religion, as he asks us to understand:

> is realisation; not talk, nor doctrine, nor theories, ... not hearing or acknowledging, it is the whole soul becoming changed into what it believes.[3]

Obviously Vivekananda puts more premium on the mystical or the realisational aspect of religious experience or life. He analyses the phenomenon of religion into three parts: philosophical, mythological and ritualistic. The first part is set forth in abstract terms, while the second and the third "concretises" the abstract formulations of the first part. Mythologies and rituals of a religion are embedded in history, society and other spatio-temporal conditions that may have played a part in the evolution of particular faiths. The philosophical part of a religion usually contains mystical intuitions and supportive theological statements. This part is more shareable with the outsiders, since it comprises judgements of life and existence, and hence are often found to be raised above the conditions of conformity dividing people into believers and non-believers. If unity is to be looked for it may be hoped to be found in the first and the most important first "philosophical" part of the phenomenon of religion. It is also significant that Vivekananda takes into account plurality of religions, and to an extent pluralism, too, of religions. Plurality is a fact of history, while pluralism is something that we may ask for. The unity view of religion demands that both plurality and pluralism of religions are reconcilable in terms of a higher order perspective and understanding of the phenomena. Phenomenology of religion distinguishes between the essence and manifestation of religion.[4] Vivekananda's idea of the philosophical part of religion belongs to the essence aspect, while mythology and rituals go to the manifestation aspect of the religious phenomena.

Vivekananda is well aware of the fact that unity is hard to find. The philosophical part of religion may and does often contain such assertions that would refuse accommodation to assertion of other religion's so-called philosophical part. These are theological statements. At this point St. Paul's distinction between the letter and the spirit of scriptures is quite significant. St. Paul said the letter killeth, while the spirit enliveneth. A literal interpretation is a form of idolatory; it ignores the symbolic nature of religious language, and gives rise to fanaticism. Vivekananda has no soft term for fanaticism, and considers it as a "dangerous disease" arousing "all the wickedness of human nature". The religious fanatic, he says, is an "irresponsible lunatic".[5] Religious harmony has its enemies within religion itself.

Yet Vivekananda argues that "a universal form of religion" "already exists".[6] The existence claim is of course precarious, and defies quantification. The claim that religion is, or that a universal form of religions exists is devoid of any descriptive content. Even in rituals there is no universal symbol. The historical manifestation of religions is so deeply embedded in history, society and material conditions that universality claims on the part of any religion is to be given up. Is there one Buddhism or one Islam, or one Christianity? Studies in comparative religion disclose facts on the contrary. Nor is there only one form of Hindutva. Vivekananda's Hindutva leans heavily on mysticism and moral purity, which he calls "chastity". It is open and awakened to the need for a religion of reconciliation, a religion marked by tolerant and benevolent universalism. It proceeds from the classical Hindu assumption about the underlying unity of the manifold, and the relative nature of all formulated creeds. It abhors exclusiveness.

Plurality of religions, at the empirical level, is a truth too hard to forget or even to ignore, and it perhaps entails exclusiveness in spite of the vacuous talks of "brotherhood", which remains a closed circle of the believers, and has to be understood always in the sectarian context.

Vivekananda therefore has to look for something ideal. He is not looking for "unity of sameness."[7] What then is "universal religion"? He takes an evolutionary view of religion in its manifestation. Truth may be timeless, yet it is manifested in time, and manifestations of truth in time conditions their individualities. Individualities of religions are the outcome of historical changes undergone by them. All religions are religions in history. Individuality of religions, or "variations" as Vivekananda calls it, has its own value, but need not be taken to represent the final truth. Religions are not to be understood apart from the people who follow them. And people do not stand still; they are taken along by the winged chariot of time. Should one desire or think it possible that she or he would live the life of the time of her or his prophet is apt to give expression to, in Vivekananda's striking phrase, "tribal self-assertion in religious matters".[8] The way to come out of mutual anger and hatred amongst the religions of the world is to uphold the idea of universal toleration. Toleration is entailed by Vivekananda's idea of civilisation, which, he says, cannot grow or flower:

> unless fanaticism, bloodshed and brutality stop. No civilisation can begin to lift up its head until we look charitably upon one another; and the first step towards that much-needed charity is to look charitably and kindly upon the religious conviction of others ... not only should we be charitable, but positively helpful to each other, however, different our religious ideas and convictions may be.[9]

Positive helpfulness is the crux of religious toleration. It is never a sort of passive indifference to the presence of religions other than mine. And at this point Vivekananda touches the ethical chord, for charity is impossible unless love be there, and love alone, he says, is the fittest thing to survive, not hatred. There is a remarkable poem by Robert Frost. He mentions the theory that the world will end in ice. And if that be so, then hate will do. And should the world end in fire, then anger would do. Vivekananda will not assent, and says that we need to have some great "life-giving idea".[10] This life-giving idea is what religion stands for: "that you and I are really one" – the idea of *Advaita*, the ideal of the oneness of all. It is the oneness which subsists beyond, and persists in and through all the religions that exist. The omnipresence of the supreme soul in all obliges one towards an attitude shift in one's action towards the believers in other faiths, and worship becomes unbounded and free.

There occurs a very moving account of the philosophy of religion that Vivekananda is formulating, and it deserves hearing: ... the religions of the world are not contradictory or antagonistic. They are but various phases of one eternal religion. That one eternal religion is applied to different planes of existence, is applied to the opinions of various minds and various races. There never was my religion or yours, my national religion or your national religion; there never existed many religions, there is only the one. One infinite religion existed all through eternity and will ever exist, and this religion is expressing itself in various countries in various ways. Therefore, we must respect all religions and we must try to accept them all as far as we can. Religions manifest themselves not only according to race and geographical position, but according to individual powers. In one man religion is manifesting itself as intense activity, as work. In another it is manifesting itself as intense devotion, in yet another, as mysticism, in others as philosophy, and so forth. It is wrong when we say to others,

> "Your methods are not right." ... To learn this central secret that the truth may be one and yet many at the same time, that we may have different visions of the same truth from different standpoints, is exactly what must be done. Then, instead of antagonism to anyone, we shall have infinite sympathy with all.[11]

There need not be any apology for the long citation. That was no empty rhetoric, but words come up from the depths of truth. The message rings sharp and simple, and so very relevant for our bigoted times: ... "making a political something out of the truths of religion – is not religion at all".[12]

Vivekananda's concept of religion is not mere talk, mere trying to believe, mere groping in darkness, mere parroting the words of ancestors. On the contrary, religion is nothing short of realisation of oneness of the humankind, and has to be founded upon love for others. Vivekananda's notion of religion has no room for any negative breaking down and destructive teaching; it welcomes and accommodates practical spirituality instead.

A couple of important features of practical spirituality may be noted. It steers clear of the vexed question of conversion, which has plagued our times. Vivekananda is quite unambiguous in saying that the "only true teacher is he who can convert himself".[13] He declared as early as 1893 that:

> the Christian is not to become a Hindu or Buddhist, nor a Hindu or a Buddhist to become a Christian. But each must assimilate the spirit of the others and yet preserve his individuality and grow according to his own law of growth.[14]

The law of growth is what the concept of *svadharma* stands for. *Svadharma* for Vivekananda is not a closed concept, and there can be enrichment of it by assimilation from others. The idea of exclusive survival of any religion by the destruction of other is a pitiable and idle dream. The idea that there shall be only one religion in the world is an absurdity. As the Dalai Lama has put it, the whole of India was not Buddhist even during the time of the Buddha. Holiness, purity and charity, says Vivekananda, are not exclusive possessions of any church in the world.

The Dalai Lama has further suggested that inter-faith dialogue is possible on the basis that it is important to appreciate the different religious traditions, and that there are sufficient reasons for respecting and appreciating the major religious traditions of the world. Inter-faith dialogue can improve closer understanding in two possible ways. One involving scholars meeting in a more academic way to clarify the differences and similarities between their traditions. The second way of dialogue is pilgrimage by followers of different religious traditions. They can go together as a group in order to make a pilgrimage to the holy places of different religious traditions. The pilgrims should pray together if possible, if not they can silently meditate. The Dalai Lama considers this a very effective way to understand the value and power of other religious traditions. His Holiness himself has gone on such pilgrimages to the holy sites of the Jews, Christians, Hindus and Muslims. His experience of spiritual friendship with benedictine monk Thomas Merton is related by His Holiness himself in *Ethics for the New Millennium*.[15]

Vivekananda's concept of religion is inspired by a humanism in which man is defined by the analogy of a "circle whose circumference is nowhere"[16], and more importantly as an open-ended potential divinity. Accordingly, religions are but embodiments of man's inspiration for holiness. In religion properly so-called man worships the infinite, not anything finite, be it a book, a temple or a mosque. Nothing that is finite would ever satisfy or comprehend man's religious inspiration. The Book of God is never closed, and the Parliament of Religions is always in session. Religions have so far or till now described or interpreted the religious situation in diverse ways, but the task is to change it. Taking the interpretations in his stride Vivekananda would prefer man to arrive:

> to the place where there is neither the Vedas nor the Bible nor the Koran, yet this has to be done by harmonising the Vedas, the Bible and the Koran. Mankind ought to be taught that religions are but the varied expressions of THE RELIGION, which is oneness so that each may choose the path that suits him best.[17]

A conception of religion such as Vivekananda's is vastly wide and open, as it stands beyond the confines of murky medievalism of churches and institutions. It is edifying to note Vivekananda's values. They are freedom and fearlessness, love and charity, and reason. This conception of religion does not brook superstition, fear, tyranny and priest-craft, hate and over-running of others' faith. Even the scriptures, in order to be authoritative, have to go by the test of reason. These values are in part called from his philosophical faith, partly from ethics, and no less from his scientific temper.

Something should be said about Vivekananda's philosophical anthropology, his distinction between the real and the apparent man. Whatever he says about religions has oblique reference to the twofold nature of man. Man lives at two levels. At one level man is *atman*, free and infinite, universal existence, the ultimate unity. At another level man is the ego, finite, bound by space, time and causality. The religion properly so-called is the religion of the *atman*, while the religions of the world are but mental formulations, diverse and sympathetically mediated, partial gleamings of the *atman*. Religions are an affairs of giving name and form to that which can never be named and formed. The scriptures of the world "are only words, external arrangement, syntax, the etymology, the philosophy, the dry bones of religion".[18] The point is "to know the spirit of the scriptures", the ultimate significance of all these, the unity sustaining the variation.

The essentialism running through Vivekananda's argument for unity amongst religions is a matter to be experienced, realised, and never to be rendered conceptual. A Buddhist is not an essentialist, and we have seen the Dalai Lama arguing the possibility of inter-faith understanding based on the mutuality of the pervasive human condition of suffering and the desire to come out of it. Since all men, irrespective of their faiths and belief, seek happiness, they are all worthy of caring and love as I am. The point is that all talk of unity need not be necessarily essentialist and any talk or language of essentialism need not be philosophically defective. Vivekananda's language of unity should not be misunderstood, even though its syntax and semantics is *Vedāntic*, and even at times anti-theological. Plurality of religions is an empirical fact of the first order. This is never denied, rather it is asserted unambiguously. Variations are real in the *vyavahārika* mode of being, how a higher order way of looking at the phenomena, the plurality can and desirably be seen as having a common purpose, function and importance for mankind. Vivekananda asked the question: "Why should I be moral?" and answers that there has to be:

some eternal principle of truth. The infinite oneness of the Soul is the eternal sanction of all morality, that you and I are not only brothers – every literature voicing man's struggle towards freedom has preached that ... you and I are really one .... This is the rationale of all ethics and all spirituality.[19]

All good, he goes on to say, comes from equality. The omnipresence of unity entails amelioration and elevation of man as duty. This humanism of a different order, based on love so wide as to embrace men of all and every denominations. One should recall what John wrote in his first epistle:

If a man says I love God and hateth his brother, he is a liar: for he that loveth not his brother whom he hath seen, how can he love God whom he hath not seen?[20]

Which secular humanist would say like this? Much of what Vivekananda has said belongs to this category. Above all his idea of the unity of religions derives its validity and viability from the lived experiences and experimentations of his master, Ramakrishna. And it is one of the contentions of Indian epistemology that the experiences of a veracious person, an *āpta purūṣa* need be taken as authoritative for working out our own freedom.

We may now turn to consider some critical observations concerning Vivekananda's thesis.

There is much in Vivekananda's concept of universal religion that reminds us of Hegel's idea of religion as a self-subsisting essence or a transcendental entity, underlying all particular historical manifestations. Schleiermacher argued that religion was not simply a theological system or a set of theories, doctrines, principles or ideas, but something to do with man's soul. To discover what religion really is one will have to turn away from arid and fossilised forms of it and look within at the pious soul. The primordial form of religion is the "soul dissolved in the immediate feeling of the Infinite and the Eternal".[21] For both Vivekananda and Schleiermacher, the starting point of religion is man. It originates in the soul's response and surrender to the Infinite. True religion is the sense and taste for the Infinite, and it cannot be equated with its outward forms, though its primordial essence does find expression in the sorry forms of earthly religions. Each historical religion is a distinct though impure form of its essence yet the multiplicity of earthly religions is necessary for the complete manifestation of the essence of religion.[22] The essentialist position, be it propounded by Hegel or Schleiermacher or Vivekananda, has one thing in common: that religion is one in essence and diverse in manifestation, that the transcendental unity of religion is a necessary pre-requisite for the existence of historical religions through which the essence of religion is manifested. But it is also true that it is not possible to nominate a particular historical religion as the perfect embodiment of the essence of religion. Hence, it is possible for God to be contemplated and worshipped in a variety of different ways, and it would be wrong of anyone to insist on religious uniformity.

Relativist thinkers would of course present a stark contrast to essentialist conception of religion argued for by Vivekananda. They would partly be in agreement over the diversity and multiplicity of religions. The relativist philosopher of religion would argue that all religions may move in the direction of unity, but individual differences are likely to remain. The modern view of history knows of no universal principle governing historical realities and no law determining the essence of religion. He would view with disquiet the thesis that an essence underlies individual religions. The relativist considers it untenable that a particular religion could be presented as the embodiment of, or the most perfect expression of the essence of religion.[23] The relativist would be in accord with Vivekananda on the question of the diversity and multiplicity of religions, but not because they are manifestations of a primordial essence. This is a view he rejects as untenable, because of its inaccessibility to historical investigation, rather because they are culturally determined.

We may not decide the issue between essentialism of Vivekananda and the relativistic counterpoint. But we can rightfully ask if the relativistic view that the quest for the essence of religion leads us away from a true understanding of particular religious traditions is right. Is there a justification for the claim that historical investigation can point to no universal principle underlying the appearance of historical realities? Does the essentialist elevate the concept of the essence of religion to the position of a norm and assign an inferior status to the discipline of historical investigation? Are we to take it for granted, on the pleading of the relativist, that such essentialists as Plato and Śamkara, Schleiermacher and Rudolf

Otto and Vivekananda have gone on the wrong track? Is immediate self-consciousness or infinitive awareness, the sense and taste of the infinite or anamnesis of no use or value concerning our judgements of life and existence? And what after all is the issue between essentialism and relativism? Is it the old and perennial battle between empiricism and idealism? No answer is possible to satisfy every one of the contenders. There must be reasons for someone's upholding the essentialist position. And Vivekananda's reasons for his version of essentialism are no less important than the relativist's. These remain valid for him to uphold his concept of universal religion.

NOTES AND REFERENCES

1. Swami Vivekananda, *Selections from the Complete Works of Swami Vivekananda*, Advaita Ashrama, Kolkata, Third edition, 1987, p. 161 (hereafter cited as S).
2. *Ibid.*, p. 163.
3. *Ibid.*, p. 174.
4. Vide G. Van der Leenw, *Religion in Essence and Manifestation*, tr. J.E. Turner, Harper and Row, New York, 1963.
5. S. 159.
6. *Ibid.*, p. 160.
7. *Ibid.*, p. 163.
8. *Ibid.*, p. 203.
9. *Ibid.*, p. 204.
10. *Ibid.*, p. 205.
11. *Ibid.*, pp. 354-55.
12. *Ibid.*, p. 356.
13. *Ibid.*, p. 356.
14. *Ibid.*, p. 18.
15. *Ethics for the New Millennium*, Little Brown and Company, London, 2000.
16. S. 78.
17. *Ibid.*, p. 535a.
18. *Ibid.*, p. 47.
19. *Ibid.*, p. 47.
20. *The New Testament*, Epistle of John, 4.20.
21. F. Schleirmacher, *On Religion*, pp. 15-16, New York, 1958.
22. *Ibid.*, pp. 211-13, 217.
23. Ernst Thoeltsch, *The Absoluteness of Christianity and the History of Religions*, London, 1972, and *Contemporary Religious Thinkers*, ed. John Macquarrie, New York, 1968.

7

Universalising Universal Religion: Reading in Vivekananda

Geeta Manakatala

As we live in the first decade of the third millennium, we are being forced by the trend of global events to address a number of issues which sometime in the distant past did not occupy the attention of our ancestors. Because of the growing power of these events and owing to the complexities they create for the average Indian, it is imperative that some attention be given to them. One of the key issues that is beginning to make life nasty, brutish and short is the conflation of two explosive issues in the human condition. These are the issues of religion and ethnic culture. Much blood has been shed in this country and elsewhere by the so-called "religious" people who believe that their violent actions serve a divine cause. We have the experience of Godhra, one of the most recent ghastly examples of man's inhumanity to man. Such tragedies, which are daily brought into our living rooms, tell us a great deal about ourselves and about the strange and sometimes bizarre psychology, which defines our identity, our self-image and our self-worth. Watching such events unravel before one's eyes forces the religiously conscious human being to ask the long-standing question: "Is religion and its message to human kind still relevant?"

This paper attempts to examine and elucidate Swami Vivekananda's views on the nature of religion and its bearing on the plurality of religions in the world, thus providing a basis for a universal religion. On the whole, Vivekananda's concept of a universal religion is a comprehensive and consistent attitude toward an explanation of what by common consent shapes the deepest concerns of the human race. It sets the most desirable goals before us: the unity of all human beings, their harmony with one another and the world in which they live, and each person's growth into that joyous freedom which is the mark of all true religions.

Much has changed in the last century since Swami Vivekananda spoke effectively and passionately at the 1893 Parliament of World Religions, "accept and understand one another". He made a clarion call for a universal religion, whose credo would be sufficiently liberal yet adequately spiritual for recognising divinity in each being, and an infinite capacity for development to be manifest everywhere. While addressing the Americans, he stated that:

> the Christian is not to become a Hindu or a Buddhist nor a Hindu or a Buddhist to become a Christian. But each must assimilate the spirit of the other and yet preserve his individuality and grow according to his own law of growth.[1]

It obviously recognises the right of each soul to choose its own path and to seek God in its own way. Swamiji was against forcible conversion.

Before we examine Vivekananda's concept of Universal Religion and how we prepare ourselves and the world for its realisation, we need to know what is meant by "Religion". The term "Religion" like many other terms cannot be defined univocally; rather it is equivocal in itself. "Religion" when used unreflectively and conventionally is said to have a clear meaning. But when used reflectively, its meaning becomes more elusive than we realise. Perhaps the best approach that we can adopt is to recognise that words do not have singular meaning. They are used contextually and it so happens that we usually succeed in communicating ideas reasonably well without having to satisfy what particular meaning we have in mind. It is exactly under such conditions of vagueness and open-texturedness that miscommunication becomes a possibility; the listener understands the term in a way that was not intended by the speaker.

Religion is an affair of the human race. With the widening horizons of knowledge, it is no more possible to reserve the term "religion" to one's own creed and practices. Today one notices certain strange incongruities like fetish-worship in Africa, Hindus chanting "Om" before the vast impersonal Absolute, Christians seeking paternal care from a highly personalised and individualised Father-God, the Muslims seeking mercy from a transcendent but personal God, the Buddhist seeking out his own salvation unaided by any supernatural beings, tribal dances and sexual orgies of *Tantra* are all vying for the name religion. In this age of religious pluralism, the term has become ambiguous and many who began by living out their creed have started wondering what it is.

Faced with the complexity of the problem, some students of religion feel tempted to look for an easy solution by offering a simple definition. They argue that if they succeed in reducing the problem to a simple basic principle, with a claim "this is the root of the whole matter, this is the essence of the thing", then their task is accomplished. But such an accomplishment is never possible in a hurry, especially when the phenomenon studied is complex. As Knight Dunlop writes, "... certainly, in the field of religion we are dealing with forests, not with a single tree."[2] It is evident that a complex and diverse phenomenon as religion will defy all attempts at arriving at a simple definition.

A cursory view of the various definitions proposed in the course of history enables us to show how difficult the task is. Mathew Arnold called it "morality touched by emotion" and Taylor, "the belief in supernatural beings". A.N. Whitehead describes it as "what the individual does with his solitariness". Ames calls it "the pursuit on the part of the community of what are thoughts to be the highest values". Straton defines it as "man's whole bearing towards that seems to him the best of greatest" while Lowie sees its essence in the sense of something transcending the expected or natural, a sense of extraordinary, mysterious, or supernatural. Solomon Reinach thinks it as the "sum of scruples which impede the free exercise of our faculties, but Hyden exalts it as the "cooperative quest for a completely satisfying life". To George Bernard Shaw religion is that which binds men to one another and irreligion that which sunders; while Havelock Ellis writes, "Now and again we must draw a deep breath of relief – and that is relgion." Freud sees in it only a passing illusion, a sublimation of sexual desires and a neurosis of primitive man, while for Marx it is the invention of man to make life on earth more bearable. For Feuerbach religion is man worshipping himself, his own subjectivity made objective, whereas for Durkheim it is man-worshipping society idealised and symbolically expressed.

According to some thinkers, religion is identified with feeling, emotion and sentiments, cult, rituals and faith. Religion begins with a simple rite but ends with the sublime realisation. In between faith and such realisation there are so many aspects with which religion is related. Therefore, it can be said that religion is generally identified with rituals, practices of one kind or another, with taboos, inhibitions and restraints of various kinds. Religion also implies worshipping and in such acts of worship the believer surrenders to the God of his belief. Since religion is said to be a blind acceptance much remains unexplained. Some religions proclaim that behind the world of nature and man, there is a reality called God. Hence, for these thinkers religion no longer remains a blind faith, but points towards an experience of the transcendent reality.

Religion, therefore, is grounded in the very nature of man characterising his essential and spiritual need. It is his yearning for a direct experience of cosmic consciousness and a desire to be in tune with the Infinite. It is his longing for transcending the world of space and time, to have a unique mystical experience of loving communion with God. Therefore, religion is the foundation of the character of the individual and provides the basis of the society within which the individual lives. If this basis is taken away the entire social structure will collapse.

> It is then both dangerous and stupid to disregard the religious foundations on which any given civilisation is built.[3]

To Swami Vivekananda every religion represents the basic principles, which are common to all religions. He exhorted men of all religions to unite on the basis of essential common principles. Over and above, Swamiji advocated the idea of a Universal Religion, which arose above all limitations and divisions. On account of external differences we do not notice the essentials. All religions reveal that the differences are only superficial and not fundamental. With the spirit of tolerance, Vivekananda called upon men of all religions to develop an attitude of understanding based on open-heartedness, tolerance, mutual respect and broad-mindedness. Swamiji writes:

> I am proud to belong to a religion which has taught the world both tolerance and universal acceptance. We believe not only in universal tolerance but we accept all religions as true. I am proud to belong to a nation which has sheltered the persecuted and the refugees of all

religions and all nations of the earth. I am proud to tell you that we have gathered in our bosom the purest remnant of the Israelites who came to southern India and took refuge with us in the very year in which their holy temple was shattered to pieces by Roman tyranny. I am proud to belong to a religion, which has sheltered of and is still fostering the remnants of the grand Zoroastrian nation.[4]

He further writes:

But their time has come: and I fervently hope that the bell that tolled this morning in honour of this conventions may be the death knell of all fanaticism, of all persecutions with the sword or with the pen, and all uncharitable feelings between wending their way to the same goal.[5]

While addressing the great gathering in the West, Vivekananda exhorted: "If one religion be true, then all the others must also be true. Thus, Hindu faith is yours as much as mine." And again in amplification of the same idea, he reiterated:

We Hindus accept every religion praying in the mosque of the Mohammedans, worshipping before the fire of Zoroastrian and kneeling before the cross of the Christians, knowing that all the religions, from the lowest fetishism to the highest absolutism, mean so many attempts of the human soul to grasp and realise the infinite, each determined by the conditions of its birth and association, and each of them marking a stage of progress. We gather these flowers all and bind them with the twine of love, making a wonderful bouquet of worship.[6]

To the heart of speaker none was foreigner or alien. For him there existed only "Humanity and Truth".[7]

Such a vision of religious faith points towards the relation of human existence to the transcendent. Accordingly, Vivekananda's philosophy is his belief in the basic oneness of existence and the essential unity of all religions according to the philosophy that there is but one life, one world and one existence God permeates all that exists from stones and plants to human beings and differences between one life and another is one of degree and not of kind. It would be contrary to *Vedāntic* teaching. According to him to claim, for instance, that animals were created in order to provide man with food.[8] Similarly, he upholds that the concept of a universal religion does not imply a single ritual, but a mythology or philosophy, for the whole of mankind, but in the sense that every particular historical religion proclaims an aspect of the universal traits according to its own insights.[9] He maintained that religion is one in essence but diverse in its manifestations and the advantage of maintaining a tolerant attitude is that it teaches us not to look for defects in religions other than our own. Accordingly, Vivekananda regarded the existence of numerous religions as a glorious dispensation of the Lord and its essence. The philosophical implications of the oneness of existence means that all men are bound together in one spirit. It follows that a life of service and sacrifice is the pre-requisite of those who would promote the religions of the spirit. It is, therefore, man's duty to create and defend those institutions that preserve the ideals of freedom, justice and truth and promote the development of a truly human life. Such an understanding of the universe and recognition of the common ground of all religions has further implications for our attitude to religions other than our own. It acknowledges that each religion takes its own path to the realisation of the goal of union with the Divine, but they are at one in their essence and in what is eternal in them. It amounts to saying that no individual religion can lay claim to exclusiveness or superiority. That being the case proselytising based on concepts of exclusiveness and superiority has to be abandoned.

Did Vivekananda mean by Universal Religion, the harmony of all religions? Did he mean the unity of all religions or the similarity and commonality of all religions? The notion of Universal Religion becomes clear if we remove the possibility of various interpretations of some of the general statements about religion, such as "all religions are paths leading to some goal" or "all people" whatever their cult, station or way of life, who are inwardly at peace attain to the same truth, as rivers (flowing into) the sea".[10] This raises a new type of question, namely, how can the interest in religious liberation/emancipation be kept alive? Undoubtedly, it can be done only by drawing upon our heritage in the manner suggested by different religions of the world. To state differently, we need to retrieve or reach back into our own religious heritage so as to find radically new resources needed for emancipation in an increasingly dominated world. Thus, Vivekananda exhorted that:

> all religions under whatever name they may be called either Hindu, Buddhist, Mohammedans or Christian have the same God, and he who derides any one of these derides his own God.[11]

The above statement points towards a common goal in every religion and it contains a number of suppositions too, some explicit and some implicit. The explicit is that the interest here is solely in the truth or rightness of individual claims of individual religions.

The implicit is that individual religions obstruct the vision in finding out the truth that binds all religions.

The religions of the East and the West are said to have originated from different premises or world-views. The only common ground, generally, is their views on the liberation of man from the clutches of birth and death. But most religions vis-a-vis religious leaders do not take cognisance of the fact that such real liberation from our most basic limitations and deceptions comes only with a conscious effort to take account of the horizon of those who differ. Such an openness is directed primarily not to other religions but to one's own religion. In other words, it is an acknowledgement that each religion has its own cultural heritage. Hence, it becomes the basis of a life that is ever, more inclusive and more rich. Such a perspectival diversity does not lead to a rejection of other religions nor does it lead to consider them as inferior. It is especially the religious sense within the various religions that can help to free people from the feeling of being absolute. Realising oneself as subordinate to God and only a partial manifestation of his truth and power opens in principle the possibility of recognising that other religions too are reflections of the divine perfection. Hence, there can be an essential similarity despite apparent diversity and it leads eventually to an inner unity among the world religions and that this unity is the progressive realisation of God as the incarnate. Vivekananda explained the task of Universal Religion in the following way:

> Religion is a realisation; not talk nor doctrine, nor theories, however beautiful they may be. It is being and becoming, not hearing or acknowledging; it is the whole soul becoming changed into what it believes.[12]

According to Vivekananda:

> There are many sects among the Mohammedans and among Buddhists, and hundreds among the Hindus ... in order to show you that any attempt to bring all humanity to one method of thinking in spiritual things has been a failure and always will be a failure. Every man that starts a theory, even at the present day, finds that if he goes twenty miles away from his followers, they will make twenty sects. You see that happening all the time.[13]

Besides, Vivekananda also accepted and upheld that:

> you cannot make all conform to the same ideas: that is a fact, and I thank God that it is so .... Now, if we all thought alike, we would be

like Egyptian mummies in a museum looking vacantly at one another's faces – no more than that whirls and eddies occur only in a rushing, living stream. There are no whirlpools in stagnant dead water. When religions are dead, there will be no more sects; it will be perfect peace and harmony of the grave. But so long as mankind thinks there will be sects. Variation is the sign of life and it must be there.[14]

And yet Vivekananda spoke of an ideal Universal Religion:

> Which does not mean any one universal philosophy, or any one universal mythology or any one universal ritual, held alike by all, for I know that this world must go on working wheel within wheel, this intricate mass of machinery, most complex, most wonderful. What can we do then? We can make it run smoothly, we can lessen the friction, we can grease the wheels as it were.[15]

This vision implies an understanding of the universal concept of God. Such a concept of God, in essence, lies in the unfoldment of man's real nature, which is pure consciousness, the Universal Spirit in man. This Universal Spirit is the very soul of the human being and as all life is the evolution of that which is within, the Universal Spirit necessarily expresses itself through various peoples and nations in different circumstances and with widely different customs and methods of life. The difference between man and man, people and people, nation and nation is not one of substance but one of expression. If every religion is the perception, realisation and manifestations of man's real nature, which is divinity itself, then it is not illogical to claim that the Universal Spirit in men express itself through infinite aspects, forms, modes and media. These forms and modes are different radii of a circle. According to Vivekananda:

> we must learn that truth may be expressed in a hundred thousand ways, and that each of these ways is true as far as it goes.... Suppose we all go with vessels in our hands to fetch water from a lake. One has a cup, another jar, another a bucket, and so forth, and we all fill our vessels. The water in each case naturally takes the form of the vessel carried by each of us.... So it is in the case of religion; our minds are like these vessels and each one of us is trying to arrive at the realisation of God. God is like that water filling these different vessels, and each vessel, the vision of God comes in that form of the vessel. Yet He is one, He is God in every case. This is the only recognition of universality that we can get.[16]

It is, therefore, clear that as for Vivekananda, religion is one in essence. Knowledge of the primordial form of religion is the result of an immediate and intuitive apprehension of the nature of reality, which is the result of *Jñāna*, gnosis or integral insight. It is the state of ecstasy; it is what is meant by saying that one is with God and an experience common to all religions. The aim of religion and religious education should be to learn about the basic principles of all religions of the world and promote international understanding and the creation of a world community and a world culture.

So far we have been explaining, among other things, the nature of religion and universalisability of a Universal Religion as propounded by Vivekananda but despite the common aspirations of the world religions, the historical records have shown that the common purpose of different religions to unite all the inhabitants of the world has really failed. The world has not been united by the search of God, rather it has been divided into religious communities by the insistence on the different ways of worshipping God.

> Even as the world is broken up into different races and nations, it is divided into different races and nations, it is divided into different religions.[17]

The Hindus and the Muslims, the Jews and the Christians are unable to come to an understanding. Even attempts to unite the Christian churches themselves into a single religious community have failed and the various sects continue to insist on their special formalities and rituals. War of religions have been there between the Hindus and the Muslims, the Protestants and Catholics. Different religions have created animosity among people and consequently there arouse a conflict and confusions which antagonised the human psyche in the conflictual world.[18]

Thus, today what is required is some sort of cooperation among world religions. This cooperation does not envisage and undergird the concept of Universal Religion. As there are differences in attitude and perceptions in particular religions and as they are based upon upholding their own religions as supreme or absolute, there remains a tension among religions. It is also noteworthy to state that there is a widespread awareness in the post-modern world that our tendencies have been out to balance in favour of a Universal Religion which has resulted in oppression and tyranny. It would be doubtful as to whether anything of value would emerge in our times by universalising tendencies, since the attraction towards a particular religion is only ethically and humanistically grounded. Therefore, what can be universally accepted is the promotion of life which requires such virtues as justice and love. But as soon as they are interpreted into concrete situations, virtues turn into vices leading to promote arrogance and a sense of superiority to those with whom specific meanings are not shared. Such partial and limited perceptions have destroyed the meaning of religion in World Religions throughout history. Hence the all to a Universal Religion seems no longer attractive as it once was.

NOTES AND REFERENCES

1. Selections from *The Complete Works of Vivekananda*, Kolkata, Advaita Ashrama, 1986, p. 18.
2. Knight Dunlop, *Religion: Its functions in Human Life*, New York, M.C. Grew Hill Book Company Inc., 1946, p. 4.
3. See Tomas Kipler, *Contemporary Religious Thought : An Anthology*, New York, Abingdon – Cokesbury Press, ...), p. 13.
4. *The Complete Works of Swami Vivekananda, op. cit.*, p. 1.
5. *Ibid.*, p. 2.
6. *Ibid.*, 1970, Vol. III, p. 32.
7. *Ibid.*, Vol. III, p. 272.
8. *Ibid.*, Vol. II, p. 297.
9. *Ibid.*, Vol. II, pp. 382-83.
10. *Ibid.*, Vol. IV, pp. 82-83.
11. *Ibid.*, Vol. 1, p. 350.
12. *Ibid.*, p. 85.
13. A *Study of Religion*, SwamiVivekananda, Kolkata, Advaita Ashram, p. 92.
14. *Ibid.*, pp. 92-93.
15. *Ibid.*, pp. 68-69.
16. *Ibid.*, pp. 69-70.
17. *Religion & Society*, S. Radhakrishnan, (London, George Allen & Unwin Ltd., 1966), p. 13.
18. *Ibid.*, p. 51.

SECTION TWO

NATURE OF MAN, CREATIVITY, LANGUAGE AND ART

8

The Nature of Man According to Swami Vivekananda

Swami Brahmeshananda

Swami Vivekananda has summarised his message in his own words: "To preach unto mankind their divinity and how to make it manifest in every movement of life." This short message finds expression in some form or other on every page of the nine volumes of his *Complete Works*. This very ideal assumes various forms in various contexts: of the twin national ideals of renunciation and service; of the man-making, character-building education; of the four *yogas*; of the motto, "for the salvation of one's own self and the welfare of the world," and so on.

To be able to appreciate the profound significance of Swamiji's message, let us first review the various prevalent concepts of man. Biologically, man is an animal with the species name *homo-sapiens*, whose fore-brain or neo-cerebrum is more developed than that of other animals. Consequently, man is less governed by his instincts than other animals, who, due to the preponderance of the lower brain or paleo-cerebrum, are primarily driven by instincts. According to medical materialists, man is a physiologically driven machine made of complex biochemical molecules. These basic concepts of man have been accepted by almost all the non-theological philosophers of the West, each one of whom has added his own adjective to the animal-man. Greek philosophers considered man a rational animal. Aristotle has defined man as a political animal, and the American philosopher Benjamin Franklin calls him *homo-faber*, or tool-making animal. Man has produced tools as extension of his own body, as it were, and has increased his productivity manifold. He has harnessed steam energy, electricity, atomic energy, etc. He has produced devices that replace thought itself (automation, artificial intelligence). E. Cassirer has emphasised that man is a symbol-making animal and the most important symbol invented by him is the "word" through which he can communicate with others.

Of the Western thinkers, special mention must be made of Sigmund Freud and Karl Marx. Freud's outstanding contribution is his discovery of the unconscious. But by laying too great a stress on sex as the most important driving force, he has reduced man into a sexual animal, the *homo-sexualis*, with far-reaching psycho-social consequences which are too evident in the contemporary society to be mentioned. The whole aim of his system of psychotherapy is to help man attain sexual maturity. Marx believes that man is driven primarily by a desire for economic gains: he is a *homo-economicus*. However, in *Das Capital* he has defined man as a social-animal. According to him, if man fails to relate himself actively with others and with nature, he loses himself, becomes alienated, his drives lose human qualities and assume animal qualities. He becomes a sick, fragmented, crippled human being. According to Marx man is driven by two sets of drives: fixed or constant and relative. Sex and hunger fall under the first category, while relative drives like hate, avarice etc. owe their origin to certain types of social organisations. This concept, to some extent, resembles the Hindu concept of man: "Eating, sleeping, fear and sex are common to men as well as animals. In human beings *dharma* (i.e. restraint by moral rules) is extra and special. Without *dharma* men are no better than beasts." According to Shankaracharya, this *dharma* is of two types: *pravritti-lakshana* and *nivritti-lakshana*. When one, observing the moral codes of conduct applicable to one's station in life and society, performs actions for enjoyment (*kàma*) and acquisition of wealth (*artha*), one is said to be following *pravritti dharma*. A time comes, however, when one gets disgusted with sense-enjoyments and acquisition of wealth and aspires for final emancipation *(moksha)*. Then one embraces what is called *nivritti dharma*, characterised by renunciation of all worldly desires and selfish actions, and resorting to spiritual practice to attain liberation. Man rises from animal to human level by accepting *pravritti dharma*, i.e. by observing social injunctions. He ascends to godhood and becomes divine by embracing the *nivritti dharma*.

This Hindu concept of liberation, in turn, is based upon another concept of an ever pure, ever free, ever perfect, ever conscious spiritual entity in man called *Atman*. According to Swami Vivekananda this *Atman* is the Real Man as against the body-mind complex which is only the apparent man. The relation between the real and apparent men has been beautifully described through an allegory in the *Katha Upanishad*:

> Know the soul to be the master of the chariot and the body the chariot. Consider the intellect the charioteer, and the mind the reins. The senses, they say, are the horses, and their roads are the sense objects. The wise call Him the enjoyer when He is united with the body, senses and mind.

From the above resume it would be evident that the Hindu concepts of the nature of man, his destiny and his drives, are far more comprehensive and vastly superior to the Western ones. For Western thinkers man is either an animal or a machine. Hindus on the other hand, believe that he is essentially divine. Secondly, whereas Western *savants* have postulated only three ultimate goals for man, viz., sensual enjoyment (*kàma*), acquisition of earthly riches (*artha*), and fulfilment of social obligations (*dharma*), the Indian philosophers have postulated a fourth and final goal: liberation (*moksha*), the state of fullest manifestation of innate divinity and perfection. Thirdly, whereas Freud thinks that man must satisfy his passions to remain whole and healthy, Marx states that man cannot truly be a man unless he actively relates with others. Swami Vivekananda, however, says that "man is man so long as he is struggling to rise above nature", both internal and external. Finally, Western philosophers say that man's evolution is governed by drives and instincts. But the Hindu sages say that man's innate perfection is constantly trying to manifest itself and every effort on our part simply acts as a remover of barriers to its manifestation.

Swami Vivekananda laid the greatest stress, in his message, on the divinity of man because he knew men are divine and since truth liberates, the only way to be free was to perceive the truth of one's divinity. Secondly, we tend to think and act according to our concept of ourselves. This has profound practical, psychological and social implications. The concepts of man as a sexual, economic, tool-making or social animal may be useful to individual or society to a certain extent, but they are restrictive. If we consider ourselves sexual animals as Freud wants us to believe, sexual shall we become. If we believe we are economically-driven machines, we shall run after money. If we think we are social animals, we shall become slaves of society. But if we consider ourselves ever free, blissful divinities, we shall enjoy freedom and bliss.

Swami Vivekananda used to illustrate this truth with the help of the story of a lion cub which was reared along with a herd of sheep from the very day of its birth. As it grew, it learnt to bleat and eat grass. Then this flock of sheep was attacked by another lion. He was surprised to find a full grown lion running away in fear. He caught hold of this younger lion, dragged it to the forest and told it that it was a lion and acting like a sheep did not befit it. To convince it the older lion showed its reflection in the lake. The young lion was convinced that it was a lion and not a sheep and in a moment gave up its fear.

Once two young sons of a devotee were playing. One was Vivek and another, Shirish. They, for the sake of fun, added "ananda" to their names and became Vivekananda and Shirishananda, and as their play demanded, started acting according to their new names. Vivek folded his arms and stood erect like Swami Vivekananda with a grave face. Shirish did the same. But then, for some reason, Shirish started weeping. Vivek was surprised, and asked his mother, "Can Shirishananda weep?" That's it! Weeping does not befit Shirish as long as he is "ananda", a dignified monk. If children can temporarily change their behaviour in play according to their assumed identity, can we not change our identity and behaviour permanently?

But there are difficulties. It is extremely difficult to impart the knowledge of our divine nature and equally difficult for another to grasp it. Hence, it is said in the *Katha Upanishad*:

> Many do not even hear about the divinity of the soul. Of those who hear, many do not understand it. Wonderful indeed is one who can speak about it; and the receiver too must be equally competent. Wonderful is he who comprehends it when taught by an able Preceptor.

The knower of the divinity of soul is so rare and extraordinary that he is more likely to be considered abnormal than normal. The experience of Swami Vivekananda, then Narendranath Dutta, on his first meeting with Sri Ramakrishna at Dakshineswar was somewhat similar. Taking him aside, Sri Ramakrishna had, with joined palms, addressed him as the sage Nara born to redeem the earth, thus alluding to his divinity. Stunned, Narendra had thought Sri Ramakrishna to be a monomaniac. For, after all, he was none other than Narendranath Dutta, the son of Vishwanath Dutta. His body-consciousness or identification with the body and through it with his father was so strong that he could not accept any allusion to his divinity. But Sri Ramakrishna was not an ordinary teacher. He was the Master of masters, an extraordinary teacher, a wonderful speaker of the *Upaniṣads*, and could impart highest knowledge through a mere touch. On Narendra's next visit, Sri Ramakrishna took him to a solitary place and suddenly touched him. Due to that powerful touch, the whole world gradually vanished and as Narendra was about to lose his ego-sense, he shouted, "Sir, what are you doing? I have my parents." At the moment of impending loss of consciousness, he remembered his parents with whom he was related through the physical body. Such is our strong body-consciousness!

Since Narendra was not ready for this direct experience of his divinity, nor had he accepted what Sri Ramakrishna had told him on the first occasion, Sri Ramakrishna adopted the third method: he treated Narendra as a divine being to such a perfect degree that the youth was convinced of his divinity in due course. Sri Ramakrishna used to behave with everyone in the same manner because the experience of divinity within himself and in others was extremely natural for him. Once Latu, his personal attendant, was meditating in the Shiva temple at Dakshineswar. He was deeply absorbed and was oblivious of his perspiring body. When Sri Ramakrishna saw this, he started fanning him. On regaining normal consciousness, Latu was highly embarrassed to find Sri Ramakrishna fanning him and protested that it was he who should fan Sri Ramakrishna and not vice versa. Sri Ramakrishna, however, replied that he was not fanning his body but the divinity which had manifested in his heart while meditating. When bohemian Girish Chandra Ghosh confessed that he was a sinner of the highest order, Sri Ramakrishna stopped him and warned him not to speak that way. For, he said, he who thinks he is a sinner becomes a sinner. Scores of such instances can be cited where Sri Ramakrishna had acted in accordance with the divinity which he saw in others.

Another difficulty is that this concept of divinity is liable to be misunderstood. Each has his own concept of the Divine and that too more often vague and confused than clear. And yet Swami Vivekananda wants it to be preached to all men and women, young and old, alike. For, it would make, as he said, a fisherman a better fisherman; a student a better student; a lawyer a better lawyer. It would instill strength, confidence and courage, and drive away doubt, weakness and hesitation. One may rightly argue that by the same logic a thief would become a better thief, and a robber an expert robber! Quite so. But it seems Swamiji was not really worried about this problem of a thief becoming a better thief by the *Vedāntic* teaching of one's divinity. Nor the present socio-economic turmoils and ethical decadence in India would have bothered him. He would have seen them as part of the process of evolution from inertia to activity and from activity to tranquillity, i.e., from *tamoguna* to *rajoguna* and finally to *sattvaguna*. Once, one of his Western disciples praised India for her low crime rate. Swamiji, however, did not consider it a sign of India's greatness. Instead, he thought it was a sign of extreme inertia, *tamoguna*, which had covered the whole length and breadth of the country.

Once Swami Vivekananda met a very dull and stupid person. He asked Swamiji what should he do to know God. "Can you tell a lie?" Swamiji asked him. "No," "he replied. "Then you must learn to do so," Swamiji said.

> It is better to tell a lie than to be a brute or a log of wood. You are inactive; you have not certainly reached the highest state, which is beyond all action, calm and serene. You are too dull to do something wicked.

That was an extreme case of course, and Swamiji was joking with him. But what he meant was that a man must be active in order to pass through activity to perfect calmness.

It is a common observation of doctors and parents alike that under-nourished children are generally dull and apathetic. But when they are given nutritious diet, they rapidly gain weight and become alarmingly active. Not able to contain their newly-acquired exuberant energy, they break things, fight with other children and create havoc in the house. But as they grow, they get used to that energy, and, with the help of affectionate parents, learn to direct it into creative channels. Something similar may happen if a dull and inactive person is told about his divine nature. He might first become anti-social and immorally active. But let the process be continued, let him continue to hear about his divine nature and sooner or later he will be transformed into a saint.

Once a thief broke into the cottage of Pavahari Baba, the saint of Ghazipur. As he was tying the bundle of stolen goods, the Baba woke up. The poor thief ran for his life. Pavahari Baba too followed him and after miles of chase caught up with him. Presenting the bundle of stolen goods to the trembling thief, the Baba, joining his palms, addressed him as "Narayana", and humbly apologised for disturbing him in his act of stealing. He then requested him to accept the offering of the bundle of goods. Swami Vivekananda bears testimony to the fact that deeply convinced of his divinity by this extraordinary act of Pavahari Baba, the thief was transformed into a saint. Swamiji actually met him during his travels in northern India.

From this, do not conclude that if ever a thief enters your apartment and tries to run away with your watch, you have only to offer, with joined palms and hymns and praises, your wallet too, and he will be transformed into a saint! No, not at all! Instead, he may transform you into a penniless beggar, saint or no saint. Such miracles of instant conversion of a sinner into a saint are possible only for saints like Pavahari Baba who saw God, always and in all creatures, even in rats, cats and dogs, and for whom a stinging cobra was a "messenger of the Beloved". We, on the other hand, are not convinced of even our own divinity. How can we convey it to others? Before making others saints, we ourselves must become saints.

Thus, we see, there are difficulties in understanding, accepting, assimilating and finally practising the concept of the divinity of man. It is difficult to convert precept into practice, theory into action. We may assert this moment that we are divine but may turn red and blue next moment if we are abused. But let us not despair. Let us repeat day and night that we are birthless, deathless, blissful, omnipotent, omnipresent spirits. It is better to falter and even fail with a higher concept of ourselves, attempting to put it into practice, than to accept a baser concept and degrade ourselves to the level of brutes.

9

Self: Appearance and Reality

Asha Maudgil

The theme of *Vedānta* philosophy is the search for unity. It is looking for the universal rather than the particular. What is that by knowing which the whole universe can be known? The answer is *Ākāśa* and *Prāṇa*. This *Prāṇa* acting on *Ākāśa* is creating the whole of this universe – Universal Thought – *Mahat*. Thought is a manifestation of the power of *Prāṇa*. This *Prāṇa* acting on *Ākāśa* is responsible for creation and dissolution.

The unity which is the reality is not displayed. In our search for reality we always come up with particulars which gives us mere appearance.

According to Wittgenstein the world and life are one. I am my world (the microcosm). Vivekananda too states that no distinction can be made between the mind and the world. The world is a combination of you and something else. Vivekananda further states that the microcosm and the macrocosm are built on the same plan.

Whenever the world of ours on account of growth, on account of added circumstances, requires a new adjustment, a wave of power comes. The waves of adjustment come on both planes, i.e., the material plane and the spiritual plane.

> It is true that external nature is majestic with the mountains, and oceans and rivers, and with its infinite powers and varieties. Yet there is a more majestic internal nature of man higher than the sun, moon and stars higher than the physical universe, transcending these little lives or ours; and it affords another field of study.[1]

Referring to this other field of study, the epistemological question raised is that: "What is that, by knowing which everything else is known?" That is the one theme. As, through the knowledge of one lump of clay all that is of clay is known, so, what is that by knowing which this whole universe itself will be known? That is the one search. Vivekananda states that the whole of this universe according to the Hindu philosophers can be resolved into one material, which they call *Ākāśa*. Everything that we see around us, feel, touch, taste, is simply a differentiated manifestation of this *Ākāśa*. It is all-pervading fine. All that we call solids, liquids, or gases, figures, forms, or bodies, the earth, sun, moon and stars – everything is composed of this *Ākāśa*.[2] Along with *Ākāśa* exists universal power, all that is power in the universe manifesting as force, or attraction. Thought is also another manifestation of power of *Prāṇa*. This *Prāṇa* acting on *Ākāśa* is responsible for the whole cycle of creation and dissolution. When the *Prāṇa* vibrates it creates; when it is in a state of rest or sleep, there is dissolution. Using scientific terminology we may say there are periods when it is static and there are periods when it is dynamic. This cycle or alteration has gone on through eternity.[3]

So far we have seen that the whole universe is resolved into two components, matter and energy, i.e., *Ākāśa* and *Prāṇa*. Both these can be further resolved into a higher entity called mind or the *Mahat*, i.e., the universally existing thought power from which these two have been produced. Thought is still finer manifestation of being than either *Ākāśa* or *Prāṇa*. It is thought that splits itself into these two. The universal thought existed in the beginning, and that manifests itself into these two *Ākāśa* and *Prāṇa*; and by the combination of these two the whole universe has been produced.[4]

Let us now analyse the psychology of perception or the process of perception. The external sensations are brought to us by the external instruments – organs like eyes, ears, nose, mouth and skin. Supporting these are the internal organs which carry the nerve impulses to the brain. Yet if the mind is not attached to the organ, i.e., if one is not paying attention one will miss out on all the information coming in from the sense organs. Only when the mind attaches itself to the organ or pays heed to it will it be possible to receive news from the sense organs. The mind now presents this news to the intellect, which groups it in relation to pre-received impression and sends a current reaction and with that reaction comes perception. The state of mind which reacts is called *Buddhi,* the intellect.[5]

What is it upon which all our different impressions are pieced together, upon which the perception as it were, comes together, resides and forms a united whole? What is that which gives unity to the changing whole of our being? This individual perceiver is the soul of man. It is to this destination all our sensations, carried by the mind and intellect, are placed and grouped and formed into a unity.

Mind is only a phase of matter, i.e., the ever-changing phenomena of which matter and mind are different states or views. There must be something in whose presence this eternal, phenomenal net is spread – that is the substance, the Brahman.

The meditative state of mind is declared by the *yogis* to be the highest state in which the mind exists. When the mind is studying the external object, it gets identified with it and loses itself. The soul of man is like a piece of crystal, but it takes the colour of whatever is near it. The colour is so strong that the crystal forgets itself and identifies itself with the colour of whatever is near it. This constitutes bondage. We have taken the colour of the body and have forgotten what we are. This leads to all kinds of difficulties. All our fears, worries, weakness, evil are from this one mis-identification that we are bodies. We are no more bodies than the crystal is red. It is by meditation, i.e., by studying the mind or concentration on mind or inner self, that we can know our true selves.

In his Master, Ramakrishna Paramahansa, living and teaching in the temple garden at Dakshineswar, the Swami Vivekananda "Naren" as he then was called, found the verification of the ancient texts which his heart and his reason demanded. Here was the reality which the books only hinted at in their description. Here was one to whom *Samādhi* was a constant mode of knowledge. Every hour saw the swing of the mind from the many to the One. Every moment heard the utterance of wisdom gathered superconsciously. Everyone about him caught the vision of the Divine. Upon the disciple came the desire for supreme knowledge "as if it had been a fever". Yet he (Ramakrishna Paramahansa) who was thus the living embodiment of the books was so unconsciously, for he had read none of them! In his Guru, Ramakrishna Paramahansa, Vivekananda found the key to life.

Wittgenstein was born in Austria and came to philosophy via the problems of the foundations of mathematics. He was a musician, an aeronautical engineer, a philosopher, etc. He occupied the chair once occupied by Bertrand Russell. It has been said that the publication of the *Tractatus* in 1921 brought about a revolution in philosophy. The Wittgensteinian and post-Wittgensteinian philosophy is quite unlike what was done in the pre-Wittgensteinian days. In his *Blue Book,* Wittgenstein comments about his own way of philosophising:

> Every particular notation stresses some particular point of view. If e.g. we call our investigations "philosophy", this title, on the one hand seems appropriate, on the other hand it has certainly misled people (one might say that the subject we are dealing with is one of the heirs of the subject which used to be called "philosophy".[6]

Wittgensteinian philosophy is a class apart and cannot be compared with the views of his contemporaries or predecessors. What has been done by Wittgenstein has no historical analogue. This, however, does not mean that there are no similarities between his thoughts and say the thoughts of Plato, Aristotle, Hume, etc.). Wittgenstein says:

> I do not wish to judge how far my efforts coincide with those of other philosophers. Indeed what I have written here make no claim to novelty in detail the reason why I give no sources in a matter of indifference to me whether the thoughts what I have had been anticipated by someone else.[7]

Just as Ramakrishna Paramahansa was the living embodiment of the *Vedic* texts even without having read them. *Similarly* Wittgenstein too has arrived at the universal truths through his independent efforts and does not wish to judge how far his efforts coincide with those of other philosophers.

I was struck by the fact that the conclusions arrived at by Vivekananda and Wittgenstein, i.e., people belonging to two totally diffeent streams could be so similar.

Wittgenstein also states his helplessness in knowing and stating the world in the following words:

5.621 The world and life are one.

5.63 I am my world (The microcosm).

5.631 There is no such thing as the subject that thinks or entertains ideas.

If I wrote a book called "The World as I found it", I should have to say which parts were subordinate to my will, and which were not, etc., this being a method of isolating the subject, or rather of showing that in an important sense there is no subject; for it alone could not be mentioned in that book.

5.632 The subject does not belong to the world: rather, it is a limit of the world.

5.633 Where in the world is a metaphysical subject to be found?

You will say that this is exactly like the case of the eye and the visual field. But really you do not see the eye.

And nothing in the visual field allows you to infer that it is seen by an eye.

5.6331 For the form of the visual field is surely not like this eye.

Eye

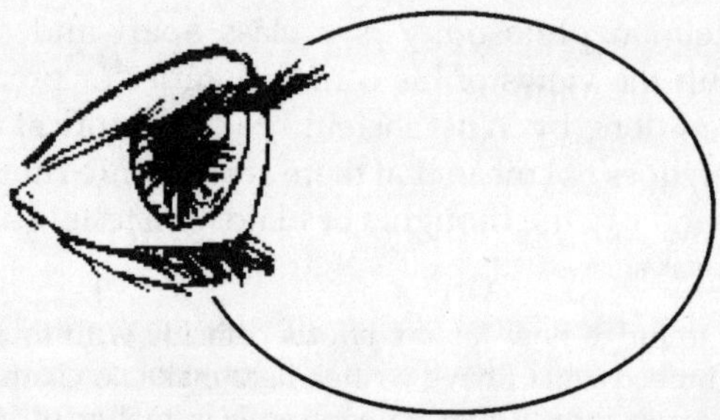

5.634 This is connected with the fact that no part of our experience is at the same time a priori.

Whatever we see could be other than it is.

Whatever we can describe at all could be other than it is.

There is no a priori order of things.

5.64 Here it can be seen that solipsism, when its implications are followed out strictly, coincides with pure realism. The self of solipsism shrinks to a point without extension, and there remains the reality co-ordinated with it.

5.641 Thus there really is a sense in which philosophy can talk about the self in a non-psychological way.

What brings the self into philosophy is the fact that "the world is my world".

The philosophical self is not the human being, not the human body, or the human soul, with which psychology deals, but rather the metaphysical subject, the limit of the world – not a part of it.[8]

Something X produces an impression on me I send a reaction Y towards that and the external object is a result of this combination. If you try to distinguish which is your mind, which is the world there is no such distinction. The world is a combination of you and something else. Vivekananda further states that the microcosm and the macrocosm are built on the same plan. Just as the individual soul is encased in the living body. So is the universal soul in the living *Prakriti* (nature) the objective universe. Shiva, i.e., Kali is embracing Shiva, i.e., Kali is embracing Shiva not a fancy. This covering of one (soul) by the other (nature) is analogous to the relation between an idea and the word expressing it: they are one and the same: and it is only by mental abstraction that one can distinguish them. Thought is impossible without words. Therefore, in the beginning was the word, etc.[9]

This dual aspect of the universal soul is eternal, so what we perceive or feel in this combination of the eternally formed and the eternally Formless.

The soul or self is in bondage in this world as it identifies itself with the world as in the case of a crystal identifying with the colour reflected in it. Similarly, Wittgenstein states that the subject does not belong to the world: rather, it is a limit of the world.[10]

Vivekananda points out that the:

"soul is separate from the body separate from the mind itself.[11]

"Every item of creation is simply a composition. No one ever saw creation come out of nothing. All that we know of creation is the combination of already existing things into newer forms."[12]

(That being so, this soul of man must be simple and must have been existing forever.

This finds a parallel in Wittgenstein's views:

1.2 The World divides into facts.

A state of affairs is a combination of objects.

Wittgenstein never repudiated the remarks about philosophy quoted earlier from the *Tractatus*. Rather, he began to understand better what was required in order to do justice to the insight that those remarks expressed, for example that there can be no such thing as a philosophical proposition, and that philosophy was entirely different from science.

Similarly, the *Vedāntists* allow one to arrive at insights into ancient views, through the meditative states rather than reading the ancient texts in which they may be expressed.

Religion is a question of being and becoming and not of believing. Stand up and reason out having no blind faith. "Do not believe in what you have heard," says the great Buddha. Similarly, Vivekananda tells us:

> do not believe in doctrines because they have been handed down to you through generations; do not believe in anything because it is followed blindly by many; do not believe because some old sage makes a statement; do not believe in truths to which you have become attached by habit; do not believe merely on the authority of your teacher and elders. Have deliberation and analyse, and when the result agrees with reason and conduces to the good of one and all accept it and live up to it.[13]

Similar views are stated by Wittgenstein when he says: "plant a seed in my soil and it will grow differently....

There is a difference between realisation and mere talking philosophies and doctrines and arguments and books and theories and religions. All these things are good in their own way; but when that realisation comes these things drop away. Those who have realised truth do not require the ratiocinations of logic and other efforts of the intellect to make them understand the truth; it is to them the life of their lives concretised, made more than tangible. Suppose we have realised this oneness we have realised oneness of the univesal, that we are the one Infinite Being and suppose we have realised that it is the same self which is manifesting in all these various phenomenal forms, what becomes of us after that. Shall we become inactive, get into a corner and die away? People are afraid that when they realise that there is but One, the foundations of love will be dried up, that everything in life will go away, and that all love will vanish for them as it were in this life and life to come. People never stop to think that those who bestowed the least thought on their individualities have been greatest workers in the world. Then alone a man loves when he finds that the object of his love is not a clod of earth, but is the veritable God himself. That man will love a holy man, who knows that the holy man is God Himself, and that very man will also love the unholiest of men because he knows the background of the unholiest of the men is even He, the Lord. Such a man becomes a world-mover for whom his little self is dead and God stands in its place. The whole universe will become transfigured to him. That which is painful and miserable will all vanish; struggles will all depart and go. Instead of being a prison-house where we struggle every day and night and compete for a morsel of bread, this universe will then be to us a playground. If all mankind today realises only one of the great truths, the aspect of the whole world will be changed and in place of fighting and quarrelling there would be a reign of peace. With it will vanish all struggle, hate, jealousy. All evil will vanish away forever. That is the great utility of divine realisation. Everything that you see in society will be changed and transformed. No more will you think of man as evil, and that is the first gain. No more will you think of jealousy and punishments. They will all vanish and love, the great ideal of love, will be so powerful that no whips and cords will be necessary to guide mankind aright. Be good and evil will vanish for you. The whole universe will thus be changed. This is the greatest gain to the human organism as well to the society.

NOTES AND REFERENCES

1. *The Complete Works of Swami Vivekananda,* Vol. IV, Advaita Ashram, Kolkata, p. 156.
2. Selections from *The Complete Works of Swami Vivekananda,* Advaita Ashram, 2001, p. 116.
3. Cf., p. 117.
4. *Ibid.*
5. *Ibid.*, Cf., p. 118.
6. Blue and Brown Books, L. Wittgenstein, p. 28.
7. *Tractatus Logico Philosophicus Preface,* p. 3.
8. *Tractatus Logico Philosophicus Preface,* Ludwig Wittgenstein.
9. Cf., Vol. 9, p. 291.
10. *Tractatus Logico Philosophicus,* 5.632.
11. See from *The Complete Works of Swami Vivekananda,* p. 120.
12. Selections from *The Complete Works of Swami Vivekananda,* p. 120.
13. *The Complete Works of Swami Vivekananda,* Vol. IV, p. 216.

10

On Symbol

Pankaj Srivastava

"Reasons, theories, doctrines, books, religious ceremonies are all help to religion: religion itself consists of realisation."[1] These are the words of Swami Vivekananda. In his view religion is a very long and slow process. One has to pass through various stages to achieve the final goal of religion.

Within every religion a difference in the level of religiosity is accepted explicitly or implicitly. At least two levels are clearly seen everywhere. Some people are regarded as deeply or highly religious and contrasted with common followers of a religious faith. There is no ontological difference between the two. The potentiality that lies dormant in everyone becomes manifest in some. Swami Vivekananda says:

> Each soul is potentially divine. The goal is to manifest this divinity within by controlling nature – external and internal.[2]

In order to realise the divine nature of self one has to pass through two phases of religious life.

Divinity is not something concrete. Although it is not merely an idea, it is the very nature of self, it cannot be presented in a tangible form. So there is no way to understand it directly. We can reach it only by associating to something concrete. The situation is somewhat similar to that of understanding number. Numbers are abstract entities. No child can ever learn counting if he is made to understand the numbers directly. But by showing two pencils, three apples and so on he can be made to learn counting easily, and when he grows old, he understands what is number. Similarly, common men cannot directly grasp what divinity is unless it is associated to something concrete.

People talk about God, soul, rebirth, etc. but when one asks, "Have you seen God?" or "What is soul?", they just repeat the words of religious scripture or what they have heard from tradition without having any direct knowledge about these matters. Very few people admit that actually they have no experience regarding these. For most people these are mere words having no clear significance and they have assented to use them without understanding them fully. For majority of people religion is nothing but an assent to what is written in religious scriptures or what is talked of in tradition. But religion is independent of our assent or dissent. Religion is a way of life and only by passing through various steps of this journey one can understand the actual meaning of divinity. The biographies of saints like Kabir, Meera, Nanak, Ramakrishna Paramahansa and others state that all of them passed through various steps in their religious journey. In fact this is the path of inner transformation. When one realises one's divine nature one rises above mundane attachments and gets transformed into a different person. Rituals, ceremonies, formal prayer, etc. which appear to be important at the initial level remain no more relevant when one reaches the higher level of religion.

The initial or lower phase of religious life, as Swami Vivekananda said, begins in relating oneself to ceremonies and formal prayers, forms and words, etc. which are regarded as helps to approach one's divine nature. These rituals have a great diversity. There are various forms of worship and prayer through which mind gradually proceeds in that direction. No single form can be idealised for everyone. My way of worshipping may not be acceptable to many people. I should not force others to follow my way. Swami Vivekananda says:

> We are looking at truth from different standpoints, which vary according to our birth, education, surrounding and so on. We are viewing at truth, getting as much of it as the circumstances will permit, colouring the truth with our own intellect and grasping it in our own mind.[3]

All the ceremonies observed and rituals performed at the lower phase of religion are symbolic in nature. Symbol is a means to envisage something that is either abstract or that is not presently perceptible. All our words are symbols which signify thoughts behind them. Swami Vivekananda says:

Symbols are associated with thoughts, and as the thought brings the symbol outside so the symbol, on the contrary, brings the thought inside. Symbol signifies something abstract that we cannot grasp in itself.[4]

In Sanskrit the word *pratīka* has been used for symbol. Etymologically, *pratīka* means coming towards or nearing. In the lower phase of religion all forms of worship are only *pratīkas*. They help one to reach near the ultimate goal of divine self- realisation. There are various types and orders of *pratīka*. Some people worship the images of saints, some worship creatures of higher order such as angels, deities, etc. who are believed to possess special powers. Swami Vivekananda says:

Bhakti Yoga does not condemn any of these various grades but they are all classified under one name – *Pratīka*.[5]

In Swami Vivekananda's view these people are not worshipping God: they are worshipping *pratīkas* of God which is a step towards Him. He emphasises that the worship of these *pratīkas* by themselves cannot lead to salvation. Only some special powers can be achieved by such forms of worship. These powers are called *Vidya* – supra-natural knowledge to do certain things miraculously or to control the course of natural events in an occult way. Normally people worship creatures of supra-human order to achieve these *vidyas* only. While these *vidyas* may be of some help in the journey of one's divine self-realisation, they become great hindrances if one is tempted to misuse them. One has to remember that these *pratīkas* are only means: they are not ends in themselves.

All the great *Acharyas* have acknowledged the importance of *pratīka*.

Acharya Rāmānuja has defined it as – *Abrahmaṇi brahmadṛṣtyānusandhānam*, Swami Vivekananda interprets it as:

joining the mind with devotion to that which is not *Brahman*, taking it to be *Brahman*.

Explaining *Acharya* Śamkara's view on *pratīka* Swami Vivekananda states:

the mind as *Brahman*, this is internal; and *Ākāsha* as *Brahman*, this is with regards to *Devas*. Mind is an internal *pratīka* and *ākāsha* is an external *pratīka*, and both have to be worshipped as substitute of God. *Upasana* means going towards, and worshipping a *pratīka* is worshipping something as substitute, which is some one or more respects, *Brahman;* more and more but not *Brahman*.[6]

Before the *Brahman,* one's ultimate divine nature is attained, symbols play a significant role in the religious life of people.

SYMBOLS AS CONTRASTED WITH SIGNS

Symbols are not the same as signs. A sign refers to something other than itself. The relation between a sign and that it points to, may be natural as well as conventional. A nimbus cloud is regarded as a sign of imminent rain. It is a natural sign. Traffic lights, on the other hand, are conventional signs which are meaningful only for those who understand the conventional rule of road traffic. Ordinarily, conventional signs are called symbols. But symbols are of many types. In some symbols the relation between them and what they point to, is only external. However, in some, this relation is not purely external or arbitrary. A national flag is deemed as the symbol of a nation. While this is a conventional sign, the relation between this and the nation that it represents is not external. In the minds of the people of a nation their national flag represents their sovereignty, dignity and unity. The relation between a national flag and the nation is not external. It essentially involves the emotions of the people of that nation. In this sense the symbol itself becomes a part of the power and dignity it stands for. It is in this sense that Paul Tillich distinguishes symbols from signs.[7] In the terminology of Tillich, a symbol "participates" in that which it symbolises.

Pratīka that we are discussing presently is a symbol in Tillich's sense of the term. A religious symbol does not merely refer to a realm of divinity beyond itself; it is believed to be possessing a touch of divinity in itself. Every religious symbol itself is regarded as holy and commands people's reverence. A religious symbol, in itself, is a material thing: it is a mundane object, but it is made sacrosanct by religious authority so that common people, in their busy life, can get a clear indication that there is something beyond the mundane affairs of the world. A religious symbol invites them to spare some time to meditate upon its ascribed holiness to envisage what holiness is like. The serenity and the bliss are the direct consequences of meditating on these symbols. These are felt by most people immediately. This effect enables and inspires them to search for the supra-mundane dimension of their life. Going to a mosque to participate in *Namaz*, or worshipping an idol of a deity or that of a saint, creates some space in the busy life of people and give them an opportunity to see that everything in life is not merely a bargain of give and take. Symbols are intended to help them understand the significance, value and blessedness of this life. The basic function of these symbolic acts is to open the door of the heart of the people to let the light of Divine enter into their life.

This life is not out and out material: there is a divine spark in it which comes from the unbound and unfathomable ocean of Divine Consciousness. To bring this truth within the reach of the people is the essential purpose of symbols in religion.

SYMBOL AND SUPERSTITION

If a person understands the message encoded in the symbol, he rises above the lower level of religion and the purpose of symbol is served. This, however, is a rare occurence.

Most people are so engrossed in their worldly affairs that even when they pray, or bow heads before the idol of a deity, their minds keep calculating the loss and gain of the symbolic act. Although physically performing the acts they are either mentally absent, or they actually begin to think how their act (worshipping, praying, etc.) is going to benefit their business. Symbol loses its significance for such people. It remains nothing more than a physical drill performed before a material object. The calculating mind associates some physical benefits to ritualistic acts. Thus, superstition comes up. Some shrewd persons begin to exploit this weakness of people by frightening them of the possible loss and assuring about unexpected gains. This is how religion becomes the captive of selfish people who spread hypocrisy and superstition in the name of religion. Given the weakness of human nature this accident is commonplace. This is very unfortunate about the history of all religions of the world. Every religion on earth descends in someone's pious heart in the encounter with the Divine but in the process of transferring it to others and to save it for posterity religious institutions are born. When the enlightened egoless soul departs, the darkness of selfishness begins to cast its shadow. Gradually, the essence of religion is lost in the detailed observance of rituals.

Swami Vivekananda has criticised superstition and hypocrisy on various occasions. While admitting the importance of symbols and allowing some room for ritualistic worship, he always emphasised the need for understanding the real meaning of religious symbols so that they can serve as means to elevate people from the mundane to the supra-mundane level of self which is Divine in nature. Enlightened souls come generation after generation and warn us against the attempts of reducing religion to rituals. While it is true that the essence of religion is so subtle that it cannot be saved for long without religious institutions, it is equally true that the institutional framework cannot save it without imposing its ritualistic dictates over its experiential contents. It can be said that understanding the real significance of symbols is the way out of this impasse. But the situation seems to be paradoxical. They who understand the real significance of symbols do not need them, and they alone need the symbols most who do not understand their real significance. This, however, should not be regarded as an argument against the utilityof religious symbols. Symbols in religion are useful indeed. Majority of people are such who can never form any idea of divinity if symbols are not provided and their potentiality to realise the divine nature of self will be lost in vain. Moreover, religious symbols become the basis of religious tradition which paves the way of a seeker of self to reach an enlightened Master who can help him understand the real significance of these symbols.

A religious tradition is formed by the dialogue between the Master and the seekers. With the passage of time religious institutions come up and the dialogue is frozen by the followers. Tradition within which, or against which an enlightened Master comes to reinterpret the meaning of religious symbols.

Ironically, it is against mechanical ritualism and small-minded understanding of religious symbols that the enlightened masters have striven to protest but these attempts at reinterpretation themselves become antiquated and obsolete due to mindless repetition.

EMOTION: ELAN VITAL OF RELIGIOUS SYMBOLS

Our understanding of religious symbols will remain incomplete if its relation to the emotion of people is not discussed. Paul Tillich has explained that symbols participate in the glory and dignity of what they signify. This participation manifests in the emotional bond that people of a religious community feel with the symbols of their religion. Accepting a religious symbol is not a matter of theoretical assent only. Religious symbols are regarded as sacred as the Supreme Divine Reality itself. No matter whether the people of a community understand the real significance of the symbols or not, they pay as much reverence to it as to the Supreme Divine Reality. Normally religious persons cannot tolerate criticism of the holy symbols of their faith. Resentment against such criticism often takes a violent turn. This shows the emotive power of these symbols; this is the most important aspect of religious symbols. Although this emotional attachment ordinarily presents itself in the form of chauvinistic ethnicity but this is also the life force of symbols. If properly nurtured, the emotional bond unfolds the real significance of symbols. Whether an act of worship and prayer is merely a ritual or an attempt to come in the proximity of the Supreme Reality, is decided only by investigating whether that act is performed with profound devotion or not. If the symbolic act touches the heart then alone can it serve as a key that unlocks the mysteries of the Divine. Before long such symbolic acts transform the person radically and the divine nature of self manifests in the encounter with the actual living form of the symbol. The materiality of the symbol dissolves and Divinity reveals itself in that very symbol.

The spiritual master of Swami Vivekananda, Shri Ramakrishna Paramahansa, in the initial stage of his *sādhanā* used to feel the divine presence of goddess Kali in the idol at Dakshineswara temple. He never took the stone idol as a material thing. For him it was a seat of Divine Mother. As such he paid his full obeisance to it. But after he reached the culmination of his devotion to the Divine Mother he never saw the idol. He saw that Divine Mother Herself was always present instead of the idol, and She was not only at the place of the idol but talking to him, laughing with him and giving him instructions. She was present always in his proximity.[8] Pure selfless devotion creates the space in which the ego-less consciousness manifests in the form of an intimate relation between the devotee and the deity. This is not a projection of imagination. It is only the realisation of that sublime emotion which constitutes the supra-mundane – divine dimension of human life. In the light of this sublime emotion the authentic religion is clearly distinguished from inauthentic or fake religion.

In the light of above discussion we find that religious symbols acquire a special feature which makes them very different from all other types of symbols. Religious symbols are, in a sense, replicas of what a person experiences when he reaches certain height or summit of religious journey. Since there is nothing in the mundane world of sense-experience that resembles supra-mundane experience of Divine, the replica of that experience as religious symbol appears to be unintelligible and paradoxical from the level of sense experience. Such paradoxes are expressed in the puzzling questions of theology.

How does the infinite enter the world of finitude? How does the timeles incarnate in time? are the questions which arise at the level of sensuous world but cannot be answered at that level. When the symbols which create such problems, are regarded as challenges for the intellect, they remain unsolved mysteries. But if they are regarded as objects before which one can open one's heart with complete humility and without hesitation, then at once the solution is attained by way of a radical change in one's outlook. Religious symbols are the means of transformation.

NOTES AND REFERENCES

1. *The Complete Works of Swami Vivekananda*, Vol. IV, Advaita Ashram, Kolkata, p. 34, 1995.
2. Swami Vidyatmananda, *What Religion is: In the words of Swami Vivekananda*, Advaita Ashram, Kolkata, p. 1, 1996.
3. *Ibid.*, p. 18.
4. *The Complete Works of Swami Vivekananda*, Vol. IV, pp. 37-38, Advaita Ashram, Kolkatta, 1995.
5. *Ibid.*, p. 48, 1995.
6. Swami Mumukshananda, *The Complete Works of Swami Vivekananda*, Vol. III, p. 59, Advaita Ashram, Kolkata, 1995.
7. Paul Tillich, *Dynamics of Faith*, Harper and Raw, New York, p. 42.
8. Swami Pavitrananda, *Life of Sri Ramakrishna*, Advaita Ashram, Almolra, 1948, p. 75.

11

A Critique of Vivekananda's Political Idiom

Kuldip Dhiman

In the past hundred years, though Swami Vivekananda's role as a Hindu revivalist and social reformer has been duly recognised, his literary talents have not been given their due place. Vivekananda was a very versatile man – singer, saint, thinker, religious and social reformer, and a great orator and writer. He had a way with words, and he used his immense literary gifts to realise his spiritual and patriotic goals. This paper aims to study his political idiom, and its impact on the freedom movement.

A towering figure of the Indian Renaissance, Swami Vivekananda not only revived faith of an enslaved and demoralised people in their own religion, but also breathed in them a fiery zeal of revolution to fight the British rule. There were other equally important figures like Bankim Chandra Chattopadhyay, Swami Dayananda Saraswati, Vidyasagar, Keshub Chandra Sen, Rabindranath Tagore, Aurobindo Ghose and Bal Gangadhar Tilak, but it was a combination of literary gift, robust oratory, and an impressive physique that made Swami Vivekananda the most inspiring icon of the freedom struggle. The revolutionaries of all shades had Bankim Chandra's *Bande Matram* on their lips and Vivekananda's clarion call "Arise awake and stop not till the goal is reached" in their hearts. He successfully employed the philosophy of *Advaita Vedānta* to infuse the spirit of heroism in his countrymen who had resigned themselves to being slaves of the occupying forces. He strongly believed that first of all people had to be educated and shown what a rich past they have had. For achieving this goal, he made full use of his extraordinary literary skills that are evidenced in poems, essays, speeches, and letters. In his literary oeuvre he used imagery, metaphors, and similies from the epics, combining them with modern metaphors. The combination was highly effective and lethal.

Vivekananda's writings, speeches, and poems, published as *The Complete Works of Swami Vivekananda* (nine volumes), can be classed into two groups. The first is his work concerning Hindu scriptures, and the second about social and national matters. In both we just cannot fail to notice the deft use of language. While he used a simple though formal style in his religious works, his speeches and poems dealing with socio-political concerns are written in a more robust style. Here he, at times, not only uses *Vedic* metaphors, highly poetic idioms and similies, but also a good deal of hyperbole and rhetoric often at the expense of consistency and accuracy. But that was expected, for most gifted public speakers know that to arouse sleeping "leviathans", you have to first give them an ideology, and to do that you often have to exaggerate things in order to drive your point home.

A born versatile genius, young Narendranath Dutta, later Swami Vivekananda, was the very embodiment of the spirit of his times. He was brought up in a traditional Bengali kshatriya household, educated at Presidency College, Calcutta where he was strongly influenced by Western thinkers like John Stuart Mill, Herbert Spencer and others, and of course his well-known spiritual guru Swami Ramakrishna Paramahansa. It was a happy combination of these influences and an inborn talent for an impressive turn of phrase that made Vivekananda's language so powerful. We must appreciate that most of his speeches were delivered at a few moments' notice with no time to prepare or rehearse, yet words seemed to flow without effort. The Swami was a gifted writer and a poet who wrote in Bengali in his early life, and mainly in English in the later.

As if these talents were not enough, Vivekananda also had a pleasing countenance, impressive physique, and a strong voice. Going through his correspondence, and various press reports in the East as well as the West, Vivekananda emerges as a fairly tall and handsome man who stood out in a crowd.

We first take up his Bengali work in brief. But before that, we must take into account the milieu in which Vivekananda grew up and worked. The spark that started in the mid-nineteenth century was first called the Bengal Renaissance, but as the fire spread to all corners of India, we can call it the Indian Renaissance. At the time young Vivekananda was getting his education, the Brahmo Samaj movement was in full swing, and reformers and thinkers like Raja Rammohun Roy, Bankim Chandra Chattopadhyay, Debendranath Tagore were transforming a decadent society with their attacks on orthodoxy. These men awakened Indians to Western ideas, democracy, science, and urged them to catch up with the rest of the world. At the same time, in order to instill self-respect in the masses, the reformers compelled them to take a renewed interest in India's glorious past, its religion and sacred books like the *Vedas* and the *Upaniṣads*, and of course the Sanskrit language.

The new-found interest in India's lost glory was such that writers, whether they wrote in Bengali, Hindi or any other language, were trying to make their language as close to Sanskrit as possible. Although immensely influenced by India's ancient texts, Vivekananda was one of the first to use colloquial Bengali in his early writings (the flavour is missing in the English translation). As I do not know Bengali, I shall depend on leading academics and litterateurs to give us some idea of his prodigal literary gifts. Historian R.C. Majumdar says that Vivekananda's Bengali writings, apart:

> from the rich store of thought and information contained in these, they are specially remarkable for the simple colloquial language in which they were written, at a time when a heavy Sanskritised style was the fashion of the day. It was the general impression that serious topics could not be discussed in colloquial language. Swamiji showed in his articles that such a thing was possible.[1]

The Bengali prose works of Vivekananda's *Paribrajak* (Traveller) and *Prachya O Paschatya* (East and West) are actually a collection of his articles that appeared in the Bengali magazine *Udbodhana*. These were very popular, but some leading thinkers and writers of the day strongly criticised Vivekananda for using street language. Scandalised by such defilement of Bengali, Pandit Sakharam Ganesh Deuskar, the sub-editor of the weekly *Hitavadi* said in disgust that *Udbhodhana* was actually *Udbhandana*, i.e., death by hanging of the Bengali language.[2] But Vivekananda stuck to his guns saying:

> Simplicity is the secret. My ideal of language is my Master's language, most colloquial and yet most expressive. It must express the thought which is intended to be conveyed.[3]

And though Vivekananda had a great admiration for Sanskrit, he knew that to awaken the masses, he had to address them in their own rustic tongue.

It was Rabindranath Tagore who first appreciated the new Bengali style introduced by Vivekananda by citing *Prachya O Paschatya* as a model for showing how colloquial Bengali can be made a living and forceful language.[4]

We now take up his work in English, a language he learnt from Englishmen, and as a result spoke and wrote like them. His uncommon command of English was acknowledged by the English and Americans themselves. *Evening News*, August 29, 1893 reported that like:

> all men who are educated in the higher Universities of India, Viva kananda speaks English easily and correctly.[5]

A news report in the *Chicago Record* of September 11 says that the: "Hindoo is of smooth countenance.... His English is very good.[6] While *Daily Iowa Capitol* of Nov 28, 1893 remarked that the:

> lecturer is an able, dignified and forcible speaker. His mastery of English is perfect, there being only the faintest indications of a foreign accent.[7]

Some even commented upon his impressive voice.

As we look into his English prose, poetry, and speeches, one thing that first comes to our notice is that unlike his work in Bengali where he used a colloquial style, here he employed a more formal style, sometimes veering into pompous English. Vivekananda's lectures collected in book form entitled *From Colombo to Almora* gripped the imagination of revolutionaries. His thundering words:

> heaven is nearer through football than through Gita. We want men of strong biceps – stirred up their minds to rise against the occupying force.

To the Awakened India, a poem written for *Prabuddha Bharata* or Awakened India, in August 1898 gives us some idea of his poetic style and diction.

> Once more awake!
> For sleep it was, not death, to bring thee life

Anew, and rest to lotus – eyes for visions
Daring yet. The world in need awaits, O Truth!
No death for thee!
Resume thy march,
With gentle feet that would not break the
Peaceful rest even of the roadside dust
That lies so low. Yet strong and steady,
Blissful, bold, and free. Awakener, ever
Forward! Speak thy stirring words.[8]

Not having any literary pretensions (some say he wrote in a meditative trance) Vivekananda gave a free reign to his imagination often writing in verse libre though he did employ iambic tetrameter, trimeter, etc., but he was not consistent in rhyme or stanza pattern. In the use of language he tried to emulate the Western masters like Keats, Shelly and Wordsworth. In most cases his religious poems appear to be thinly disguised patriotic poems. For instance, take these lines from *Kali the Mother*:

Who dares misery love,
And hug the form of Death,
Dance in Destruction's dance,
To him the Mother comes.[9]

At times his poetic style spilled over his prose work. For instance, in a letter to Mrs. G.W. Hale from Detroit on 10 March, 1894, he wrote:

If the Himalayas become the inkpot, the ocean ink, if the heavenly eternal Devadaroo becomes the pen, and if the sky itself becomes paper, still I would not be able to write a drop of the debt of gratitude I owe to you and yours.[10]

And like a good awakener of conscience, he also instilled an urgency in his call to his "brave boys":

The work has begun well in India, and it should not only be kept up, but pushed with the greatest vigour. Now or never is the time.[11]

He tirelessly tried to drive the point home that there cannot be any growth without liberty for liberty is the first condition of growth.[12] In *The Song of the Sanyasin* which he composed in 1895 in America, he once gain stresses the importance of freedom:

Strike off thy fetters! Bonds that bind thee down,
Of shining gold, or darker baser ore.

For fetters though of gold, are not less strong to bind;
Then, off with them, Sanyasin bold![13]

In order to be free the first step is education and material progress. We cannot talk about religion and other higher goals if the masses are starving. Vivekanada here goes back to the scriptures and uses the metaphor of the tortoise which is supposed to be the god of the stomach.

Now understand what religion means. The first thing required is the worship of Kurma .... Until you pacify this, no one will welcome your words about religion.[14]

Attacking glorification of poverty and overemphasis on spiritualism by Indians, he argued that there were about a hundred thousand really spiritual men and women, but for the spiritualisation of these, must three hundred millions be sunk in savagery and starvation?

Material civilisation, nay, even luxury, is necessary to create work for the poor. Bread! Bread! I do not believe in a God, who cannot give me bread here, giving me eternal bliss in heaven! Pooh! India is to be raised, the poor are to be fed, education is to be spread, and the evil of priestcraft is to be removed. No priestcraft, no social tyranny! More bread, more opportunity for everybody![15]

Vivekananda was aware that his speeches and writing could be seen by the British as seditious, but he wondered why nobody ever arrested him. He was prepared to go to any length to usher in the revolution, and at times he even expressed a great longing that the English government would arrest and shoot him.

It would be the first nail in their coffin... and my death would run through the land like wild fire.[16]

Having gone through his literature, it is clear that though he had renounced the world and become a monk, he felt that he could not sit by and watch his country raped by invaders. His immediate task was to overthrow the British rule.

Vivekananda stressed again and again that Indians had lost their freedom and become slaves, and because of our slave mentality, we have lost our manliness. At such a time spiritualism could only be a distant goal, our immediate effort ought to be to instill martial spirit in the masses so they could break their shackles and first become free. For this, he advocated aggression spiritual, material and even physical if something came in the way. A careful study of his correspondence shows that although he was merely laying the groundwork for the revolution through peaceful means, he was not opposed to using militant methods; he was prepared to use force if the need arose. In *Swami Vivekananda: Patriot Prophet,* Bupendranath Datta writes that after his second tour of the West, Vivekananda told one Prof. Kanankkshya Mitra that "what India needs to-day is bomb".[17] From Surendra Nath Sen's private diary we learn that when it was pointed out to him that instead of aggressive force, shouldn't he consider the course of Radha love advocated by Chaitanya, he burst out:

> Look at this nation and see what has been the outcome of such an attempt. Through the preaching of that love ... the whole nation has become effeminate .... The whole of Orissa has been turned into a land of cowards; and Bengal, running after the Radha-prema, these past four hundred years, has almost lost all sense of manliness![18]

He rued the fact that the refrain of Bengali literature for these four hundred years had failed to produce poetry which breathes a true heroic spirit. Aghast at the state of affairs he cried out in verse:

> O Thou Lord of Gauri, O Thou Mother of the Universe, vouchsafe manliness unto me! O Thou Mother of Strength, take away my weakness, take away my unmanliness, and make me a Man![19]

Vivekananda was himself a regular at the gyms and wrestling *akharas* of Calcutta. He wanted his countrymen to do the same and become physically strong. "A dozen of such lions will conquer the world, and not millions of sheep ...."[20] To achieve this goal, he even encouraged young men to eat meat, for he felt that the idea of non-violence and vegetarianism had made Indians weak in body as well as spirit. Justifying it he said:

> Do you think that a handful of Englishmen could rule India if we had a militant spirit? I teach meat-eating throughout the length and breadth of India in the hope that we can build a militant spirit![21]

He reminded his listeners that there was a place for struggle in the *Vedānta,* but not fear.

> All fears will vanish when you begin to assert your own nature. If you think that you are bound, bound you will remain. If you think you are free, free you will be.[22]

The cause of our weakness in his opinion was that being a conquered race for centuries, Indians had lost *Shraddha* or faith in their own selves.

> Strength is life, weakness is death.... It is by losing this idea of Shraddha that the country has gone to ruin. The idea of true Shraddha must be brought back once more to us, the faith in our own selves must be reawakened, and, then only, all the problems which face our country will gradually be solved by ourselves.[23]

As he did not actually use the bomb or the gun to overthrow the British, though he might have inspired others to do so, we see that he used a lot more potent weapon, that is his pen, and with what mastery. In order to appreciate his revolutionary idiom, we shall also as we go along try to grasp his religious and political ideas, for he used the former to achieve the latter. Religion in his opinion ought to be central to our lives, because in order to avoid degeneration and attain perfection, everything had to be done with devotion, even business and politics. India had lost its ancient glory because its people practised only rituals, not religion. Though he often stressed that all religions basically had the same teachings, he for reasons of his own believed that all other religions somehow owed a debt to Hinduism. Vivekananda saw it as his life's mission, to reawaken the masses and restore India's lost glory. This is because, according to the Indian tradition, whenever there is a decline of morals or when there is a social crisis, a yogi cannot just sit by and watch passively. He has to act in accordance with the times. He bemoaned the fact that Indians were concerned with their own personal salvation with utter disregard to their social responsibilities. He was the first modern Indian, says Amiya P. Sen, to challenge this traditional orientation.[24] He believed that though there are various paths to achieve supreme bliss, at present times when *Tamas* is predominant, action was the need of the hour.

> Jñāna, Bhakti, Yoga and Karma – these are the four paths which lead to salvation. One must follow the path for which one is best suited; but in this age special stress should be laid on Karma – yoga.[25]

Vivekananda argued that at present in India, the quality of *Rajas* was almost absent as is *Sattva* absent in the West. Unless we overcame *Tamas* by *Rajas*, its opposite, we shall never gain any worldly good or welfare in this life or the next.[26] By putting action at least on the same footing as ascetic contemplation, Vivekananda seems to have not only departed from the negative work ethic of his Master but also implicitly suggested a fresh look at traditional (Hindu) value systems.[27]

Vivekananda's analysis of socio-political history was that society is ruled in turns by the four castes. The priestly class assumes power first, and at such a time there is great intellectual activity. In this age *Sattva* is dominant. This is followed by the supremacy of the Kshatriya caste which rules by the sword, and in this age *Rajas* prevails. Later Vaishyas begin to rule, as is the case in modern times; at such a time business flourishes and there is great generation of wealth. Finally, the Shudra class rules, that is the rule of the working class; at such a time *Tamas* is everywhere. We must here bear in mind that to Vivekananda the four castes were a kind of division of labour. A person belongs to a particular caste owing to the kind of work he chooses, not because of his birth in a particular caste. Thus, on his view, caste should not be made hereditary, it should change according to one's station in life. Even the general composition of society changes in different ages, so does its dominant national character.

> In the mighty course of time, the Brahmin and the other higher castes, too, are being brought down to the lower status of the Shudras, and the Shudras are being raised to higher ranks. Europe, once the land of Shudras enslaved by Rome, is now filled with Kshatriya valour. Even before our eyes, powerful China, with fast strides, is going down to Shudra-hood, while insignificant Japan, rising with the sudden start of a rocket, is throwing off her Shudra nature and is invading by degrees the rights of the higher castes.[28]

No matter which class assumed power and which *guna* prevailed, the first condition of life according to Vivekananda was freedom, freedom of the soul and the freedom of the body, without which everything else was meaningless. In his short life, that is what he tried to tell his people through his powerful language.

> From dreams awake, from bonds be free!
> Be not afraid. This mystery,
> My shadow, cannot frighten me!
> Know once for all that I am He![29]

CONCLUSION

Vivekananda was a yogi in true spirit. He was well-educated, well-versed in ancient scriptures and philosophy, was well acquainted with the arts and sciences, did selfless work for society, and all his life he was a model to others for he practised what he preached. Having had the talent to use language, he used it to further the two aims of his life – spiritual and political freedom of his countrymen. Thanks to his writings, speeches and poems, he very eminently achieved that goal, though it is not duly recognised.

NOTES AND REFERENCES

1. Majumdar, R.C., *Swami Vivekananda: A Historical Review*; Advaita Ashram, 1999, first published by General Printers and Publishers Private Ltd., 1965, p. 84.
2. Dutta, Bhupendra, *Swami Vivekananda Patriot Prophet*; Navbharat Publishers, 1954, p. 290.
3. *The Complete Works of Swami Vivekananda*, Advaita Ashram, Vol. V, 1995, p. 259.
4. Majumdar, R.C., *Op. cit.*, Advaita Ashram, 1999, first published by General Printers and Publishers Private Ltd., 1965, p. 85.
5. *Swami Vivekananda in the West: New Discoveries*, Advaita Ashram, p. 51.
6. *Ibid.*, Before the Parliament, Advaita Ashram, p. 60.
7. *New Discoveries*, Advaita Ashram, Vol. I, pp. 200-202.
8. *The Complete Works of Swami Vivekananda*, Advaita Ashram, Vol. IV, 1995, p. 387.
9. Selections from *Swami Vivekananda*, Advaita Ashram, p. 617.
10. *The Complete Works of Swami Vivekananda*, Advaita Ashram, Vol. IX, 1995, p. 13.
11. In a letter written to Justice Sir Subrahmanya Iyer from Chicago, 3, January 1895, *The Complete Works of Swami Vivekananda*, Advaita Ashram, Vol. IV, 1995, p. 371.
12. *The Complete Works of Swami Vivekananda*, Advaita Ashram, Vol. IV, 1995, p. 367.
13. Selections from *Swami Vivekananda*, Advaita Ashram, 1946, p. 613.
14. *The Complete Works of Swami Vivekananda*, Advaita Ashram, Vol. V, 1995, p. 379.
15. *Ibid.*, Advaita Ashram, Vol. IV, p. 368.
16. *Swami Vivekananda in the West: New Discoveries*, Advaita Ashram, p. 34.
17. Datta, Bhupendranath, *Swamy Vivekananda: Patriot Prophet*, Navbharat Publishers 1954, p. 212.
18. *The Complete Works of Swami Vivekananda*, Advaita Ashram, Vol. V, 1995, p. 345.

19. *Ibid.*, Advaita Ashram, Vol. IV, 1995, p. 480.
20. *Selections from the Math Diary; The Complete Works of Swami Vivekananda*, Advaita Ashram, Vol., V, 1995, p. 315.
21. *The Complete Works of Swami Vivekananda*, Advaita Ashram, Vol. IX, 1995, p. 404.
22. *Ibid.*, Vol. V, 1995, p. 286.
23. *From the diary of Surendranath Sen; The Complete Works of Swami Vivekananda*, Advaita Ashram, Vol. V, 1995, p. 332.
24. Sen, Amiya P., *Hindu Revivalism in Bengal: Some Essays in Interpretation*; Oxford University Press, 1993, p. 312.
25. *The Complete Works of Swami Vivekananda*, Advaita Ashram, Vol. V, 1995, p. 414.
26. *Ibid.*, Vol. IV, 1995, p. 406.
27. Sen, Amiya P., *Hindu Revivalism in Bengal: Some Essays in Interpretation*, Oxford University Press, 1993, p. 320.
28. *The Complete Works of Swami Vivekananda*, Advaita Ashram, Vol. IV, 1995, p. 468.
29. *The Song of the Free; The Complete Works of Swami Vivekananda*, Advaita Ashram, Vol. VII, 1995, p. 164.

12

Vivekananda's Aesthetics

Rekha Jhanji

If one cannot appreciate the harmony in nature, how can one appreciate God, the summation of all harmony, sublimity and beauty.

— Swami Vivekananda

The present paper* is devoted to an exposition of the much neglected but important subject of Vivekananda's aesthetics. It is surprising that despite Vivekananda's deep interest in both beauty and art, not much has been written on it. I have been trying to figure out the reasons for this lacuna, perhaps it is either due to the fact that he did not write any separate treatise on this subject or it is due to the commonplace association of the aesthetic with the sensuous. Ordinarily the pursuit of beauty is associated with persons who are deeply entrenched in bodily pleasures. Since a *sanyasi* is understood to have renounced all concern for sensuous pleasure, and the aesthetic experience is steeped in the sensuous experience, it is presumed that one who has taken *sanyasa* has no interest in the aesthetic. Usually, one associates a saint with austerity, renunciation and indifference towards beauty and ugliness. But this is more a myth than a reality. There is great poetry written by sages. If we look at the life of Swami Vivekananda and his master Ramakrishna Paramahansa we realise that both were deeply sensitive to the beauty of nature and art. Natural beauty often generated trances in Ramakrishna; he acted in plays and danced with joy while taking the name of God. He held the aesthetic sense to be a necessary pre-requisite for the development of spirituality. Vivekananda's disciples tell us that:

He was an ascetic and artist in one. He never merged his nature in physical experience; he was constantly the witness, the poet, the great dreamer who meditated on the phenomena of experience and saw the spiritual even in the physical.[1]

Vivekananda was very sensitive to the beauty of nature and its representations through art. He travelled extensively and had keen observation of the subtleties of natural landscapes as well as the variety of art traditions of the world. He defines art as a representation of the beautiful. He writes:

... true art can be compared to a lily which springs from the ground, takes its nourishment from the ground, is in touch with the ground, and yet is quite high above it. So Art must be in touch with nature – and wherever that touch is gone, Art degenerates – yet it must be above nature. Art is representing the beautiful. There must be art in everything.[2]

From the above citation it becomes clear that Vivekananda gave precedence to the following two parameters for evaluating art:

a) that art must always remain closely associated with nature. Even though it may not imitate nature, it must remain rooted in it.
b) Art must be a representation of the beautiful.

Let us go deeper into these parameters and see their implications for Vivekananda's aesthetics. The first point that becomes important is the recognition that without its connection with nature, art would have no life in it. In fact, Vivekananda gave a lot of importance to observation of nature and faithfulness to details observed. Despite his great admiration of Kālidāsa, he could not help criticising him for his inaccurate description of the sea shores in *Raghuvamsham*. He very candidly states in his *Memoirs of European Travel*:

with all my respect for the great poet, it is my belief that he never in his life saw either the ocean or the Himalayas.

Although, he later revised his opinion regarding Kālidāsa's acquaintance with the Himalayas but his comments on the sea remain and they tell us how much importance he gave to the necessity of travelling and a keen observation for a poet. Since Vivekananda himself had great passion for travelling, he was well aware of the benefits of travelling. He was clear that an artist who does not have a keenness of observation will not be able to represent the content and form of his art work with authenticity. However, he was also clear that mere faithfulness of representation does not make a great work of art. For art is not simply a duplication of nature. Despite his admiration of Phidias, he was critical of the over-emphasis on imitation in Greek art. Contrasting Greek art with its Indian counterpart he writes:

> The secret of Greek Art is its imitation of nature even to the minutest details; whereas the secret of Indian Art is to represent the ideal. The energy of the Greek painter is spent in perhaps painting a piece of flesh, and he is so successful that a dog is deluded into taking it to be a real bit of meat and so goes to bite it. Now, what glory is there in merely imitating nature? Why not place an actual bit of flesh before the dog?[3]

Thus, it becomes clear that despite his love of observation Vivekananda thinks it necessary for art to transcend mere imitation and blend within its form a harmony between faithfulness to nature and commitment towards an idea. Without the idea it will have no lasting value. As Vivekananda puts it:

> Art has its origin in the expression of some idea in whatever man produces. Where there is no expression of idea, however much there may be a display of colours and so on, it cannot be styled as true art.[4]

We have already stated that Vivekananda held art to be a representation of the beautiful. He did not allow the grotesque to be accommodated in the domain of art. The full meaning of this contention would become clear only when we first delineate his conception of beauty. His conception of beauty is deeply spiritual; its physical manifestation is only a reflection of its spirit. Like all the great *Bhaktas*, Vivekananda saw God as the real embodiment of beauty, every beautiful object in the world partakes of His beauty. He writes:

> What is the beauty in the human face, in the sky, in the stars, and in the moon? It is only the partial apprehension of the real all-embracing Divine Beauty. "He shining, everything shines.[5] .... He is the most beautiful, the most sublime, He is beauty itself, sublimity itself. Who in this universe is more beautiful than He?"[6]

It is obvious that such a conception of beauty has no place for the grotesque.

Vivekananda's approach towards art is quite in tune with the classical Indian aesthetics. As against the folk traditions which are more mundane in their content, the Classical Indian aesthetics is deeply entrenched in a spiritual weltanschauung. The *Upaniṣadic* view of the organic relationship between *rasa* and Brahman seems to have had an indelible imprint on Vivekananda, his aesthetics seems to be charged by the same spirit. He saw the *Upaniṣads* as some of the most beautiful poems ever written. He refers to the famous *Śloka* which describes Chaos – तम आसीत्तमसा गूढमग्रे etc.— "When darkness was hidden in darkness", so on it goes. One reads and feels the wonderful sublimity of the poetry "... outside of India, and inside also, there have been attempts at painting the sublime. But outside, it has always been the infinite in the muscles, the external world, the infinite of matter, or of space ... our forefathers ... were bolder in declaring the utter hopelessness of the senses to find the solution .... In the *Ātman* they found the solution – the greatest of all *Ātmans*, the God, the Lord of the universe, His relation to the *Ātman* of man, our duty to Him, and through that our relation to each other. And herein you find the most sublime poetry of the world.[7]"

Vivekananda quotes many passages from the *Upaniṣads* to substantiate his view of beauty and sublimity and his own poems also embody this *Vedāntic* spirit. The basic thrust of all these remarks is the belief in the spiritual nature of beauty. He found it necessary to capture this spirit in art. Through his own poetry he has tried to envision this essential character of beauty. In one of his poems he writes:

It is joy that never spoke,
And grief unfelt, profound,
Immortal life unlived,
Eternal death unmourned.
It is not joy nor sorrow,
But that which is between,
It is not night nor morrow,
But that which joins them in.
It is sweet rest in music;
And pause in sacred art;
The silence between speaking;
Between two fits of passion –

It is the calm of heart.
It is beauty never seen,
And love that stands alone,
It is song that lives un-sung,
And knowledge never known.[8]

These lines seem to echo the statement from *Taittariya Upaniṣad*: *raso vai sah.* They indicate Vivekananda's faith in the all-pervasive Absolute Being as the source of all beauty and aesthetic joy. His is a wholistic view of life in which every pursuit is meaningful only in terms of illuminating the Absolute. No pursuit is an end in itself because the primary purpose of human existence is self-knowledge. Art is valuable to the extent that it helps us reach that goal. The three *yogas* of *jñāna, bhakti* and *karma* are nothing but the three paths to reach the goal of self-realisation. Ultimately, all three are different facets of the same pursuit, thus highlighting the inherent unity of *styam, śivam, sundaram* (truth, goodness and beauty).

In Vivekananda's world-view there was no place for art for art's sake. He looked upon human life as an organic whole in which all actions must have an organic relation to each other. Such a view presupposes a complete harmony between theory and practice. Thus, any artistic pursuit must contribute to the wholeness of the life of its creator, without this objective there would be no harmony between the different pursuits of man. If the pursuit of beauty does not go hand in hand with truth and goodness then it will turn into an aberration. And, however attractive and enticing it may be, it will be poisonous for any culture. Similarly, the pursuit of knowledge and truth without goodness and beauty would only generate a culture of wolves – totally lacking in compassion for fellow beings. Vivekananda admired poets like Vyāsa and Vālmiki who envisioned such characters that became paradigms for the posterity. He appreciated classical Indian painting and sculpture for its concern for the idea behind the sensuous image. By bringing out this aspect of Indian visual arts, he provided an appropriate view-point for looking at these arts in a time when Western critics were literally denigrating Indian arts as creations of monstrosity. Much before Coomaraswamy and Havell, Vivekananda had the ingenuity to see Indian art from its own parameters and give an appropriate response to Western art critics. Vivekananda saw a connection between art traditions and world views. For instance, a materialist world-view generates art forms which are mainly realistic in nature while idealist world views give rise to symbolic art. This is how he explains the concern for the visible appearance in modern European art as against the deep commitment to the presentation of an ideal behind the image in classical Indian art. Thus, for a sculptor who set out to sculpt the image of Buddha, it was not so important to faithfully represent his physical appearance as it was to render the qualities of compassion (*karuṇā*), non-violence (*ahiṃsā*) and friendship (*maitri*) through his image of the Buddha.

His understanding of world literature becomes quite obvious from his letters, travelogues and lectures. His own writings – both prose as well as poetic ones – give us an idea of the power of his pen as well as the inspiration behind it.

He had a deep understanding of classical Indian music. Apart from his gift of musical talent and a sonorous voice, he had also the ability to compose music. Many of the tunes composed by him are still sung in Ramakrishna *ashrams*. He had a deep understanding of the theoretical aspects of both Western and Indian music.

Vivekananda's work on the Bengali text *Saṅgīta Kalpaturu* published by Chandicharan Basak gives an evidence of his expertise in musicology. As a dancer, musician and singer he was well known amongst the spiritual followers of Sri Ramakrishna. Had he the time, he could have developed this talent on a much larger scale. A vivid description of Vivekananda's aesthetic sense is found in *The Life of Swami Vivekananda* by his Eastern and Western disciples. It states:

> .... Narendranath ... had a strong, beautiful body, and more than that, a beautiful mind and a highly developed aesthetic sense. Thus, when he was dancing and simultaneously singing, every movement of his limbs scintillated beauty, and the eyes and ears of those who watched would be filled with a unique experience of gracefulness.[9]

The above passage does give a glimpse of Vivekananda's natural aesthetic sensibility. It was a sensibility very close to the medieval European fathers who saw beauty in the whole of nature and its human pursuit being essentially a pursuit of divinity. Thus, anything that violates the moral or the spiritual sensibility could never be acceptable to him, however "creative" it might pretend to be. For beauty, if it only titillates the senses, would take one away from one's real self into the abyss of *Māyā*. Such a creation had no place for the objective he had set out to achieve. This is the reason why one finds almost an echo of Plato in Vivekananda's critique of certain art forms. Any art that evokes indolence and titillation of sensory pleasures is to be shunned because it divests one of manliness. Manliness for Vivekananda is not gender-centred but quality-centred; it refers to the pursuit of fearlessness and non-covetousness. An art-form that evokes desire, violates the very norm of aesthetic excellence which aspires to lead human beings towards joyfulness born of detachment and disinterestedness. Aesthetic experience in its proper sense helps one to live life joyfully because it inspires detached and disinterested contemplation. Vivekananda thought it necessary to extend this attitude of disinterested contemplation towards our whole life because he was convinced that:

> Only to the soul that has attained to this contemplative state that the world really becomes beautiful. To him who desires nothing and does not mix himself up with them, the manifold changes of nature are one panorama of beauty and sublimity.[10]

The freedom from involvement, which the work of art generates in the spectator, becomes a cue for an individual to free himself of desires. For, if we want to enjoy life then we need to cultivate desirelessness. To a spectator of art desirelessness comes quite effortlessly because of the clear recognition that what is happening before him is an imaginary creation and not a real one. To a Vedantin the mundane world is like a dream, thus any involvement with it is futile. It contributes nothing to one's understanding of reality; it rather distracts and misleads an aspirant and traps him in the vicious circle of desires of ephemeral phenomena. Since art is a reflection of life, participating in it we can vicariously go through an imaginary life and see how enjoyable detachment is. The story of Yayāti in the *Bhāgavata Purāṇa* very well recounts the ephemerality of all worldly experiences. After experiencing worldly pleasures for a thousand years, Yayāti realised that one is not satiated by them, rather one's desires keep increasing and with each desire one gets more and more restless. It is only through renunciation that one can go beyond this vicious circle.

One discerns two levels in Vivekananda's aesthetics: in the first level there is the pursuit of art in harmony with morality and knowledge, for he upholds the intimate relationship of truth, beauty and goodness. In the second level art goes beyond good and evil and truth and falsehood. It is in this stage that the aesthetic experience reaches equanimity and becomes the twin of mystical experience. Once one has become a true *sahṛdaya* the whole world looks beautiful. Such was Vivekananda's aesthetic vision that he saw the world itself like a beautiful painting of the Divine Creator. Just as many unpalatable things look appealing when rendered in a painting, if one looks at the whole world with the eyes of a true *rasika*, then everything gets imbued with a sense of beauty and one starts to marvel at the Creator.

Thus, for a true *Sahṛdaya*, everything gets imbued with a sense of joy. All the different *bhāvas* lead to *śānta rasa*. However, this joyfulness does not mean complicity with evil and advocacy of the status-quo. It enables one to invoke the eternal witness in oneself; it also refers to a *karma yogi's* detachment towards the fruits of any *karma*. This aesthetic detachment embodies within it the fearlessness born of the unity of *karma*, *jñāna* and *bhakti* and not the apathy of passivity and the fearful acquiescence of the status-quo.

Swami Vivekananda embodies his whole vision of life in terms of his idea behind the design of the seal of the Ramakrishna Mission. He explains the symbolic meaning of this visual form as follows:

The wavy waters in the picture are symbolic of *Karma*; the lotus, of *Bhakti*; and the rising – sun, of *Jñāna*. The encircling serpent is indicative

of Yoga and the awakened *Kundalini Shakti*, while the swan in the picture stands for the *Paramātman* (Supreme Self). Therefore the idea of the picture is that by the union of *Karma, Jñāna, Bhakti*, and Yoga, the vision of the *Paramātman* is obtained.[11]

From the foregoing it becomes clear that for Vivekananda genuine art (as against mere trendiness) generates in the beholder a quest for the Absolute. It performs two roles – one of warning us against the ephemerality of all worldly pleasures and the second of giving us a glimpse of the Divine. However, it will depend on the beholder's own effort what he receives from art. As Bhartṛhari writes:

> The same knowledge which is conducive to extripate the existence of vain conceit from the minds of good is also productive of vanity and pride into those of others. A lonely place which frees those who have obtained complete control over the senses from attraction to world likewise become the cause of lustful excitement in passionate hearts.[12]

> ज्ञानं सतां मानमदादिनाशनं केषांचिदेतन्मदमानकारणम्
> स्थानं विविक्तं यमिनां विमुक्तये कामातुराणामतिकामकारणम्।।१२।।

One can understand what Bhartṛhari wants to say here if one looks at some of our ancient temples like Khajuraho. The erotic sculptures on the outer façade of the temple are seen by the licentious as an invitation to see sexually exciting sculptures, while those who have realised the limitations of worldly pleasures see their attraction due to the reflection in them of the transcendental joy. Consequently, the latter turn towards the *garbha gṛaha* (the sanctum sanctorum) because that symbolises the need to begin one's journey within. We can conclude from the foregoing that if we want to have an aesthetic experience then we need to cleanse ourselves of the dross, only then would we be capable of disinterested contemplation. A *Sahṛdaya* is like a *jīvanamukta* who sees beauty in both good and evil; for he finds nothing alienated from the divine play. As Hiriyanna puts it:

> This beauty is the characteristic of the reality taken as a whole is immanent in every part of it, so that we may "spy some shadow of eternity" in every object or every situation in it .... If we do not usually discern this intrinsic beauty, it is because we are distracted by personal and practical concerns with which we have long become accustomed to associate them .... That is, the absence of selfish desire is the sole

condition for the perception of beauty in nature; and when that condition is satisfied, there will be nothing to prevent one from seeing the beauty that is presented.[13]

NOTES AND REFERENCES

* An earlier version of this paper was published in the Bulletin of the Ramakrishna Mission Institute of Culture, Kolkata, Nov, 2004.

1. *Vivekananda: The Man and His Message by His Eastern and Western Disciples*, Advaita Ashram, Kolkata, 2004, p. 43.
2. *Complete Works of Swami Vivekananda*, Advaita Ashram, Kolkata, Vol. I, 1996, pp. 258-59.
3. *Ibid.*, Vol. V, p. 258.
4. *Ibid.*, Vol. VII, p. 201.
5. *Ibid.*, Vol. III, p. 74.
6. *Ibid.*, Vol. III, p. 98.
7. *Ibid.*, Vol. III, pp. 330-31.
8. *In Search of God and Other Poems*, p. 29.
9. C.W., Vol. I, p. 54.
10. *Ibid.*, Vol. I, pp. 186-87.
11. *Ibid.*, Vol. VII, p. 204.
12. Bhartṛhari, *Vairagya sataka*, tr. Purohit Gopi Nath, Bombay, 1914, *sloka*. 88.
13. M. Hiriyanna, *Indian Conception of Values*, Kavyalaya Publishers, Mysore, 1975, p. 321.

Section Three

INDIAN PHILOSOPHICAL SYSTEMS

13

Vivekananda on Buddha and Buddhism

Manjulika Ghosh

There are numerous mentions of, and references to, the Buddha in Vivekananda's writings. Of these, two stand out as most significant and remarkable. Vivekananda looked upon the Buddha as a "God-man" and "the ideal *Karma Yogin.*[1] It will be a part of the contention of this paper to look into the religious and socio-cultural import of Vivekananda's estimation of the Buddha. I propose to proceed in a twofold manner. First, I shall consider the cultural attitude prevailing in respect of the Buddha, and in some context towards Buddhism, at least in West Bengal; and secondly, look for the reason for Vivekananda's high esteem of the Buddha.

There is a currency of the idea that Śamkara had ousted Buddhism from India, which is a historical howler. Śamkara had his own axes to grind in refuting (?) or rebutting or arguing against various philosophical points of view. These included *Hindu* (*āstika* or ways of thinking which went by *śabda pramāṇa* of the *Vedas*), philosophies such as *Samākhyā, Vaiśeṣika, Nyāya, Pāśupata,* and *Pancarātra* or the *Bhāgvata.* Śamkara philosophically contested two non-Hindu (?) or non-*Vedic* systems, the Jaina and the Buddhist. None of the views argued against by Śamkara got lost from the Indian subcontinent, except of course Buddhism. There have been reasons, other than philosophical, for the disappearance of Buddhism from the Indian scene. The Turko-Afghan invasions, in particular, were the hardest of blows that led to the destruction of Buddhist monasteries of North India, and then the kingdoms and traders that donated wealth to those monasteries had disappeared eventually. Buddhism was primarily a monastic religion, and without the monasteries, the faith could not sustain itself. There were large-scale conversions to Islam, and this is reported by Udayana in his *Tattvacintāmani*. It should be taken into account that the real antagonism to the Buddbhist way of thinking came not from Śamkara, but from Kumārila Bhatta, the *Mīmāṃasaka*, and the antagonism, more often than not, is couched in unphilosophically emotive terms. Kumārila called the Buddhists "dogs".[2] The content of Kumārila's remark is that the Buddhist code of conduct emphasising *ahiṃsā* is a noble one (this is admitted honestly by using the term *kṣīra* or milk), though its repudiation of the *Vedas* is ignoble. Hence Kumārila compares Buddhism to milk put up in dog's skin: *śvā-carma-kṣipta-kṣīra-vad*. As regards Śamkara's anti-Buddhist dialectics, it should be noted that it goes un-responded, since no Buddhist philosopher of the stature of Nāgārjuna or Dingnāga were any more there to take up the cudgels for Buddhism. Śamkara has argued against both the realist and the idealist trends of Buddhist thought, and finally the negative absolutism or *śūnyavāda* of the Mādhyamika. Has it all been a fair play? The question still remains open. The profound development of Mādhyamika point of view took place in Tibet and this has not yet been taken into account by the historians of Indian thought. However, it has come to be gradually acknowledged that Mādhyamika *śūnyavāda* is not nihilism *simpliciter*. The *Prasannapadā* of Candrakirti has a definite undoubted thrust towards a positive non-dualist ontology of Śamkara's type. This has been openly exhibited in the annotated translation of Śamkara's *bhāṣya* or the *Brahmasūtras* by Swami Visvarupananda of Ramakrishna-Vivekananda order.[3]

Vivekananda, as per his Master, Ramakrishna's initiation, belonged to the Puri order of monks founded by Śamkara himself. But as a radical he did not go the entire miles with Śamkara. His practicalisation of *Vedānta* is an instance. Moreover, Vivekananda was a bit of socialist and looked at the philosophies of India as "class philosophies", formulated to serve the interest of the socio religious establishment. This is reported by no less a person than Dr. Bhupendranath Datta, the younger brother of Vivekananda, who was, by training, a social anthropologist. Datta mentions also that Vivekananda considered both Kumārila and such *Vedāntins* as Śamkara, Rāmānuja and Madhva to have prioritised Brahminical interest as against the Jaina and the Buddhist. According to Datta, Śamkara's borrowings from the two heretical schools can hardly be profaned. The appellation of being a crypto-Buddhist applies to Śamkara in no uncertain or unfair sense. The theses of rebirth and law of *Karma* are typically Buddhist in intention and import. Śamkara had usurped the theses and passed them off as though they were essentially *Vedic*. The Brahmins usurped much of the Buddhist heritages and let it have currency under new names. The Buddhist trinity of the Buddha, the *Sangha* and the *Dharma* were reintroduced as the trinity of the Jagannath temple at Puri. This is contended by no less a knowledgeable person than Haraprasad Shastri. Even Nivedita had endorsed the thesis in her *Footfalls of Indian History*. The resurgence of Brahminism around AD 800 was not without its sad tales of extermination of Buddhists in the most unkind fashion. This had happened in Maharashtra at the instance of Kumārila, and when Śamkara had besieged the temple of Puri similar incidents were recorded. The social anthropologists might ask about the lot of the Buddhist masses in the eastern Bengal. In order to escape from the oppressive tyranny of the caste elite the people at the lower rung of the social hierarchy espoused Islam.

It was against the authority of the Brahminical order under the *Vedic* flag that the Buddha protested. Yet the canonisation of the Buddha as the ninth *avatāra* of Vishnu was finalised by the time of the Guptas. Not only Jayadeva did sing of him as the embodiment of compassion there are other sources, both *Vedic* and *Tantric,* which also join in the adoration of the Buddha. Even Śamkara himself had composed a poem in praise of the Buddha whatever animus he had against his followers. Radhakrishnan quotes the verse on p. 38 of his translation of the *Brahmasūtra.* Śamkara hails the Buddha as the King of the Yogis in *Kaliyuga: ya āste kale yogināṃ chakravarti.*[4] It appears that Śamkara distinguished between the person of the Buddha, his wonderful purity and enlightenment from the dialectics of his followers divided between several schools and practices. It is alleged in Śamkara's *bhāṣya* that the *Saugatas* owing to the defective intellect (*manda buddhi*) misunderstood the teachings of Sugata (the Buddha). Jayadeva in adoring Buddha as Vishnu's *avatāra* refers to his vilification of the *Vedas* on the ground of enjoying animal sacrifices. This is somewhat misleading in the light of what the Buddha himself is reported to have said in the *Anguttara Nikāya.*

I do not praise every sacrifice. Yet I do not withhold praise for every sacrifice. In whatever sacrifice cows are slaughtered, goats and sheep, fowl and swine, and where diverse living creatures come to destruction

– such sacrifice, as involves butchery, I do not praise. Why is this? To such a sacrifice, involving butchery, neither perfected ones nor those who have entered on the way to perfection draw near. But I do praise such sacrifice as a long established charity, an oblation for the welfare of the clan. Why is this? Because to such a sacrifice both perfected ones and those who have entered on the way to perfection draw near.[5]

The Buddha used *yajna* as a term for commanding actions to be performed, and he defined it persuasively by replacing the old, descriptive meaning with new ones. A similar device is observable in *Gītā* with regard to the term. The umbrella condemnation of the Buddha as *Veda nindukah* is certainly unreasonable and a pre-meditated strategy to eliminate his followers.

Vivekananda grew up in a metropolis which was agog with discoveries relating to Buddhism. The British enterprise in this direction was exemplary. The Pali Text Society published translations of *Pali Canons of the Buddhistic Lore*. The Mahabodhi Society was founded by the the Sri Lankan monk Anagarika Dharmapal (who also had gone to the Parliament of Religions at Chicago in 1893); restoration work of the *Mahabodhi* temple was undertaken by Rajendralal Mitra; Satish Chandra Bidyabhusan was editing works on Mahayana Logic and Haraprasad Shastri was publishing on the theology of later Mahayana sects and practices. The house of Tagores contributed a lot in popularising Buddhism in Bengali. At least some of these achievements should have come to Vivekananda's notice, and had touched a deeper chord of his heart. His numerous references to *Lalitavistara*, the poetical biography of the Buddha, held a peculiar charm for him. So had *The Light of Asia* by Sir Edwin Arnold.

We may now turn to considering what Vivekananda thought of the Buddha and his creed. But it will be worth our while to see if Vivekananda's mentor and master, Ramakrishna had something to say about the Buddha. Our source in this regard shall be the *Gospel of Sri Ramakrishna Kathamrita* by Mahendranath Gupta. This monumental work represents Ramakrishna in dialogue with his admirers and disciples. My reference will be to the original Bengali book in the one-volume edition.[6] However, in keeping with Ramakrishna's wide and catholic religious sympathies we are informed that his room at Dakshineswar had a stone image of the Buddha along with a painting depicting Christ rescuing Peter, besides other Hindu deities. These were venerated by

Ramakrishna.[7] In conversation with his disciples Ramakrishna proclaimed the Buddha as an *avatāra*[8] and approved Swami Abhedananda's adoration of the Buddha.

In 1986, Vivekananda (then Narendranath) visited Bodh Gaya and on 9th April the talks turned on the issue of the imputation of atheism to the Buddha. When Vivekananda remarked that the Buddha will not advance any positive ontological view regarding Divine Existence, Ramakrishna took up the issue and clarified it as follows. He resented imputation of atheism with the remarks that the Buddha's silence over the issue did not amount to spiritual failure. On the contrary, it bespoke of a deeper spiritual realisation. What is Buddhahood? he asked and clarified the matter with the remarks that it was realising, by uninterrupted meditation, the essence of enlightenment. The realisation of essence is a poise intermediate between the concept of existence as well as non-existence. *Buddha ki jano? Boddhaswarupake cinta kore kore tayi haoya ... yekhane swarupke bodha hoya sekhane asti-nastira maedhyera abastha.*[9]

It appears that Ramakrishna did not go by the commonly held simplistic definition of the term *nāstika*. Nāgārjuna held that the enlightenend person restrains himself from the categorical manner of speaking with regard to transcendental objects. He maintains the *tusni* attitude. Such had been the dramatic import of the silence of the Buddha. It is worth noting that Ramakrishna maintained a sort of analytic impossibility between one's becoming enlightened and being a nihilist or an atheist. "The fools say to themselves that there is no God," so goes the Psalm no. 14, and commenting upon it Saint Anselm built his ontological argument. Ramakrishna was no ordinary theist, and could take on his stride various stages of realisation. The question whether there is a Creator God or not had never been of paramount importance in the Hindu spiritual tradition. There was the quest for a deeper affirmation that would assert itself in an altered quality of life and action. What Sri Aurobindo says of the Buddha deserves hearing. It was

> possible for the Buddha to attain the state of Nirvaṇa and yet act puissantly in the world, impersonal in his inner consciousness, in his action the most powerful personality that we know of as having lived and produced results upon earth.[10]

Did Sri Aurobindo echo Vivekananda's description of the Buddha as the ideal *karma yogi*?

In his conversation with his disciple Sarat Chandra Chakraborty, Vivekananda disclosed the experience of having had a vision of the Buddha in his early youth, and that he had been overtaken by awe.[11] It is also a highly significant event that when Ramakrishna was terminally ill and was being looked after, among others by Vivekananda, he escaped without notice to Bodh Gaya along with Swami Shivananda and Swami Abhedananda. The latter has reported that Vivekananda wept bitterly sitting beneath the Bodhi tree while he tried to invoke the spirit of the Buddha.[12]

For the disciples of Ramakrishna, the Buddha was the ideal of renunciation. We find that Vivekananda had emphatically asserted that Hinduism had become a greater religion only by absorbing the ideal of Buddhism. The Buddha had breathed a new life into monasticism in India.[13] Keeping this fact in mind Vivekananda thanked his audience at the Parliament of Religions at Chicago in 1893, "in the name of the most ancient order of monks in the world", and the length of "Buddhism, the fulfilment of Hinduism."[14] So great was Vivekananda's admiration of Buddhism that he did not spare chastising Śamkara for exterminating the Buddhists and called him a fanatic on that score.[15] He suggests that the Buddha was the real embodiment of *Vedānta* practicalised, *tini-I yathartha vedantera sfuranamurti*.[16] Here are the words with which he concluded one of his lectures at Chicago:

> Hinduism cannot live without Buddhism ... the separation between the Buddhists and the Brahmins is the cause of the downfall of India.[17]

And earlier he had said, the Buddha:

> was the fulfilment, the logical conclusion, the logical development of the religion of the Hindus.[18]

It appears that Vivekananda distinguished the Buddha and the historical development of Buddhism. He holds somewhat in Śamkara's vein that the Buddha's disciples did not understand him properly. He came like Jesus, to fulfil and not to destroy. Referred to as Śakya Muni, the Buddha, says Vivekananda, brought out the truths of *Vedānta* and "threw them broadcast all over the world".[19]

The truth of *Vedānta*, for Vivekananda, is primarily practical, and hence of the Buddha he speaks in ecstatic admiration: "the heart, the noble soul, the wonderful humanising power of the

Great Master."[20] Vivekananda has much to say about the Buddha as the ideal *Karma Yogi*. It may be that Vivekananda's assessment would lead us to consider the thesis of *Gītā* in a new way. First let us hear Vivekananda about the:

> one man who actually carried [the] teaching of Karma-Yoga into practice. The man is Buddha. He is the one man who carried this into perfect practice. All the prophets of the world, except Buddha, had external motives to move them to unselfish action. Buddha is the only prophet who said, "I do not care to know your various theories about God. What is the use of discussing all the subtle doctrines about the soul? Do good and be good." He was in the conduct of his life absolutely without personal motives; and what man had worked more than he? Show me in history one character who has soared so high above all. The whole human race has produced but one such character, such high philosophy, such wide sympathy. This great philosopher, preaching the highest philosophy, yet had the deepest sympathy for the lowest animals, and never put forth any claims for himself. He is the ideal Karma-Yogi, acting entirely without motive, and the history of humanity shows him to have been the greatest man ever born, beyond compare the greatest combination of head and brain that ever existed. The greatest soul-power that has ever been manifested.... This man represents the highest ideal of Karma-Yoga.[21]

This passage cited above leaves us wondering why on the *Gītā*, except Tilak and Sri Aurobindo, no commentator could get over their sectarian blindness concerning the ideal *Karma Yogi* and considered the Buddha as one. No ethical theory, however profound, sounds convincing without possible exemplars. The *Gītā* had mentioned Janak and others as those who had practiced *loksamgraha*.[22] Even Kant had to admit in discussing "respect for the law", that "respect for a person is properly only respect for the law" of which he gives us an example.[23] This is not very far from what the Buddha himself had announced: "one seeing *dhamma* sees me; seeing me he sees *dhamma*."[24] We must not be taken away by the similarity between Kant's thesis and the Buddha's assertion. The similarity is only on the surface, and hardly does go any deeper. In Kant's case there is the ontology of the will of moral person. For the Buddha, there being no core self, but only a procession of thoughts and dispositions hanging together for empirical purposes of life, the self-hood is quite fluid and evanescent. The Kantian ideal of escaping from self-interest, even though under the sovereignty of reason, is not morally enough for the Buddha. Kant goes by the principles or laws of reason, while the Buddha proceeds by the practice of virtues till they become spontaneous, and spread over the entire field of moral ecology. The concept of loving kindness to all beings is foreign to Kant's universe of discourse. When the Buddha says that he is one with *dhamma* he escapes not only for self-interest, but from personality altogether, he is well-gone (*Sugata*) from ego-hood. The Buddha's way is the way of witlessness, and not the determination of the will by reason. But there remains another part of the story, the thesis of *anātmā*. Did Vivekananda take care of it when he said that the Buddha was the ideal *Karma Yogi*? The thesis of *Karma Yoga* is built upon the reality of the *ātmā*, the indestructible core of the moral agent. For the Buddha *anātmā* and *anitya* are cognate truths of empirical existence. Whatever cannot stay for a while cannot be said to have any essence, or *ātmā*. If nothing abides, if everything is on fire, as the Buddha himself has said in one of his famous sermons, nothing remains for one to identify oneself with. And yet the Buddha exhorted his audience to go along having the Self as lamp, the Self as refuge. It is through the Self that the self is saved. We may consider three sayings of the Buddha in this context, and see how *Upaniṣadic* they are. Udyotkara was right in remarking that the Buddha's views were based on the *Upaniṣads*.

a. Not to consider "I am this" that is freedom.[25]
b. Rejecting the notion "I am".[26]
c. What is impermanent, that is ill; what is ill is not the Self, what is not Self, that is not mine, that I am not, that is not my Self....[27]

The citations point to a distinction of two selves: the great self and the little self, one transcendent that cannot be spoken of, and the other empirical. In *Brahma jāla-sūtra*, the Buddha steers a middle course between enternalism and annihilism. *Anātmāvāda* is an empirical thesis. The perfect view, or *Samyak dṛṣṭi,* consists in rejecting any metaphysical thesis about the empirical notion of the self, and remaining silent about the transcendent self. Everytime Gautama was asked: is there Self? he became silent. It was Vivekananda's great insight to have identified the Buddha as the ideal of *Karma Yoga*. This *Yoga* is intended, after all, to save the little self by the great self, the empirical by the transcendent. *Karma Yoga* is not a matter of speaking about a self, rather getting into the way of action by which the traces of passion and egoity that constitute the little self are eradicated once and for all.

Vivekananda's acquaintance with Buddhism was primarily with the Pali variety Buddhism. We can venture to saying this since in his works we do not find references to what is called Sanskrit Buddhism. Again, he was highly critical of the Tantric Buddhist schools, which he regarded as decadence that had set in religion of the Buddha. Vivekananda was never inclined to any esoteric doctrines in religious matters, and the Buddha himself is reported to have said that he did not teach with closed fists, that he did not have esoteric and exoteric doctrines. However, the recent religious studies are essentially non-essentialist in character. It can be doubted if there is one Christianity, or Islam, and for that matter, one Buddhism. But Vivekananda was an essentialist thinker and looked for the essential Buddhism in the life of the Buddha. He somehow discredits the historical developments of Buddhism across centuries and countries. The post-modern account on the historical was not for him. He always looked at the naked peaks and the glaciers, and quite to an extent cared for the streams that flowed down from there conditioned by time and terrain. But this is another story. The fact remains that Vivekananda was singular in rehabilitating the Buddha in the heart of Hinduism. And that is one of lesson.

No one understood Vivekananda better than Nivedita, as none did Ramakrishna better than Vivekananda. Nivedita has noted Vivekananda's "passionate personal adoration of Buddha"[28] and she adored her Master's "Buddha-like dignity and calm of bearing"[29] and had chosen for her own personal emblem the *dorje (Vajra)* of Tibetan Buddhism. There is the sense in which Vivekananda found the Buddha in Ramakrishna, and according to him two things mark the Master in an outstanding manner: absolute purity of character and universal love and compassion. Even a casual visitor to the Belur Math cannot fail to notice the presence of the image of the Buddha in Vivekananda's bedroom, in front of which he used to meditate, and in front of which he initiated Nivedita into monastic order by asking her to offer flowers to the image. In her own words:

> he first taught me to perform the worship of Shiva, and then made the whole culminate, in an offering of flowers at the feet of Buddha![30]

Nothing can better round off the contention of this paper than the chapter on "The Swami Vivekananda and His attitude to Buddha" in Nivedita's masterly account of her Master. She writes, and I quote: "Chief of intellectual passions with the Swami, was his reverence for Buddha."[31] And

> the moment he [Vivekananda] was initiated into Sannyas ... his first act then was to hurry to Bodh-Gaya, and sit under the great tree, saying to himself "Is it possible that I breathe the air He breathed? That I touch the earth He trod?" At the end of his life again, similarly, he arrived at Bodh-Gaya, on the morning of his thirty-ninth birthday and this journey, ending with a visit to Benaras, was the last he ever made.[32]

Nivedita informs us that Vivekananda has studied the great Mahayana text *Prajñā Pāramitā*. As regards this one may not be sure since there is nothing in evidence in Vivekananda's own writings. But the fact that he delighted in playing off Śamkara against the Buddha, behoves us to take the matter seriously. How can one disregard history and forget Gaudapada's *Kārikā* and retain Śamkara, who was third in order of discipleship of Gaudapada? What is more important is that Vivekananda constantly tallied Ramakrishna's life with Buddha's.

> In Buddha, he saw Ramakrishna Pramahansa; in Ramakrishna he saw Buddha.[33]

Once Vivekananda was relating the last moments of Buddha's life – how the Buddha "raised himself on his elbow and taught," and said, in brief parenthesis, "I saw this, you know, in the case of Ramakrishna Pramahansa!"[34] Teachers teach till the last moments of their lives. It is no wonder that Vivekananda would say that "I am the servant of the servants of the servants of Buddha."[35]

NOTES AND REFERENCES

1. Selections from *The Complete Works of Swami Vivekananda*, Advaita Ashram, Kolkata, 1987, pp. 35-36 & 83.
2. *Tantra Vārttika*, I. 3.6.
3. *Vedānta Darsana*, in Bengali, Udbodhan, Kolkata, 1996, See Vol. II, p. 450.
4. George Allen & Unwin, London, 1960.
5. *The Living Thoughts of Gautama the Buddha*, ed. A.K. Coomaraswamy and I.B. Horner, Cassell and Company Limited, London, 1948.

6. Anada Publishers, Kolkata, 1983.
7. *Ibid.*, p. 69.
8. *Ibid.*, p. 399.
9. *Ibid.*
10. *The Life Divine*, The Grey Stone Press, New York, 1949, pp. 29-30.
11. *Swami-Sishya Sambād*, Udbodhan, Kolkata, 5th edition, Bengali era 1389, pp. 72-73.
12. *Sri Ramakrishner Antyalilā*, Vol.-II, Swami Prabhananda, Udbodhan, Kolkata, Bengali era 1401, pp. 268-270, Prabhananda reproduces the account of the incident given by Swami Shivananda.
13. *Swami-Sishya Sambād*, p. 46.
14. Selections from *The Complete Works of Swami Vivekananda*, Advaita Ashram, Kolkata, 1987, pp. 1 & 15.
15. *Swami-Sishya Sambād*, Udbhodhan, Kolkata, 5th edition, Bengali era 1389, p. 114.
16. *Ibid.*, p. 115.
17. Selections from *The Complete Works of Swami Vivekananda*, Advaita Ashram, Kolkata, 1987, p. 17.
18. *Ibid.*, p. 16.
19. *Ibid.*
20. *Ibid.*, p. 17.
21. *Ibid.*, pp. 35-36.
22. Chapter III, 20.
23. Footnote, *Fundamental Principles of the Metaphisic of Ethics*, tr. T.K. Abot, Longmans, Tenth Edition, London, 1965, p. 21.
24. *Samyutta Nikāya*, I. 71, quoted in *The Living Thoughts of Gautama the Buddha*, ed. A.K. Coomaraswamy and I.B. Horner, Cassel and Company Limited, London, 1948, p. 199.
25. *Udāna*, 74.
26. *Majjhima – Nikāya*, I. 139.
27. *Samyutta Nikāya*, III 83. These three sayings are quoted in *The Living Thoughts of Gautama the Buddha*, ed. A.K. Coomaraswamy and I.B. Horner, Cassell, London, 1948.
28. *My Master as I saw Him*, Udbodhan, Kolkata, 1987, p. 171.
29. *Ibid.*, p. 30.
30. *Ibid.*, p. 133.
31. *Ibid.*, p. 210.
32. *Ibid.*, p. 215.
33. *Ibid.*, p. 216.
34. *Ibid*, pp. 216-17.
35. *Ibid.*, p. 215.

14
Vivekananda – An Advaitin

Godabarisha Mishra

Śamkara left this Advaita Philosophy in the hills and forests, while I have come to bring it out of these places and scatter it broadcast before the workaday world and society.

Complete Works of Swami Vivekananda, VII, p. 162 (Advaita Ashram), Calcutta, 1922.

It was Śaṅkaracarya, who firmly rehabilitated the *Advaitic* non-dualism back to the rails of traditional *Upaniṣadic* ethos after the historical onslaught of the Buddha who decried the *Vedic* precept and practice. Buddha's aversion for the *Vedas* was so massive that he took up a posture antagonistic to anything that was *Vedic*, even though he seemed to be only against rituals. It was not certain whether Gautama really wanted to reject non-dualistic reality as we find that he propounded *śūnya* in the model of *Advaita* Brahman.[1] In the history of *Vedānta*, Śaṅkara has been criticised as a Buddhist in disguise whereas in reality he appears to have challenged Buddhism. While bringing back the *Upaniṣads* into the lively thinking of Indians, Śaṅkara is very clear about the fact that it is by knowledge alone one can be freed from the fetters of transmigratory existence and such knowledge would arise from *Śruti* and *Śruti* alone. He asserted that the final liberation depends on the knowledge of attributeless Brahman which is the true nature of the cause of the world. Without resorting to the *Śruti-pramāṇa*, it is impossible to conceive of this reality on account of its excessive abstruseness.[2] In post-Śaṅkara period, this idea is reiterated many times in different ways. Vidyāraṇya calls it *prabala-*

mana, a stronger means of knowledge. It was during this period that *Vedānta* streamed out into many schools and the Indian philosophical history witnessed the emergence of the systems like *Viśiśtadvaita*, *Dvaita*, *Śuddhadvaita* and the like. All through these, there is continuity, consistency and novelty in the *Vedāntic* thinking in its propagation and practice, and it still continues to be a living school. Thinkers after thinkers have enriched this system by their contributions, systematic study and elucidations.

The theistic schools, which were opposed to the *Advaita*, questioned its *Vedic* validity from various angles, from the concepts like *māyā-avidyā*, Brahman and the nature of the world. Rāmānuja and Madhva, who were the proponents of *Viśiśtadvaita* and *Dvaita* respectively, refuted the views propounded by Śaṅkara and claimed their schools to be superior in logic having *Upaniṣadic* basis. In post-Vidyāraṇya period, Vyāsatīrtha, a *Dvaita* exponent attacked the *Advaita* tenets in his famous *Nyāyamṛta*. The tradition of *Advaita* responded to his challenges with the advent of Madhusūdana who in his *Advaita-siddhi*, stood up to reply to the philosophical interventions of Vyasatīrtha. Caitanya's Gaudīya Vaiṣnavism, with its theistic tenets developed a sharp criticism of *Vedic* ritualism and *Vedāntic* non-dualism.

Though there are certain principles common to all schools of thought in *Vedānta*, Śaṅkara stands on a different pedestal as he champions the idea that in the journey towards truth one has to gain the discerning knowledge as given in the *Śruti* texts and see the truth beyond worldly appearances. The culmination of such knowledge is the realisation that he is not different from Brahman. In the interaction between *Vedānta* and Buddhism, there is massive influence of the former on the latter, and there are also strong differences. The Mādhyamika Buddhism, with which the thinking of the Buddha came to be identified later on, treated the world and worldly experiences as totally illusory. Śaṅkara, on the other hand, maintained that this illusory world was pervaded by the absolute truth in every sense. Śaṅkara, like Buddha, was addressing his philosophy for the benefit of the people; it was not meant for a particular caste or creed since under the holistic banner of *Advaita* no such distinctions can be really sustained.

The modern period, which saw the revival of the *Vedāntic* ethos, tried to come to terms with the apparent complexities that were felt in Śaṅkara's thinking. Raja Rammohun Roy, who led the renaissance movement followed by Vivekananda, tackled this problem in a different way, and while accepting Śaṅkara in his broad postulates, disregarded the transcendental character of the reality in attempting to develop more clearly the idea of reality, the non-qualified Brahman, as the focus of all human effort and activity. Here for the purpose of this article, I shall deal with the contribution of Vivekananda who enriched the *Advaitic* thought through his speeches in English to meet the needs of the contemporary generation.

VIVEKANANDA AND HIS INTERPRETATION OF ADVAITA VEDĀNTA

In expounding and restructuring *Vedānta*, Vivekananda started with the teachings of Śaṅkara and allowed adequate space to dissenting opinions of other schools. There are two things which catch the attention of any serious reader of Vivekananda, and these are: 1. his notion of *Śruti* as a means to liberation, and 2. discovering the practical dimension of Śaṅkara's thinking. Early in his life, he was influenced by Ram Mohun Roy in his understanding of *Vedāntic* thought. He admired the Brahmo Samaj for its reformative ideas, and attitude towards caste, creed and sex, but was dissatisfied by its anti-scripture and anti-idol worship stances as they ran counter to his yearning for divinity. All through his life, he championed the idea that *Advaita* saved India from materialism twice, once through the teachings of the Buddha and the second time through the teachings of Śaṅkara. He said:

> By Buddha the moral side of the philosophy was laid stress upon and by Śaṅkaracarya, the intellectual side. He worked out, rationalised and placed before Indians the wonderful coherent system of Advaita.[3]

A comparison between Ramakrishna and Vivekananda suggests that Vivekananda was a more committed *Advaitin* than his Guru, who was sympathetic and also encouraged theistic worship. Though Ramakrishna did not deny the transcendental Brahman, he believed that the Absolute could be equally manifest as the immanent God. Vivekananda was attracted to *Advaita* as a school of philosophy fused with its non-sectarian and trans-social character. In *Advaita*, Vivekananda discovered enormous humanistic concern and immense space for accommodating diverse schools of thought. In doing so, his understanding also allowed worship, and we could see that it lies somewhere in between Ram Mohun, who decried Hindu polytheism and Ramakrishna who enunciated various forms of worship. In his *Lectures and Discoveries*, Vivekananda says:

> .... there is more merit in the dualistic method; it helps many men who are weak. But then I think of the other side, how long will the world have to wait to reach the truth if it follows this slow, gradual process.
>
> ... pure truth cannot be realised by all. Men have to be led to it generally. In India I work both ways. In Calcutta I have these images and temples .... but on the height of the Himalayas (the Advaita Ashram at Mayavati) I have a place where nothing else shall enter but pure truth.[4]

This reminds us of two paths: fast-track *vihaṅgama-mārga* and the long and time-consuming, *pipilikā-marga* discussed in *Vedāntic* texts. The fundamental premise for him was that non-duality is the unavoidable goal of the human religious quest and that movement in religious thought is a growth not from error to truth, but from lower truth to higher truth. Vivekananda distinguishes between the path and the goal. In the light of this broad position, he sees the possibility of accepting all religious doctrines, not as an act of patronizing, but with full conviction that they all lead to the same conclusion.[5] He believed that reason and usefulness are important in the sustenance of religious faith. He was also aware of the fact that reason always shifts its base whereas realisation lasted forever. That is why he maintains that the realisation of God comes through being and becoming; through experience and *not theoretical knowledge* (born of *Śruti*). He was of the opinion that the realisation of God was more valuable than the mere knowledge of God. Here he seems to have been influenced by the Yoga school which deals with the limits to knowledge. While knowledge may be deemed to lead to God, God-realisation is untranslatable into human cognizable language. For Vivekananda, the idea of oneness suggested by *Advaita Vedānta* has implications for the individual as well as the cosmos. Individualistically, it is intuitive in nature and at the cosmic level it is the immanent spirit of the universe.

VIVEKANANDA ON ŚRUTI PRAMĀṆA

With the emergence of the Renaissance, the scientific temper gained adequate prominence, and old beliefs and practices were thoroughly questioned. Raja Ram Mohun Roy, Keshub Chandra Sen and others, in their practices and predilections, strongly favoured rationalism, and it resulted in the denial of authoritative nature of the *Vedas* and such other texts. Its other consequence was that it also denied the role of reason and the intellect in the religious quest of a person, upholding personal experience as unquestionable. Vivekananda, being a product of that age, was not free from such influences. In keeping with the idea of *apauruṣeya*, Vivekananda asserted that Rsis are not the creators of the truth in the *Vedas*; they are but seers or discoverers of truths. The *Vedas* embody a collection of spiritual laws discovered at different times. He drew a comparison between *Vedic* truth and scientific truth. Just as the law of gravitation existed before it was discovered and continues to exist even if it is forgotten, so is it with the *Vedic* laws that govern the spiritual world. In order to bring home this idea of immanence and to commend that the *Vedas* contain the eternal laws existing in all souls, he described the *Vedas* as "expired" than "inspired".[6] In the spiritual journey of an aspirant, Vivekananda asserted that scripture works as a map. According to him, the *Vedas* document the spiritual discoveries of others and the methods by which such discoveries are made, and they need to be subjected to close scrutiny before being accepted. He said:

> The man who asks you to believe everything, degrades himself, and if you believe, degrades you too. The sages of the world have only the right to tell us that they have analysed their minds and have found these facts, and if we do the same we shall also believe, and not before. That is all there is in religion.[7]

The proof of the truth is the direct knowledge of the individual, and if verified it gains in validity. Time and again he calls for the verifiability of the religious truths, notwithstanding the *Vedas*. He considered verification to be the only proof of religious truth. He said:

> Each must verify for himself; and no teacher who says, "I have seen but you cannot", is to be trusted, only that one who says, "you can see too." All scriptures, all truths are Vedas in all times, in all countries; because these truths are to be seen, and anyone may discover them.

(*CW*, 3.253) He is a man who sees religion, to whom religion is not merely book learning, not argumentation, nor speculation, nor much talking, but actual realisation, a coming to face to face with truths that transcend the senses.[8]

He was of the opinion that even as one person's eating has little value for another, so is the experience of one person to the other. He was of the strong view that there is a necessity of everyone becoming a *Ṛṣi* and making a first-hand verification of the experiences of others recorded in the *Vedas*. These texts were not written for the intellect or for the understanding through a process of rational enquiry and analysis. He was firmly rooted in his opinion that it was only the *Vedas* which assert the need for going beyond them as per the *Vedic* dictum, *yatra vedaḥ avedaḥ bhavanti*. They are written for the adult who is in the childhood state of his religious growth, and hence he must outgrow reliance on them.[9] He compares the *Vedas* to the hedges around a small plant the confines of which it must eventually outgrow.

Vivekananda did make a distinction between scriptural knowledge (or revelation) and realisation. For him, the knowledge of *Śruti* cannot be the means to liberation.[10] He said:

We can read all the Vedas, and yet will not realise anything, but when practise their teachings, then we attain to that state which realises what the scriptures say, which penetrates where neither reason, nor perception nor inference can go, and where the testimony of others cannot avail.[11]

He strongly felt that textual knowledge is not adequate, but must in some way or the other be further applied to produce the desirable end. While interpreting *śravaṇa*, *manana* and *nididhyāsana*, he felt that the first two are only preliminary. Once he said:

You may reason it out and understand it intellectually, but there is a long way between intellectual understanding and the practical realisation of it. Between the plan of a building and the building itself, there is quite a long distance.[12]

So in order to realise one need to have meditation, this is *nididhyāsana*. He says:

It must be heard, apprehended intellectually and lastly realised. Cogitating is applying reason and establishing this knowledge in ourselves by reason. Realising is making it a part of our lives by constantly thinking of it. Realisation will come as a result of this continuous cogitation.[13]

Regarding the fourfold requirements (*sādhanā-catuṣtaya*) he holds a view which is different from that of Śaṅkara. He says:

The pure heart is the best mirror for the reflection of truth, so all these disciplines are for the purification of the heart. And as soon as it is pure, all truths flash upon it in a minute; all the truth in the universe will manifest in your heart, if you are sufficiently pure.

The great truths about atoms, and the finer elements, and the fine perception of men were discovered ages ago by persons who never saw a telescope, or a microscope, or a laboratory. How did they know these things? It was through the heart; they purified the heart.[14]

Vivekananda seems to have entertained different and at times opposite views on the authority of the *Vedas*. In his speeches in the West, he seems to have been motivated by a more liberal and scientific attitude whereas in India he endorsed the tradition. An example of the latter is as follows:

In India, everything necessary for the perfection and freedom of the human beings could be found in the *Vedas*. Śruti is presented as the final word on spiritual truth, beyond which there is nothing to be known or said. There is no religious idea anywhere, he claims, that cannot be found in the Vedas. All that needs to be done is to apply the dicta of the Śruti to the changing needs and conditions of societies.[15]

There are several instances of his varying stances in regard to the *Vedas* which make it difficult to conclusively state his considered view on the *Vedas*. As Rambachan says:

This is not surprising in the light of his contention that conclusive and liberating knowledge is not gained by enquiring into the texts of the *Upaniṣads*. The closest he comes to a justification of such texts is in his view that they tell us of the spiritual findings of others and the processes by which we discover and verify such findings for ourselves. The difficulty is that in some of his extreme assertions, he even denies them this limited value and function. This becomes apparent in his argument that the *Vedas* are properly understood only when one has lifted oneself to the same level of direct perception as its authors that they were not written for the intellect and cannot be understood through reasoning. Such statements negate their preliminary value, which one assumes to depend on the possibility of some understanding of their claims and methods. If such an understanding cannot be sought through the faculty of intellectual reasoning, then scripture seems to be totally deprived of usefulness.[16]

REASON, REVELATION AND REALISATION

Vivekananda seems to be obsessed with the fact that even the religious propositions can be certified only through actual realisation. He wanted to uphold the supreme value of this realisation and thought that the highest point of the *Advaitic* truth lies in its realisation. He wrote:

> Talking is one thing, and realising is another. Philosophies, and doctrines, and arguments, and books, and theories, and churches, and sects, and all these things are good in their own ways; but when realisation comes, these things drop away. For instance, maps are good, but when you see the country itself, and look at the maps, what a great difference you find! So those that have realised truth do not require the ratiocination of logic and all other gymnastics of the intellect to make them understand the truth; it is to them the life of their lives, concretised, made more tangible.[17]

To conclude this part of the essay, I would like to point out that in doing *Advaita*, Vivekananda owes a lot to Śaṅkara. Vivekananda took Śaṅkara's philosophical position as the foundation and built a modern edifice through a creative reinterpretation. However, such an exercise throws up certain points of divergence, not in the fundamentals, but mostly in the domain of application. For Śaṅkara, the appearance of the world is due to ignorance and the knowledge gained through the inquiry of the *Śruti* is the only means to counter the ignorance. Such knowledge is possible for a person equipped with *sādhanā-catuṣtaya*. The knowledge derived from *Śruti* is simultaneous with the advent of knowledge, and there is no need to invoke any other action apart from that. Here is the first difference between Śaṅkara and Vivekananda. While the former treats the *Śruti* knowledge to be final, for the latter it is only a hypothetical knowledge awaiting confirmation. For Śaṅkara, the relation between Brahman and *Śruti* is like that of a misconceived object and the appropriate means for knowing it. For Śaṅkara, all other *pramāṇas* have for their field of operation the objects outside the domain of the Brahman. Each *pramāṇa* has its own field of operation, and is capable of generating knowledge which does not require another pramāṇa. In the same way, *śabda* or *Upaniṣads* as *pramāṇa* gives rise to Brahman-knowledge which does not require any other source of action. For Vivekananda, however, the *Vedic* statements are to be confirmed by direct realisation. Here he makes a distinction between theoretical religion and its practical implications, *Śruti* and *anubhava* respectively. For Vivekananda, the *Vedānta* constitutes a method rather than a *pramāṇa*. When Vivekananda says that one can go beyond *Vedas*, what he means is that there exists a superior means of understanding, and that is realisation. Whereas for Śaṅkara, the transcendence means that for a person who has attained the liberating knowledge, the *Śruti* ceases to be a *pramāṇa*.[18] For Śaṅkara, once, the world is understood as empirical and transcended; *Śruti* which is a part of the world is also transcended. For Vivekananda, in the process of understanding itself one transcends *Śruti*, since the aspirant moves forward to realise Brahman after hearing the *Śruti* and its contents.

I also draw upon the idea of the traditional *prasthānas* in *Advaita*, *Vivaraṇa* and *Bhāmatī*, in order to evaluate the position of Vivekananda as a post-Śaṅkara *Advaitin*. As is well-known, the *Upaniṣads* prescribe *śravaṇa*, *manana*, and *nididhyāsana* to be the direct means of Brahman-realisation. That is, one has to undertake hearing, reflection and contemplation of *Śruti* for attaining the knowledge of Brahman. According to Vivaraṇa, the *śravaṇa* (hearing) of the passages aided by *manana* and *nididhyāsana* is the cause of the immediate knowledge of Brahman. He holds the view that since the self is always immediate, the *Śruti* text gives rise to the immediate knowledge or direct realisation of Brahman. The hearing will give us the mediate knowledge if the object is mediate, and since the self is the most immediate one, Śruti would give rise to the direct realisation of the self. According to Vacaspati, the *Śruti* passages can give us only the mediate knowledge of Brahman, and it becomes immediate through mind. For Vacaspati, the true nature of Brahman-Atman could be known from the *Upaniṣads*, but that could only be mediate; and they become immediate through mind. Hence it is only in the state of *nididhyāsana*, there is direct realisation of the self. In the light of the discussion given above, we find that Vivekananda can be more on the side of Vacaspati than that of *Prakāśātman*. Through the example of map and almanac, Vivekananda seems to suggest that the *Śruti* knowledge is only symbolic and that it becomes concrete when realised.

VIVEKANANDA AND PRACTICAL VEDĀNTA

In a series of four lectures he delivered at London in November, 1896, Vivekananda developed the idea of practical *Vedānta* which was conceived as a social gospel and concrete plan of action. For Vivekananda, *Vedāntic* idealism without social relevance is empty, and social life without *Vedāntic* idealism is blind.[19] He points out that *Advaita* worked so far on the spiritual plane only and this is the time for making it practical. In this, he saw the action plan of a realised soul, a *jīvanamukta*. He conceived of a God in the service of man. In one of his letters, he writes:

> ... millions of rupees have been spent only so that the temple doors of Varanasi and Vrindavan may play at opening and shutting all day long; now the Lord is having his toilet, now he is taking his meals; all this while the living God is dying for the want of food, for the want of education.[20]

Thus, we may safely conclude that the humanism preached by Vivekananda is rooted in *Advaita*. It is strengthened by the *Vedāntic* premise that self-realisation is tantamount to the realisation of God. This stems from the understanding that a person should respect the divinity both within himself and in others. A transformed consciousness reached its fruition only in transformed inter-personal relationships.

The theory of evil was a deep-rooted philosophical question in the mind of Vivekananda from his early childhood and he found an answer in the system of *Advaita*. *Advaita* made him believe that the world was a mirror of ourselves; neither good nor bad, but a bit of both. A.P. Sen, explaining Vivekananda's views on practical *Vedānta*, says:

> Human actions simultaneously produced good and bad results which in effect meant that there could be no good without evil, no pleasure without pain. Philosophically, this led to a position where one was forced to accept either the relativity of phenomena or their utter falsity. At one level, the good and bad were only relative experiences; at another level, this very relativity made them ultimately meaningless.[21]

The idea of God in *Advaita* as immutable and impersonal has implication to ethics according to Vivekananda. For him, an overwhelming sense of right or wrong should not in any way dilute man's search for God. Man is always capable of sinning and also capable of rising above it. This comes from the realisation that he is essentially divine, an integral part of the reality, the Brahman. Echoing the ideals of Ramakrishna, Vivekananda points out, "say not man is a sinner; tell him that he is God."

Another practical application for monism, which differed from traditional *Advaita*, was suggested by the German indologist, Paul Deussen, who thought himself to be a disciple of Arthur Schopenhauer. Schopenhauer thought that *Advaita* alone could provide a solid foundation for moral philosophy. Vivekananda was influenced by such thinking and held the view that the *Vedāntic* ideal of *Karma-Yoga* was the most prominent moral relativism. He says:

> Why should we do good to the world? Apparently to help the world, but really to help ourselves. ...The only help is that we get moral exercise. The world is a grand moral gymnasium wherein we have all to take exercise so as to become stronger and stronger spiritually.[22]

Vivekananda vouchsafed that it was *Vedānta* which contains the roots of ethics. In his Wimbledon lecture he said:

> The Vedānta philosophers discovered the basis of ethics. Though all religions have taught ethical precepts, such as "Do not kill, do not injure; love thy neighbours as yourself," etc., yet none of these has given the reason. Why should I not injure my neighbour? To this question there is no satisfactory or conclusive answer forthcoming, until it was evolved by the metaphysical speculations of the Hindus who could not rest satisfied with mere dogmas. So the Hindus say that this Atman is absolute and all-pervading, therefore infinite. There cannot be two infinites, for they would limit each other and would become finite. Also, each individual soul is a part and parcel of the universal soul, which is infinite. Therefore in injuring your neighbour, the individual actually injures himself. This is the basic metaphysical truth underlying all ethical codes.[23]

VIVEKANANDA AS A CONTEMPORARY ADVAITIN

Unlike Sri Aurobindo who denigrated Śaṅkara's model of *Vedānta*, Vivekananda found that this philosophy alone is the most sublime accomplishment of the human mind and could provide a promising basis for a reinstatement of Hinduism. He saw in *Advaita Vedānta* the bond that linked together the diverse varieties of Hinduism. He interpreted *Advaita* as co-terminous with Hinduism itself. He restated the doctrines with some differences. The phenomenal reality is a mere appearance, the inexplicable product of nescience or *māyā*. The sole reality is Brahman, which is pure spirit, identical with man's true self. The realisation of this is final emancipation and the end of transmigratory existence. Like Śaṅkara, Vivekananda strongly asserted that renunciation is required to achieve such an end since one has to abandon all secular as well as religious ceremonies in pursuing spiritual life. But his greatness lies in discovering the ethical dimension of *Advaita Vedānta* and its practical applicability to individual and society. For him, a man having Brahman-realisation will have unlimited potentialities like Brahman itself. This will give him boundless self-confidence and irresistible power. He will thus become capable of working efficiently for the spiritual recovery of India, and this will bring about a national reconstruction.[24] In this way Vivekananda derived a practical consequence from *Advaita* centring on nationalism.

We also notice the influence of positivism on Vivekananda. He not only repeated the *Vedānta* doctrine of individual identity with God or Brahman, but also taught that mankind as a whole is God. This implies that man's service for humanity is the true form of worship. Satprakasananda, a renowned monk in Vivekananda order, says:

> It is Śaṅkara's Advaita philosophy that he accepted and expounded in modern terms and found its widest application in modern life. So far as the basic ideas of Advaita Vedānta are concerned he does not differ from Śaṅkara, but there are some differences in his way of presentation and the emphasis laid by him on its practical aspects. He lived about twelve centuries after Śaṅkara under altogether different circumstances. He has aligned the spiritual outlook of Śaṅkara with the modern outlook upon life and the world. He has explained from the Advaita position how to spiritualise the modern view and the way of life. His aim has been the reconstruction of humanity on a spiritual outlook of Śaṅkara with modern outlook upon life and the world.[25]

EVALUATION

Here I have attempted to discuss two ideas of Neo-Vedānta of Vivekananda. Firstly, for him, it is *Anubhava* which is the most important means of realisation of reality rather than *Śruti*, which is the position adopted by Śaṅkara. Vivekananda gave more importance to immanence of the Brahman than the transcendence which is prominently brought out by Śaṅkara. As far as ethics is concerned, Vivekananda evolved a human-centric ethics rather than Brahman-centric ethics. He felt the need for assimilating *Advaita* with other systems and in doing so he might have said certain things which are against his views presented earlier, but the historical situation necessitated such thinking. Like Śaṅkara, Vivekananda too addressed the conspicuous needs of the society he was confronted with.

For Vivekananda, philosophy seems to be a means and not an end in itself. He was not like Śaṅkara who was a philosopher by choice. Vivekananda's main aim was to bring about a social reformation, to make people realise the divinity within them; and for this he did not do any speculative philosophy and kept himself confined to his intellectual cell. Since his aim was to galvanise people to work for the emancipation of the oppressed, he modelled his thinking accordingly and talked about an immanent God in all beings rather than doing a beyond-world philosophy. Most of what we know of him is from his speeches which he delivered on different occasions to different audiences. Since he spoke much and wrote little, there ought to be certain inconsistencies and variations as per the need of those circumstances. But one thing that strikes a serious reader of Vivekananda is that he had been influenced considerably by Śaṅkara. As per the oft-cited criticism of his apparent inconsistency of views, A.P. Sen, puts it in perspective by bringing out the complex background of his forceful utterances. He says:

> A trait that close friends and followers observed in Vivekananda was his inconsistency, for which he appeared to show no particular concern or anxiety. Neither did he try to reconcile his often contradictory points of view. The inconsistencies frequently apparent in his statements may be explained in two ways. In the first place, it has to be accepted that Vivekananda was a multi-layered personality speaking from multiple reference points. He also grew irritable in his later life and was given to enormous mood-swings. Moreover, the Swami was always an eager learner, never ashamed to admit that he has either changed or outgrown his earlier views. His active public life brought Vivekananda in contact with a wide variety of people and cultures and he was constantly reframing and reformulating his ideas in the light of new revelations and experiences. The social environment in which he lived and worked was itself riddled with many incongruities and contradictions.[26]

In the long journey of Hinduism, Vivekananda stands as a prominent milestone who dedicated whole of his life for the preservation of the sacrosanct nature of Indian culture and philosophy. He was a power house of creativity and tried to analyse Indian tradition in a more scientific way to suit the needs of the modern man. In doing *Vedānta*, he found it difficult to accept anything dogmatic and that is the reason why at times, he seems to have entertained different views, sometimes deviating from Śaṅkara. On most of his stand points, he accepts Śaṅkara and *Advaita*, but at places when he feels that the modern mind would find it difficult to accept such a position, he offers an alternative analysis so that it is comprehensive to address modern predicaments and becomes acceptable to the contemporary mindset.

NOTES AND REFERENCES

1. *Amarakosa* treats the Buddha as a proponent of *Advaita* (*advayavādin*) and who did not believe in the theistic principle (*vināyakaḥ*). Refer *advayavādi vināyakaḥ*.
2. In his *Bhāṣya* to the *sūtra*, 2.1.11.
3. Swami Satprakasananda, *Swami Vivekananda's Contribution to the Present Age*, The Vedānta Society of St. Louis, Missouri, 1985, p. 87.
4. *Swami Vivekananda in the West*: *New Discoveries*, ed., Marie Louise Berke, Advaita Ashram, Kolkata, 1996, Vol. 4, p. 257.
5. *Complete Works* (CW), 2.347.
6. *Ibid.*, 3, p. 409.
7. *Ibid.*, 2.163.
8. *Ibid.*, 3. 175.
9. *Ibid.*, 3.283, 5. 311.
10. Anantanand Rambachan, *The Limits of Scripture, Vivekananda's Reinterpretation of the Vedas*, University of Hawaii Press, Honolulu, 1994, p. 46.
11. CW, 1.232.
12. *Ibid.*, 504.
13. *Ibid.*, 7.37–8, 3.25.
14. *Ibid.*, 1.414.
15. *Ibid.*, 3.248, 6.105.
16. Anantanand Rambachan, *op. cit.*, pp. 61-62.
17. CW, 2. 284.
18. *Aitareyopaniṣad-bhāṣya* of Śaṅkara, Introduction and the *Bhagavadgītā-bhāṣya* of Śaṅkara on verse 2.46

19. R. Balasubramanian, "Text, tradition, and Theory-Practice problem" in *Swami Vivekananda: A Hundreds Since Chicago*, ed. by R.K. Dasgupta, R.K. Math, Belur, Howrah, 1994, p. 830.
20. *CW*, 6.264.
21. Amiya P. Sen, *Swami Vivekananda*, OUP, New Delhi, 2000, p. 55.
22. *CW*, 1.73.
23. *CW*, 1, p. 383.
24. Wilhelm Halbfass, *Philology and Confrontation*, "Aspects of Neo-Hinduism," SUNY, 1995, p. 240.
25. Swami Satprakasananda, *op. cit.*, p. 70.
26. Amiya P. Sen, *op. cit.*, p. 1.

15

Vivekananda on Rāja Yoga

Rekha Jhanji

Vivekananda's exposition of Patanjali's *Yoga Sūtras* is especially noteworthy because of its relevance to the contemporary times. He had a deep understanding of the different philosophical currents of classical India. Since his interest in them was not merely theoretical his concern was always to look upon their significance in revealing the transcendental reality. This very objective is the inspiration behind his delineation of *Rāja Yoga*. Vivekananda holds on to the original meaning of the Sanskrit term *Yoga* which means to join ourselves to our reality. He later classifies it into four – *Karma Yoga*, *Jñāna Yoga*, *Bhakti Yoga* and *Rāja Yoga*. *Karma Yoga* is the path of purification through work, *Bhakti Yoga* focuses upon love and worship and attempts to reach realisation through it. *Jñāna Yoga* has three components – hearing the truth (*śravaṇa*); reflecting upon it (*manana*); and "giving up all further argumentation and realising the truth" (*nididhyāsana*).

Vivekananda holds that *Rāja Yoga*

> ... fits inquirers of all classes with or without any belief, and it is the real instrument of religious inquiry.... Its chief parts are the *prāṇāyāma*, concentration and mediation.[1]

Although Vivekananda's exposition of all the four *Yogas* is very original and modern, yet I have focussed on *Rāja Yoga* because of its special importance in the present times. Each age has its predominant ways of looking upon man's mission in this world and our age has its own peculiar view towards it. Nothing to my mind could epitomise this mission better than this "ritualistic" celebration of the body. I have deliberately used the word "ritualistic" because any action sacred or profane becomes a ritual when each step involved in it becomes valuable in itself. The several ventures that extol the body like fashion shows, advertisements for enhancing bodily appeal and the celebration of sexuality are all to my mind ritualistic extolments of the body. *Rāja Yoga* of Vivekananda is especially significant in our age because it begins from the body and attempts to reach the goal of self-realisation through the mastery over the body-mind complex. It does not deny the body but attempts to attain mastery over the body and mind by becoming a witness. Vivekananda holds that the human body is the highest form of creation because that alone is capable of experiencing the Truth. The whole method of *Rāja Yoga* is to discipline the individual in order to become capable of experiencing higher Truths.

Vivekananda makes it very clear that there is nothing esoteric about *Yoga*; its methodology is scientific and hence completely transparent. He is against all secrecy in the pursuit of knowledge. In fact, he constantly insists on accepting nothing that is not based upon experience and potentially accessible to one and all. *Yoga* is essentially based on a practice which aims at preparing the individual to develop skills to experience the real nature of the self. This practice begins by a certain way of life which is a necessary condition for this preparation. The eightfold path of *Yoga – yama, niyama, āsana, prāṇāyāma, pratyāhāra, dhāraṇā, dhyāna* and *samādhi* – prepares the individual for realising his true self and attaining the highest liberation which is the goal of human existence.

The opening *sūtra* of Patanjli defines *Yoga* in terms of restraining the mind – stuff from taking various forms so that

> at that time (the time of concentration) the seer (*Purusha*) rests in his own (unmodified) state.[2]

Vivekananda explains this *sūtra* further. He writes:

> As soon as the waves have stopped, and the lake has become quiet, we see its bottom. So with the mind; when it is calm, we see what our own nature is; we do not mix ourselves but remain our own selves.[3]

The above passage makes it clear that the yogic discipline presumes that the mind holds the key to our path of realisation; when the mind is silenced it facilitates the experience of our real self. Our real self is not our psycho-physical being because that is ever-changing and ephemeral and hence cannot be called real. For any entity or object to be qualified as real, it must fulfil at least two conditions: i) changelessness and timelessness. Actually they are two aspects of the same attribute.

Vivekananda based his entire discussion of *Rāja Yoga* essentially on Patanjali's *Yoga sūtras* which he also translated into English but since he was not a mere theoretician but a person who gave the highest importance to experience, his ideas on *Yoga* have the originality of a practitioner (*sādhaka*). For instance, he was quite aware of the power of the mind and the need to harness its energy for the experience of higher states of consciousness. For him matter is nothing but energy of a certain frequency; although matter looks gross and mind abstract, both are nothing but different forms of energy.

Vivekananda says:

> The external and internal natures are not two different things; they are really one. Nature is the sum total of all phenomena. "Nature" means all that is, all that moves, we make a tremendous distinction between matter and mind; we think that the mind is entirely different from matter. Actually, they are but one nature, half of which is continually acting on the other half. Matter is pressing upon the mind in the form of various sensations. These sensations are nothing but forces.... Both matter and mind are really nothing but forces; and if you analyse them far enough, you will find that at root they are one.... The difference between the subtlest mind and the grossest matter is only one of degree.[4]

Vivekananda sees the self in its essential sense totally free of nature because it is immortal and infinite. In that sense it is neither mind nor matter. But to know its true nature the chatter of the mind and the restlessness of the body have to be quietened because they generate distractions in the pursuit of the Self.

The whole of yogic discipline which is motivated by the quest for self knowledge starts first with a way of life that stipulates certain "dos" and "donts". The practice of the eight limbs (*aṣṭaṅga*) of *Yoga* in their order is important because both Patanjali and Vivekananda see this as a practice that implies living certain values and rigorously following a certain daily routine.

The order of *aṣṭāṅga yoga* is important because it implies that before starting with the bodily and mental discipline of *Yoga* a certain value system as well as a daily routine must be pursued by an aspirant. In the absence of that, no silencing of the mind can be achieved. The first part of *Yoga* (*yama*) is further seen to have five constituents –

> 1st: Not injuring any being by thought, word or dead.
> 2nd: Non covetousness in thought, word or deed.
> 3rd: Perfect chastify in thought, word or deed.
> 4th: Perfect truthfulness in thought, word, or deed.
> 5th: Non-receiving of gifts.[5]

Niyama refers to the daily routine of "internal and external purification, contentment, mortification, study and worship of God."[6]

Patanjali clearly sees violence and lying as impediments in the path of *Yoga*. Vivekananda writes:

> If I tell a lie, or cause another to tell one, or approve of another doing so, it is equally sinful. If it is a very mild lie still it is a lie. Every vicious thought will rebound, every thought of hatred which you may have thought, in a cave even, is stored up and will one day come back to you with tremendous power in the form of misery here. If you project hatred and jealousy, they will rebound on you with compound interest. No power can avert them, when once you have put them in motion, you will have to bear them. Remembering them this will prevent you from doing wicked things.[7]

Vivekananda has made it clear that the practice of *Yoga* does not merely involve exercising the body. Although certain bodily postures are an important part of the practice of *Yoga* but all these *āsanas* and *prāṇāyāmas* must be preceded by a certain way of living which is based on non-violence, austerity, purity and truth. In the absence of this way of life, *Yoga* would become merely a bodily training. However, it is interesting to note that even these bodily exercises, if done with total unflinching regularity, would have an impact on one's way of life but they alone will not bring out the whole effect of *Yoga* in one's life because the ultimate objective is the experience of our real nature and that can be possible only if we pursue a way of life conducive to this goal.

Vivekananda thinks that while it is possible to scientifically study any part of nature without bringing into its study our own personal life, it is not possible to do so in the practice of religion. By religion here he simply means a search for the ultimate truth and not any particular creed. The proof of having realised the ultimate truth comes from one's experience which again is related to a way of life. He writes:

> A man may be wicked, and yet make an astronomical discovery, but in religion it is different, because no impure man will ever have the power to reach the truths of religion .... All these conditions must be fulfilled; you must first see that the man is pure, and that he has no selfish motive: that he has no thirst for gain or fame. Secondly, he must show that he is superconscious. He must give us something that we cannot get from our senses, and which is for the benefit of the world. Thirdly, we must see that it does not contradict other truths; if it contradicts other scientific truths, reject it at once. Fourthly, the man should never be singular; he should only represent what all men can attain.[8]

Thus, we see that the path of *Yoga* starts essentially with moral practices that are never abandoned even when one has attained the highest truth. For spiritual attainment is not a licence to abandon either the moral or the mundane life.

In the sequential order of the eight parts of *Yoga*, after the *yama – niyama* are discussed; *āsana* and *prāṇāyāma* which centre upon the body; *āsanas* refer to the different postures of the body that enhance the bodily well-being and makes it suitable for entertaining higher states of consciousness. One pre-requisite of all these postures is the necessity of keeping the spinal column free and the chest, neck and head in a straight line. Vivekananda recognises the fact that this part of *Rāja Yoga* is similar to the *Haṭha Yoga* because like the latter it focuses on the physical body but unlike *Haṭha Yoga* it is not confined to it. After the control of body through the practice of different yogic postures, *prāṇāyāma* has to be practised. Vivekananda makes it clear that:

> *Prāṇāyāma* is not, as many think, something about breath; breath indeed has very little to do with it, if anything. Breathing is only one of the many exercises through which we get to the real *Prāṇāyāma*. *Prāṇāyāma* means the control of *Prāṇa*.[9]

Referring to Classical Indian thinkers, Vivekananda states that:

> they saw the universe as a composition of *Ākāśa* and *Prāṇa*. *Ākāśa* is the omni-present, all penetrating existence. Everything that has form, everything that is the result of combination, is evolved out of this *Ākāśa* .... At the beginning of creation there is only this *Ākāśa*. At the end of the cycle the solids, the liquids and the gases all melt into the *Ākāśa* again, and the next creation similarly proceeds out of this *Ākāśa*.

At the beginning of the next cycle they start up, strike again upon the *Ākāśa*, and out of the *Ākāśa* evolve these various forms, and as the *Ākāśa* changes, this *Prāṇa* changes also into all these manifestations of energy.[10]

Prāṇāyāma according to Vivekananda is not confined to the control of breath but it is knowledge and control of this energy. Once a person is able to achieve this, one would have control over the whole of creation. Vivekananda looks upon *prāṇa* as the vital force in all beings and thought is its highest expression and instincts the lowest. He holds that if the *prāṇa* is trained, it can help one go beyond thought to realise super-consciousness. Vivekananda sees all creativity as a manifestation of the control of *prāṇa*. He holds that all the great prophets who have realised unusual states of consciousness and control over matter have achieved this due to their control of *prāṇa*. Vivekananda sees the universe as a sea of ether having several layers of vibration under the action of *prāṇa*. The centre has the highest vibration and gradually there is a decrease towards the periphery. One order of vibration makes one level of existence and beings of this level can reorganise one another but are incapable of recognising beings of another level of vibration. The yogic activity changes the vibration of beings. *Samādhi* is nothing but an attempt to bring the mind under a higher vibration. We can see that Vivekananda has a very comprehensive interpretation of the term *prāṇāyāma*. For instance, he writes:

> That part of *Prāṇāyāma* which attempts to control the physical manifestations of the *Prāṇa* by physical means is called physical science, and that part which tries to control the manifestations of the *prāṇa* as mental force, by mental means, is called *Rāja Yoga*.[11]

In an individual's body, *prāṇa* gets manifested by the movement of lungs; consequently, in the context of an individual's life *prāṇāyāma* is achieved by the control of breath. Breath has an intimate connection with mental states that is why we find that measured breathing harmonises the psyche. Vivekananda states that:

> When all the motions of the body have become perfectly rhythmical, the body has, as it were, become a gigantic battery of will.[12]

The aim of *prāṇāyāma* is to arouse the *Kundalini* which is coiled up in the sacral plexus. This generates tremendous power in the

Yogi because it strengthens his will and enables him to experience super-conscious states which finally lead him to inculcate wisdom.

The next step in *Yoga* is *Pratyāhāra* which Vivekananda defines as an act of "gathering towards" or checking the outgoing powers of the mind and freeing them from the senses. In our ancient texts, it is time and again mentioned that the senses by themselves are incapable of associating pleasure or displeasure with any experience; it is the mind which when associated with them that generates the attraction of the senses. *Pratyāhāra* dissociates the connection between the mind and the senses. Once an individual can free his mind from its involvement with the sensory experiences, one becomes autonomous. One is then capable of moving on to the next step in *Yoga* – *dhāraṇā* which is essentially the act of holding the mind to certain points. Vivekananda defines it as the confining of mind stuff or *chitta* to a certain place. *Dhāraṇā* is practised primarily to help focus and concentrate the mind so that its energy is optimally utilised. When the mind is not focused, its energy gets dissipated and consequently it becomes restless and agitated. *Dhyāna* is possible only after having practised *dhāraṇā*. There are several levels of *dhyāna* which move from the concrete to the abstract. The aim of *dhyāna* is to reach the state of *samādhi*–superconsciousness. One experiences the *samādhi* when one has intensified the *dhyāna* to such an extent that the external world ceases to have an impact on one's psyche and there is an undisturbed flow of concentration.

All these steps of *Yoga* gradually prepare the aspirant towards a state of superconsciousness where the ego is not operative. Having reached this state of mind one becomes suffused with unbounded love and joyfulness because the sorrows are all caused by one's identification with the ego and the desires associated with it.

Although the objective of all the four paths of *Yoga* is the same but *Rāja Yoga* seems the most systematic and scientific of them all. Vivekananda writes:

> ... in the study of the Rāja-Yoga, no faith or belief is necessary .... The study of Rāja-Yoga takes a long time and constant practice. A part of this practice is physical, but in main it is mental. As we proceed we shall find how intimately the mind is connected with the body .... We have very little command of our minds. Therefore to bring that command about, to get that control over the body and mind, we must take certain

physical help. When the body is sufficiently controlled, we can attempt the manipulation of the mind. By manipulating the mind we shall be able to bring it under our control, make it work as we like, and compel it to concentrate its powers as we desire.

According to the Rāja-Yogi, the external world is but the gross form of the internal or subtle.[13]

Now, one may still not be convinced about the relevance of this laborious practice. Vivekananda constantly states that the proof of all religious practices is in experience. The relevance of the practice of *Rāja Yoga* is evident by the physical and mental well-being it generates. Since it involves no esoteric practices, all one needs is to experiment with one's body and mind and then test for oneself whether these states are within the reach of all human beings or not.

Furthermore, like any other pursuit of religion it does help in satisfying one's curiosity about the mystery of this vast universe and man's place in it. Some of these questions cannot be answered invoking reason for despite its great contribution in generating order in our life, it can take us only up to a certain point. It does not help us in answering our queries about the meaning and purpose of human existence and the necessity of preferring good over evil. Vivekananda convinces us and takes us out of the impasse of reason by reason itself. He says:

The Yogi teaches that the mind itself has a higher state of existence, beyond reason, a superconscious state and when the mind gets to that higher state, then this knowledge, beyond reasoning comes to man. This state of going beyond reason ... may sometimes come by chance to a man who does not understand its science, he as it were, stumbles upon it .... To get any reason out of the mass of incongruity we call human life, we have to transcend our reason, but we must do it scientifically, slowly by regular practice, and we must cast off all superstition.[14]

We can see from the above exposition that the method of *Rāja Yoga* is the most scientific of all the four *Yogas* because it begins with the bodily experiences that are accessible to all of us. It enables us to go deeper and deeper into our consciousness by the control of our body and breath. The control of the breath enables us to attune ourselves with the cosmic energy and experience, the inherent tranquility that characterises our real self. Vivekananda's exposition of *Rāja Yoga* is very important because he has given the basic terminology of *Yoga* a very modern interpretation that is particularly relevant in our times when body and bodily experiences have so much significance.

NOTES AND REFERENCES

1. *The Complete Works of Swami Vivekananda*, Advaita Ashram, Kolkata, 2003, Vol. 8, p. 1, 154, heareafter cited as C.W.
2. *Yoga Sūtras* of Patanjali, *Ślokas* 2 and 3.
3. *Raja Yoga* (hereafter cited as *R.Y.*), p. 120.
4. *C.W.*, Vol. 8, pp. 245-46.
5. *Ibid.*, Vol. 8, p. 41.
6. *Yoga Sūtras* of Patanjali, 2, *Śloka* 32.
7. *Ibid.*, pp. 207-08.
8. *Ibid.*, pp. 123-24
9. *Ibid.*, p. 33.
10. *Ibid.*, pp. 33-35.
11. *Ibid.*, 52.
12. *Ibid.*, p. 56.
13. *Ibid.*, pp. 11-12.
14. *Ibid.*, pp. 87-89.

16

Sages of Ages and Ages

C.V. Babu

An understanding of Vivekananda's study of Indian scriptures culminates into an analysis of truth in its manifold aspects. According to him, there are two dimensions of truth, temporal and non-temporal. He sought to explain the two different levels of truth by a close analysis of scriptures. Scriptures are divided into two kinds, viz., the *śrutis* and the *smṛtis*. If the *śrutis* are said to be eternal, authoritative, supreme and impersonal, the *smṛtis* are temporal, unauthoritative, secondary and personal.

Śrutis are said to be eternal because they unravel eternal truths regarding the nature of soul and God. According to Vivekananda, when *Tat Tvam Asi* was discovered, religious knowledge came to an end. It is the perfect unity which is the goal of all knowledge, this has reached in the *Vedas* and hence the *Vedas* contain knowledge per se. According to Vivekananda it is impossible to go beyond this unity that is portrayed in the *Vedas*. Beyond this there is nothing more to say about spiritual life. Nothing more to be known also. The framework of destiny and goal of a man has been systematically delineated in the *Vedas*. They give general directions for spiritual life so as to lead the soul to perfection. In *śrutis*, these absolute laws are complete. What is to be supplemented to this wealth of knowledge is certain particular directions according to the needs of particular time and place. In the view of Vivekananda, what remained is its social accomplishment. The revealed spiritual truth is to be established in society, that requires the effort of spiritual activists instead of reclusive yogis. They guide people from time to time providing particular directions. Thus, there arises the necessity of spiritual leaders; they lead the society through new phases of cultural evolution creating new history.

The particular directions are shown by spiritual masters who lead the people in society. Their teachings are embodied in *smṛtis*. Hence, *smṛtis* are complied under particular circumstances, time and places. In history, it may be seen that there arose different religions in different times and different places in the name of different religious personalities. Though the eternal truth is one and the same, diversity of paths got established to reach that single truth. It has also paved the way for different sects in one and the same religion. We can see several examples of sects in Hinduism founded by eminent spiritual activists. Those religious leaders guided people according to different circumstances and situations.

Vivekananda says that *smṛtis* are not as authoritative as *śrutis* are. *Vedas* are the supreme authority of Indian spiritual knowledge. *smṛtis* are only subordinate to them. For Vivekananda, the eternal truth is that which is truly authoritative. Its eternal nature itself is the guarantee for its authority. The temporal truth is subordinate to that authoritativeness. If it is of secondary authoritativeness, it is valid only if it is in conformity with the eternal truth proclaimed by the *Vedas*.

The eternal principles have their own foundations. No amount of reasoning is needed to defend them. Besides, they do not depend upon the authority of even the sages who revealed them. The *Vedic Ṛṣis* have no personal authority over what is revealed through them. Hence, *śrutis* are perfectly impersonal. They preach impersonal laws. Most of those sages who recorded these laws are unknown. Absolute principles do not require any such personal authority. Their authority stems from the eternal nature of man, not from particular personalities. Their ethics are based upon the eternal spiritual solidarity of man. This truth is already discovered by those sages. Such a truth cannot be discovered anew. It does not mean that human beings are already liberated. There are masses in blindness and darkness of ignorance. It is due to the lack of social establishment of spiritual truth. Consequently, there arise social evils in the form of inequality, poverty, religious conflicts, wars, étc. These social problems may be solved by means of spiritual emancipation of the ignorant. This is the mission alloted to the spiritual leaders. This was not the mission of the

Vedic Ṛṣis. This is one of the reasons for the personal charisma of religious leaders. Consequently, the spiritual personalities of *smṛtis*, such as *Avatāras*, (incarnations of God), prophets and so forth are more in evidence. They are dominant figures in *smṛtis*, *purāṇas* and the *tantras*. They are said to be the startling, gigantic, impressive, world moving persons. They are said to be the living illustrations of their own teachings. Most of the times their personalities were more magnified in their teachings as they were the living embodiments of their teachings.

Hence, within the impersonal religion like Hinduism, personal worship is found from the very earliest times. According to Vivekananda, the personal God is necessary. Though there are impersonal eternal principals of ultimate truth, it is not enough for the spiritual elevation of the common masses. Common people require a spiritual leader for their spiritual upliftment. The activities of the spiritual leaders help them to come out of their ignorance in practical life. Accordingly, new codes of conduct and new modes of worship surface. Sometimes, quite surprisingly, the followers themselves unite together and start worshipping their spiritual master as a personal God.

In this connection, Vivekananda makes a distinction between true spiritual leaders and the gods of imagination. For him, only a spiritual master is acceptable as a personal God. Others are vain creations of human psyche. They are not worthy of human worship; they are mere conceptions of our imagination. The actual personal God is more worthy of worship than any idea of God that man can form. The personal gods are the living gods here and now. They appear in the midst of people with their messianic missionary promise and the people experience spiritual truth beyond any set of principles. It is a face to face interaction of the mass with spiritual divinity. This interaction is not possible by a god of imagination.

> Shri Krishna is much greater than any idea of God you or I can have. Buddha is a much higher idea, a more living and idolised idea, than that ideal you or I can conceive of in our minds; and therefore it is that they always command the worship of mankind, even to the exclusion of all imaginary deities.[1]

Those incarnations are but living illustrations of what they preach.

There is no doubt about the fact that Vivekananda always privileged the impersonal absolute idea over the relative one like the personal God or image. Glyn Richards in his essay "Vivekananda and essentialism" draws a parallel between Vivekananda and Gandhi. He writes:

Vivekananda's claim that the impersonal God is Being itself, the only reality, all else being manifested by the power of māyā, corresponds also to Gandhi's insistence on the isomorphism of Truth and Reality or God and given the great measures of agreement between them on a variety of different issues it is difficult to believe that Gandhi was not thoroughly acquainted with the thought of Vivekananda. Both distinguished between personal and impersonal concepts of God, for example, and both had significant things to say about the relation between Truth and God. For Vivekananda, however, as for Gandhi, it is the impersonal concept of God that has the greater appeal since the impersonal concept is infinite while the personal concept is limited. God is beyond the limitations of space and time when we conceive of him as impersonal Being, but he is limited when we conceive of him in personal terms. But the similarity between Gandhi and Vivekananda goes even further than the distinction between personal and impersonal concepts of God. Gandhi points to personifications of the ultimate as an indication of man's desire for symbols. In the same way Vivekananda, after the fashion of Advaita, refers to forms and images as external symbols manifesting man's endeavour to apprehend the absolute or the eternal.[2]

This study leads to Vivekananda's view that the Hindus have discovered that the absolute can only be realised, or thought of or stated through the relative.[3]

His vision of "universal religion" recognising the *Vedāntic* truth is not merely conceptual but includes practical aspect also. The practical aspect is closely related to the essence of universal religion, i.e., universal love. It is the "universal love" that makes the "Vedāntic truth practical Vedānta". Tapan Raychaudhuri in his essay, "Construction of Hinduism" explained Vivekananda's Indian agenda in the following words:

Vivekananda's Indian agenda, more than his personal faith and his mission abroad, does up to point provide evidence in support of the thesis which projects him as a hero of neo-Hinduism, albeit a reformist one. His chief handiwork back home, the Ramakrishna Mission, did have in practice a strong Hindu orientation, both in its ideological pronouncements and in the section of the population it actually served.

Swamiji's self-conscious and persistent efforts to counterbalance this bias however needs to be emphasised. In a letter dated 1897, he states specifically that from the very beginning the Mission did not discriminate between the different communities of India in their programme of service. His plans for national reconstruction gave a priority to Hindus, but chiefly in a chronological sense. In his view the decline of India was the end result of its culture of discrimination, its long tradition of contempt for others. That decline began the day the contemptuous epithet, "mleccha" was invented. To reverse that process, it was first necessary to raise the entire Hindu community from its fallen state and then revitalise the whole of mankind. The process of regeneration for the Hindus has to proceed step by step. First, the division within each caste had to be abolished, then all castes had to be given the sacred thread until every Hindu had attained the status of Brahmins "because all Hindus were brothers". Despite the revolutionary implication of such a programme as spelt out by Swamiji ("... the Brahmin and the Chandal must be placed on an equal footing") it does sound like an agenda for Hindu communal solidarity.[4]

In the same essay Tapan Raychaudhuri described Vivekananda's strong passion for practical *Vedānta* in equally strong language:

Interestingly while he continued to write on philosophical themes, there was no repetition in India of his Vedāntic lecture tours. He explained in answer to a question that India, sunk in abject poverty, was a land of "tamas" the brutish inertia which was the least worthwhile quality in Human beings. Spirituality was not for the weak nor possible on a hungry stomach. Indian's veins must throb with this-worldly virtues, with "rajas", before the country could absorb the heroic message of non-duality.[5]

We can rightly say that, when Vivekananda speaks about the impersonal gods, he emphasises the vision of practical *Vedānta*. *Ṛṣis* of *śrutis* are the proclaimers of *Vedāntic* truth; the *Avatāras* of *smṛtis* are the masters of practical *Vedānta*. According to *Bhāgavata* the world-moving sages are infinite in number. It is the peculiarity of India that she has been producing sages from the very beginning. It is the continuous stream of Indian spiritual tradition without any break. Vivekananda speaks about a few of those epoch-makers such as Rama, Krishna, Buddha, Śankara, Rāmānuja, Chaitanya, Ramakrishna Paramahansa, etc. In the words of Vivekananda:

Ram is an ideal hero who combines the ideal facets of personality. He was the ideal son, the ideal husband, the ideal father and the ideal king. He was the embodiment of truth and morality.[6]

Vivekananda speaks about Krishna with a twofold approach to his divine personality. Vivekananda explains it as two contradictory characteristics of the life of Krishna. On the one hand, he lived a life of attachment. He was the most characteristic figure of *rajas*. He exercised his power as a perfect king. Krishna was the most wonderful house-holder too. Nonetheless, he was the most wonderful *sanyasi*. He lived with a total sense of renunciation. He was the greatest illustration of non-attachment. Vivekananda's analysis of Krishna shows that he had two contradictory phases in his life. These two contradictory aspects of his life, according to Vivekananda, necessarily merge into the most marvellous aspect of episodes, it is the episode of love, the life of Vrindavan.

According to Vivekananda, the true passage of Krishna's life is the life of Vrindavan. One can understand it only when one becomes perfectly pure and chaste. The most marvellous expansion of love is allegorised and expressed in that beautiful play with the Gopis. It is the very ideal of love, love that wants nothing. This love is the greatest landmark in the history of religion, so to say, the ideal of love as "love for love's sake". It culminates into the peak of religious truth of "duty for duty's sake".

Vivekananda's understanding of Krishna enabled him to solve the conflict between the personal God and the impersonal God. In order to solve this philosophical problem he takes into account the fact of "love" between Krishna and the Gopis. Personal God is the highest point of human life; it is the highest conception of human nature. Reason stands aghast at such an idea. Impersonal God is a rational principle. One way we argue that it is immanent in the universe. We argue that everything is but its manifestation. According to Vivekananda, logically impersonal God is founded on a philosophical belief, a belief based on philosophical/rational principles. At the same time, we also argue that it is transcendental. The Gopis of Vrindavan never cared for such a belief. Their true involvement was in love for him. That experience was the true nature of his being. The Gopis never directed their attention to philosophical speculations. They never cared for the superlative qualities of Krishna such as whether he is a king or a seer or, whether he is immanent or transcendent. Krishna, for the Gopis, was just Krishna, a shepherd with a flute singing the song of love, leading innocent animals – cows. This unconditional love of the

Gopis shows that so long as there is selfishness in the heart, love of God is impossible.

According to Vivekananda, Krishna as the preacher of *Gītā* is of lower status comparing to the Krishna in Vrindavan as the ideal lover. For him, to consider in reverse order is to put the cart before the horse. Some people find it unsuitable to think of Krishna as the lover of Gopis. According to Vivekananda, it is a stupid attitude. It is a disgrace to the true being of Krishna. Vivekananda says that even the *Gītā* is nothing but a commentary on the *Vedas*. Nevertheless, the essence of *śrutis* or the *Upaniṣads* is difficult to understand. There are many commentators interpreting the ancient texts in their own ways. But Krishna himself is the inspirer of *śruṭis;* it was the true being of Krishna that the Gopis experienced in Vrindavan. But the world is after the method of interpretation. For Vivekananda, that interpretation is inadequate to establish the love that unites mankind. Only the higher form of Krishna can establish the true love. The Lord harmonises them all. He is the greatest preacher as well as the embodiment of harmony, "In me they are all strong like pearls upon a thread" – the real love that unties.

According to Vivekananda, Gautama Buddha is the boldest preacher of morality that the world ever saw. He broke the bondages of all, the chains of all, and declared liberty to all. He made everyone reach the highest goal. He exemplified himself as the noble. He gave up his throne in search of truth. He taught them what he had experienced in his life. He lived with beggars, the poor and the downcast. He broke himself of all bondages and attained *nirvaṇa*. It was not a mere personal achievement for him. He worked for the society to enable each and every individual to attain this freedom. He worked for the poor and the miserable. He even rejected the language of gods, i.e., Sanskrit and spoke the language of people, Pali. This made it possible for him to reach the hearts of the people. Amiya P. Sen described Vivekananda's frame of mind towards Buddha as follows: "'The Buddha is my Istha [special ideal],' Vivekananda would often say. For him, the Buddha's greatest qualities were this–worldliness. Ultimately, even the great Śankara was no match for the Buddha for he had not the latter's heart. For Vivekananda, the great humanism of Buddha also made him the embodiment of practical *Vedānta*. If Śankara had banished *Vedānta* to the hills and jungles, it was the Buddha who brought it back to life and humanity. The Buddha, Vivekananda pointed out did not have to think of God, he was God."[7]

Vivekananda's study of Buddhism shows that, though Buddha was pure and glorious, certain defects crept into his followers and made India suffer a lot even till today. Buddha's high ideals could not be well assimilated by his followers. It is Vivekananda's conclusion that the degradation happened in establishing big temples for idol worship and using them as places for sacrifice. According to Vivekananda, it is not Hindus that established idol worship and sacrifice but the degraded Buddhists. He disagreed with the established view that Brahmins destroyed Buddhism. He says that it is the degraded Buddhists themselves who destroyed Buddhism. The earliest Buddhists had denounced the sacrifice of the *Vedas*. They were against the killing of animals and such activities. These forms of sacrifice used to be held in every house at that time. There was a fire burning and that was all the paraphernalia of worship. These sacrifices were obliterated. But, in their places, the degraded Buddhists established gorgeous temples, ceremonies and priests and it culminated into the present circumstances of Indian religious practices. Vivekananda does not agree with the opinion that Buddha was the destroyer of Brahmanical idolatry. According to him, it is Buddhism that created Brahmanism and idolatry in India. To prove this connection, Vivekananda brings out an example of the temple of Jagannath. It is written by a certain Russian archaeologist that Jesus Christ went to the temple of Jagannath for spiritual practice with Brahmins. There he became disgusted with their exclusiveness and their idol worship. So he went to the Lamas of Tibet and sought to become perfect. But Vivekananda contradicts this view saying that the temple was an old Buddhistic temple. They were not of Brahmins but of Buddhists.

> He (Buddha) is pure and glorious, but unfortunately such high ideals could not be well assimilated by the different uncivilised and uncultured races of mankind who flocked within the fold of the Aryans. These races, with varieties of superstition and hideous worship, rushed within the fold of the Aryan, and for a time appeared as if they had become civilised, but before a century had passed they brought out their snakes, their ghosts, and all the other things their ancestors used to worship, and thus the whole of India became one degraded mass of superstition.[8]

In such a time of degradation history produced Śankara as the manifestation of true religiosity. He was a Brahmin from the South. He was such a great intellect that at the age of sixteen Śankara had completed studies on *Vedas* and *Upaniṣads* and had written treatises on them. The state of things that existed in India awaiting such a personality was very pathetic as Indian life was camouflaged with horrible and bestial customs. That was inheritance which Śankara got from the Buddhists. The horrors what were to be reformed were the outcome of reign of degradation. He wanted to bring back his mother country to its pristine purity. He used *Vedānta* to re-conquer the Buddhistic degradation. As a great philosopher, he showed that the real essence of Buddhism and that of *Vedānta* are not very different rather they are one and the same. He proved that the latest Buddhists degraded themselves to the status of atheists. They denied the existence of God due to the ignorance of real sense of Buddha's teachings. When this was revealed, the Buddhists began to come back to their old religion, the religion of *Vedānta*, or Hinduism, but by then, they had become accustomed to all those forms of false worship.

According to Vivekananda, Śankara was a man of great intellect but not a man of great heart. Vivekananda opines that, in comparison to Śankara, Rāmānuja was a man of great heart. Unlike Śankara, Rāmānuja felt for the down-trodden and he sympathised with them. He tried to purify them as far as they could be and instituted new ceremonies among them. He reformed the accretions that they were practising. He established new methods of worship in order to make them more cultured and civilised. He opened the door to the highest spiritual worship both for upper castes and lower castes. Since the time of Rāmānuja, the door of spirituality was opened for everyone. It was his preaching and practice that each and every individual, as a human being is meritorious to worship God irrespective of gender, caste, colour and creed. Vivekananda says that, since the time of Rāmānuja, it has been the watchword of all the prophets in India.

The task of Rāmānuja was later taken up by Chaitanya in the North during the Mohammedan rule. Chaitanya was born in a Brahmin family which was one of the most rational families of the day. He was a great admirer of tradition and followed it very strictly. He studied logic with great interest and became a professor of logic. He was excessively interested in defeating others in arguments. He cherished it as the highest ideal of his life and tried incessantly to achieve it from his childhood. But it is commonly believed that due to some blessing from certain Guru, Chaitanya changed his nature. He left logic and arguments and became one of the greatest teachers of *Bhakti*. He became a man of large heart instead of big head. He gave up his fight, quarrels, professorship of logic and started emulating the mad love of the Gopis. Chaitanya's *Bhakti* rolled over the whole land of Bengal bringing solace to everyone.

According to Vivekananda, if Śankara was a man of great intellect, then Rāmānuja and Chaitanya were men of great hearts. Vivekananda says that in his Guru, Sree Ramakrishna Paramahansa one can see the embodiment of both, the great head and the large heart. Vivekananda claims that his Guru has the brilliant intellect of Śankara and infinite heart of Chaitanya. His heart was large enough to include the poor, the weak, the outcases, the downtrodden. He loved every human being both inside and outside of India. On the other side, his grand brilliant intellect could conceive the subtle metaphysics of *Vedānta*. Those higher thoughts were not a hard lesson for his intellect to read and study. He could talk of *Vedānta* in a simple manner to common people and convince them of its veracity. He practised it himself as the true nature of his being and enabled others to live accordingly. He envisioned, the same spirit working in everyone, in every sect and every being. His teachings were of a universal religion of both head and heart.

It was the same with Vivekananda. He was also a man of both heart and brain in a perfect manner. He was the true spirit of his Guru. We see a striking evidence in Vivekananda's own life as is explained by Romain Rolland who was one of his French disciples. He writes:

It was wonderful that he kept in his feverish hands to the end the equal balance between the two poles: a burning love of the Absolute (the Advaita) and the irresistible appeal of suffering Humanity. And what makes him so appealing to us is that at those times when equilibrium was no longer possible, and he had to make a choice, it was the latter that won the day: he sacrificed everything else to Pity, to "poor suffering Humanity", as Beethoven, his great European brother, said.

The beautiful episode of Girish is moving example:

It will be remembered that this disciple of Ramakrishna – the celebrated Bengali dramatist, writer, and comedian, who had led the life of a "libertine" in the double sense of classic age until the moment when the tolerant and mischievous fisher of Ganga took him upon his hook – had since, without leaving the world, become the most ardent and sincere of the converts; he spent his days in a constant transport of faith through love, of Bhakti-Yoga. But he had kept his freedom of speech; and all Ramakrishna's disciples showed him great respect for the sake of their Master's memory.

One day he came in while Vivekananda was discussing the most abstract philosophy with a disciple. Vivekananda broke off and said to him in a mockingly affectionate tone, "Well, Girish, you did not care to make a study of these things, but passed your days with your "Krishnas and your Vishnus'."

Girish replied, "Well, Naren, let me ask you one thing. Of Vedas and Vedānta you have read enough. But are there remedies prescribed in them for these wailings, these cries of hungry mouths, these abominable sins ... and the many other evils and miseries that one meets with every day? The mother of the house there, who at one time fed daily fifty mouths, has not the wherewithal to cook even for herself and her children for the last three days! The lady of such-and-such a family has been violated by ruffians and tortured to death. The young widow of so-and-so has succumbed from causing abortion to hide her shame!... I ask you, Naren, have you found in the Vedas any preventive for these evils?..."

And as Girish continued in this vein of sharp irony, depicting the dark and dismal side of society, Vivekananda sat speechless and deeply moved. Thinking of pain and misery of the world, tears came into his eyes and to hide his feelings he walked out of the rook.

Girish said to the disciple, "Now, did you see with your own eyes what a large heart your Guru possesses? I do not esteem him so much of being of a scholar and intellectual giant, as for the large-heartedness which made him walk out shedding tears for the misery of mankind. As soon as he heard it, mark you, all his Vedas and Vedānta vanished out of sight as it were, all the learning and the scholarship that he was displaying a moment ago was cast aside and his whole being was filled to overflow with the milk of loving kindness. Your Swamiji is as much a Jnani as a Pandit as a lover of God and humanity."

Vivekananda returned, and said to Sadananda that his heart was gnawing with pain and poverty and distress of his countrymen, and exhorted him to do something by opening small relief centres at least. And turning to Girish, he said: "Ah, Girish, the thoughts come to me that even if I have to undergo a thousand births to relieve the misery of the world, ay, even to remove the least pain from anyone, I shall cheerfully do it!..."[9]

Afterwards Vivekananda became a perfect embodiment of love for fellow beings; this was the beginning of his concept of "universal love". In the conclusion of a study of Vivekananda, Shamita Basu observed:

> Haunted by the picture of underdevelopment and abject poverty and moved by selfless love for the underprivileged, Vivekananda was convinced that the way to modernity must necessarily lie through development. He unequivocally preached the uplift of women, underprivileged caste groups, and the downtrodden masses through social service for the uplift of the underprivileged. If the ideology of development was to be advocated on behalf of modernity then nationalist actions must take the initiative to enable the people to have an experience of this development even if it had to be only in half measures. Vivekananda was convinced that spiritual liberation was necessary to inspire the elite to activate economic liberation. Unlike Gandhi, his proposals to bring in the Enlightenment was largely interventionist in intent. It was the economic liberation of the capitalist kind that made the public use of reason imperative. However, in a society under domination economic liberation can only come about through a form of rigorous social service, which he sought to advocate as the ultimate spiritual act.[10]

His concept of "universal religion" is based on his concept of universal love, it focuses on the love for all human beings irrespective of caste, race, and colour. It includes all religions upon earth. It approves all spiritual texts throughout the history. It respects all spiritual leaders of all parts of the world. It proclaims respect for all of them in order to remove suffering in the society in different places and times.

Vivekananda's concept of "universal religion" does not seem to cohere with his earlier understanding of "*Vedic* authority". According to the concept of "*Vedic* authority", in its absolute sense, no individual truth seeker can go beyond it or depart from it. On the other side, according to the concept of "universal religion" each and every spiritual leader is absolute truth revealer. If we take into account the former concept, the diversification of individual experiences are negated privileging the *Vedic* absolute authority. These differences in vision of reality occur not only in accordance with spatio-temporal cultural differences but also in the metaphysical sense. Some of the prophetic experiences go certainly against the *Vedic* outlook of reality. In such cases, how can the *Vedas* claim absolute authority on all systems. After all, the *Vedas* are interpreted in different ways leading to the visions of monism, dualism, etc. How can there be a common criterion to judge other streams of visions?

Vivekananda's concept of universal religion is based on an unending process and continued through Rama, Krishna, Moses, Buddha, Jesus, Mohammed, Ramakrishna Paramahansa, etc. In this everlasting stream, Vivekananda says, *Veda* is but one text. Apparently, it contradicts the view of *Vedic* absolute authority. Accordingly he says:

> I accept all religions that were in the past, and worship with all; I worship God with everyone of them.... Is God's book finished or is it still a continuous revelation going on? It is a marvellous book, these spiritual Revelations of the world. The Bible, the Vedas, the Koran, and all other sacred books are but so many pages, and infinite number of pages remain yet to be unfolded.... We stand in the present, but open ourselves to the infinite future. We take in all that has been in the past, enjoy the light of the present, and open every window of the heart for all that will come in the future. Salutation to all the prophets of the past, to all the great ones of the present, and to all that are to come in the future![11]

Nevertheless, these great words are not to be quoted for their implicit contradiction with some other concept. This conceptual difference can be considered as part of evolution of his vision.

Vivekananda's analysis of scriptures established a hierarchy of truth as eternal and temporal or impersonal and personal. The eternal aspect of truth is privileged over the temporal. The impersonal phase of truth is centred whereas the personal phase of truth is marginalised. This is very clear in the following words: "Krishna is not the authority of the Vedas, but the Vedas are the authority of Krishna himself."[12] But this marginalisation is not successful when we go deep into the theme of Vivekananda's study of scriptures. In the same lecture he says:

> From the ideal lover we came down to the lower stratum of Krishna, the preacher of the Gita. Than the Gita no better commentary on the Vedas has been written or can be written.[13]

Who will judge the conformity of Krishna with *Vedas*, except Krishna himself, i.e., a seer of experience. Hence, personal experience of a seer is primarily important; it cannot stand as something secondary. Nothing else can validate it. Nothing can replace it. According to Vivekananda, the dynamic force of society transforms the personal authority of time. It is the mission endowed to personal gods. It is not impersonal authority that makes social mobility. From the standpoint of social mobility, it itself validates the spiritual leader. If the truth is not to practise in society for its well maintenance, then it is not truth but only verbalism. If they do not lead to the spiritual emancipation of people, then they cannot be spiritual principles but only jargon. Only social mobility can judge or test a spiritual leader and not some external text.

It does not mean that the *Vedāntic* truth is to be undermined. We can see the original lesson of *Vedānta* is so profound as denoted by Vivekananda. It is not the theoretical assurance of *Vedānta* that is of primary importance but its potential lesson. This potentiality of *Vedas*, we can see in his own words and from his citations from *Vedānta*:

> Religion is not in books, nor in theories, nor in dogmas, nor in talking, not even in reasoning. It is being and becoming. Ay, my friends, until each one of you has become a Rishi and come face to face with spiritual facts, religious life has not begun for you. Until the superconscious opens for you, religion is mere talk, it is nothing but preparation. You are talking second-hand, third-hand, and here applies that beautiful saying of Buddha when he had a discussion with some Brahmins. They came discussing about the nature of Brahman, and the great sage asked, "Have you seen Brahman?" "No," said the Brahmin; "Or your father?" "No, neither has he"; "Or your grandfather?" "I don't think even he saw Him." "My friend, how can you discuss about a person whom your father and grandfather never saw, and try to put each other down?" That is what the whole world is doing. Let us say in the language of the Vedānta, "This Atman is not to be reached by too much talk, no, not even by the highest intellect, no, not even by the study of the Vedas themselves."[14]

It may appear to the feeble-minded people as a negation of the *Vedas*, but the true fact is that it is the potential lesson of the *Vedas*.

NOTES AND REFERENCES

1. Swami Vivekananda, *Lectures from Colombo to Almorah*, Advaita Ashram, Kolkata, 1956, p. 201.
2. Edit. William Radice, *Swami Vivekananda and the Modernization of Hinduism*, Oxford University Press, New Delhi, 1998, p. 215.
3. *Complete Works of Swami Vivekananda*, Mayavati Memorial Edition I, p. 17.

4. Edit William Radice, *op. cit.*, Oxford University Press, New Delhi, 1998, p. 8.
5. *Ibid.*, pp. 12-13.
6. Swami Vivekananda, *Lectures from Colombo to Almora*, p. 207. Advaita Ashram, Wellington Lane, Kolkata, 1956.
7. Amiya P. Sen, *Swami Vivekananda*, Manzar Khan, Oxford University Press, New Delhi, 2000, p. 60.
8. Swami Vivekananda, *Lectures from Colombo to Almora*, Advaita Ashram, Wellington Lane, Kolkata 1956, p. 218.
9. Romain Rolland, *The life of Vivekananda and Universal Gospel*, Advaita Ashram, Wellington Lane, Kolkata, 13, pp. 129-31.
10. Shamita Basu, *Religious revivalism as nationalist discourse*, Manzar Khan, Oxford University Press, New Delhi, 2002, p. 201.
11. Romain Rolland, *op. cit.*, Advaita Ashram, Kolkata 13, p. 266.
12. Swami Vivekananda, *Lectures from Colombo to Almora*, Advaita Ashram, Kolkata, 1956, p. 199.
13. *Ibid.*, pp. 214, 215.
14. *Ibid.*, p. 205.

Select Bibliography

The Complete Works of Swami Vivekananda in 9 vols., Mayanati Memorial Advaita Ashram, Kolkata, 2003 edition.

The Life of Swami Vivekananda by his Eastern and Western Disciples, Advaita Ashram, Kolkata, 2003.

Selections from the Complete Works of Swami Vivekananda, Advaita Ashram, 1987.

Swami Vivekananda, *Lectures from Colombo to Almora*, Advaita Ashram, Wellington Lane, Kolkata, 1956.

Swami Vivekananda in the West: New Discoveries, Advaita Ashram.

Basu, Shamita, *Religious Revivalism and Nationalist Discourse*, Oxford University Press, New Delhi, 2002.

Dasgupta, R.K. (ed.), *Swami Vivekananda: A Hundred Since Chicago*, Ramakrishna Math, Belur, Howarah, 1994.

Datta, Bhupendranath, *Swamy Vivekananda: Patriot Prophet*, Navabharaṭ Publishers, 1954.

Majumdar, R.C., *Swami Vivekananda: A Historical Review*, Advaita Ashram, 1999, first published by General Printers and Publishers Private Ltd., 1965, p. 85.

Radice, William (ed.), *Swami Vivekananda and the Modernisation of Hinduism*, Oxford University Press, 1999.

Rambachan, Anantanand, *The Limits of Scripture, Vivekananda's Reinterpretation of the Vedas*, University of Hawaii Press, Honolulu, 1994.

Rolland, Romain, *The Life of Vivekananda and Universal Gospel*, Advaita Ashram, Wellington Lane, Kolkata.

Sen, Amiya P., *Hindu Revivalism in Bengal: Some Essays in Interpretation*, Oxford University Press, 1993.

Sen, Amiya P., *Swami Vivekananda*, Oxford University Press, New Delhi, 2000.

Swami Satprakasananda, *Swami Vivekananda' Contribution to the Present Age*, The Vedanta Society of St. Louis, Missouri, 1985.

Index